THE STRUCTURE OF SOCIAL THEORY

DILEMMAS, STRATEGIES AND PROJECTS

The Structure of Social Theory

Dilemmas, strategies and projects

Terry Johnson
Christopher Dandeker
Clive Ashworth

St. Martin's Press   New York

© Terry Johnson, Christopher Dandeker and Clive Ashworth 1984

All rights reserved.
For information, write: St. Martin's Press, Inc.,
175 Fifth Avenue, New York, NY 10010.
Printed in Hong Kong
Published in the United Kingdom by
Macmillan Publishers Ltd.
First published in the United States of America in 1984

ISBN 0-312-76833-8
ISBN 0-312-76834-6 (pbk.)

Library of Congress Cataloging in Publication Data
Johnson, Terry.
    The structure of social theory.
    Bibliography: p.
    Includes index.
    1. Sociology–Methodology.   I. Ashworth, Clive.
II. Dandeker, Christopher.   III. Title.
HM24.J635 1984   301'.01'8   84–13285
ISBN 0-312-76833-8
ISBN 0-312-76834-6 (pbk.)

For all the students who participated in the preparation of this book

Contents

Preface

This book is the culmination of a co-operative venture which began some years ago when a group of teachers who had the responsibility for teaching theoretical sociology – from introductory to post-graduate levels – in the Department of Sociology at the University of Leicester collectively accepted that the 'crisis' of sociology heralded by Alvin Gouldner in 1971 had arrived. As teachers of theory we found ourselves at the sharp end, attempting to pass on to students a body of knowledge, the basic assumptions of which were under attack from a variety of directions and whose contents were undergoing radical changes, seemingly from month to month. It was becoming increasingly difficult to 'keep up' with this burgeoning and critical literature and still retain a secure framework of issues which made sense of the discipline for students. The danger was to bombard students with critique and counter-critique to the point of self-destruct: a disillusioning process for those who came to sociology looking for solid achievement and knowledge. In short, a major and traditional function of theory courses, to provide a sense of disciplinary unity, was no longer being fulfilled.

In order to cope with these problems that we commonly faced, and in order to sustain some continuity of approach at each level of teaching, we agreed collectively to rework the courses. Unfortunately, our own views of what constituted sociology were very nearly as disparate as the competing perspectives and schools that we confronted in our attempts to 'make sense' of the literature, and we soon discovered that before we could collectively respond to the problems of teaching we had to reach some agreements about the nature of social theorising ourselves. Out of these dilemmas and goals the basic ideas and perspectives for the book emerged. Our discussions led us to seek for conditions of unity underlying the divisions and fragmentation which appeared to characterise the enterprise of sociology.

The text which follows seeks primarily to clarify the nature of these disputes, by providing a systematic framework which understands both present and past controversies as a persisting *dialogue* between four strategies of theorising. We do not provide a history of social theory, though the text does provide the basis for such a project. Rather it is an enquiry into the 'systematics' or structure of theorising about the social, using a number of classical and modern sociological writings as vehicles for the illustration of what we take to be the perennial dilemmas of theory – what is the nature of social reality and how can we best gain knowledge of it? Finally, we also, in our concluding chapter, set out the conditions under which disputes over these questions might be resolved: why we should prefer one theoretical perspective to another, and how we might evaluate those attempts at synthesis which recognise a disciplinary unity in sociology.

University of Leicester
December 1983

TERRY JOHNSON
CHRISTOPHER DANDEKER
CLIVE ASHWORTH

Acknowledgements

We are in the debt of our colleagues in the Department of Sociology at Leicester who have provided the arena for discussion in which the idea for this book emerged. In particular, we are more than usually indebted to John Scott, who was crucial in the early development of the perspective which is presented. Also we are grateful to have the opportunity to thank Doreen Butler, Judith Smith, Annie Brown and June Lee who saved us from some of our errors and responded to our impossible deadlines in preparing the manuscript. Finally, our thanks go to Tony Giddens for his encouragement and tolerance.

Acknowledgements

1
Theoretical Sociology: The Conditions of Fragmentation and Unity

A decade ago it was normal practice for teachers of sociology to confront new students with the question: Is sociology a science? Apart from the implicit demand that the newcomers should commit themselves to a positive evaluation of the discipline in advance of getting to know what it was about, the question assumed that there was some unity of purpose and practice in sociology, and that there was a more or less agreed set of criteria as to what constituted science – natural or social. Experienced teachers of sociology would have difficulty in setting such a question today, as developments in the subject during the last ten years have undermined the consensus which made such a question possible. We have experienced what may be called a crisis of fragmentation. It has been a crisis with two major dimensions: fragmentation through specialisation and fragmentation through theoretical confrontation. Let us consider each of these in turn.

During the 1960s and 1970s the academic discipline of sociology expanded greatly, as measured by the proliferation of university and polytechnic departments, numbers of students, and the number of teachers of sociology. This process was not confined to Britain, it occurred to a greater or lesser extent throughout Western Europe and the United States and had less vigorous parallels in the underdeveloped world. Coinciding with the increase in the amount of sociology taught, there was an even more remarkable expansion in the specific areas of social life to which sociologists turned their attention. There is no doubt that with the confidence born of the rapid expansion in the numbers who wished to learn the 'sociological perspective', sociology became a discipline with a well-developed imperialist ambition and the mounting ranks of researchers moved into more and more fields of specialism: from the sociology of education to the sociology of the curriculum; from the sociology of literature to the sociology of language; from the sociology of medicine to the sociology of death, etc. As has been the case with all empires created on the basis of a rapid deployment of forces over wide areas, sociology both scared and bewildered the colonised 'natives' and created great strains on its own resource base and logistical capacities. That is to say, the proliferation of specialist areas has resulted in specialists developing their own 'local' ways of doing things, developing their own methods and styles of procedure, gradually losing systematic contact with any unified core conception of what the subject is in a general and unifying sense.

One peculiarity of this fragmentation process has been the persistence and entrenchment of a specialist area variously referred to as 'theory', 'social theory', or 'theoretical sociology', as if the sociological analysis of particular areas of social life had at best an indirect, and at worst a tenuous, link with the specialism, 'theory'. It is as though our imperial sociological army marched off to its colonial adventures leaving at home-base all the maintenance services, to retool and refine their procedures. It is this 'peculiar' division of labour in sociology that has reinforced the potentialities for fragmentation. Specialist research has to a large extent produced what one would expect, area-specific knowledge. As a result, there are those who would make a virtue out of necessity, claiming that we must be content with fragmented specialisms, so finally abandoning any vestiges of the imperial ambition and its goal of creating 'grand' theoretical schemes encompassing social science as a whole. This view may be practical, but its underlying assumption that there are no systematic forces operating in society and history which can be known, is still very much contested, as we shall see.

The second source of the fragmentation which has come to characterise contemporary sociology is that which operates within theoretical sociology itself. The specialism 'theory' has been subjected to an increasing subdivision of schools and perspectives, to the degree that the protagonists have been encouraged to spend more time on internal debates and consolidations than they have on constructive confrontation with competing schools of theory. Thus, structuralists, phenomenologists, ethnomethodologists, action theorists, symbolic interactionists, functionalists and Marxists (including as many perspectives within it as there are schools outside it) have generated an increasing number of internal divisions, such that we get ethnomethodologists who cannot 'talk to another' let alone communicate with action theorists or structuralists. Once combined, these two sources of fragmentation – specialisation and theoretical division – have proved capable of producing a reinforcing trend, in which areas of specialised study become the preserves of different schools of theory, so creating further problems of communication and replication.

To speak of a 'crisis of fragmentation' affecting sociology over the last decade and more, does not mean that from our present vantage point we look back nostalgically on a 'golden age' in which a unified theoretical framework provided a consensual intellectual basis for the progressive and controlled extension of sociology into diverse areas of concern; although it is the case that something approaching just such a situation did characterise the discipline in the post-war period – until, that is, the mid-1960s. All that glisters is not, however, 'golden'.

It was in this post-war period, against the backcloth of the political dominance of the United States, that Western academic sociology was largely underwritten by the approach known as structural functionalism. Its major features were fashioned by American sociologists from diverse sources, not least the body of social anthropological knowledge generated out of the British colonial experience. Despite the importance of undercurrents of opposition from traditions deriving in the main from Marx and Weber and the American pragmatist position of symbolic interactionism – these were in many respects successfully incorporated into structural functionalism, albeit in modified forms – structural functionalism served as the 'paradigm' in terms of which the early expansion of the subject was directed. Structural functionalism defined the central, explicit debates in sociology centring on such issues as: the extent to which Western industrial societies, construed as institutional systems, were consensual, and destined to progress to a peaceful, affluent future based on the application of advanced technology; or whether this progress was problematic because of divisions of interest within society, stemming from differential access to privileged social statuses. In this second view, conflict was a more significant social phenomenon than mainstream functionalism was willing to acknowledge – both as a feature of society, and as a mechanism of social change – although, for the most part, such conflicts were regarded as resolvable through the further and beneficent extension of the Welfare State. More significantly, 'Third World' societies were regarded generally as 'developing' societies, which in the fullness of time would come to share the fruits of industrial technology and political democracy.

A further major issue arose out of the centrality of 'role theory' for structural-functionalist analysis; an approach that conceived of social action as patterned by shared expectations, internalised by individuals in the course of their upbringing or socialisation. The issue in contention was represented by the claim that such an approach presented an 'oversocialised' conception of the actor; overemphasising the extent to which we act in accordance with received social prescriptions; taking on roles like a chameleon takes on colour. The alternative view, 'action theory', rejected the idea of the individual as a passive recipient of social order and sought to argue that structure was itself an outcome of individual action.

These matrices of debate – conflict/consensus, actor/system – never became fundamentally divisive in so far as the protagonists shared a good many assumptions about the nature of social reality and the appropriate means of gathering knowledge about it. Of central significance to this consensus was the assumption that whatever the nature of the dispute it could be resolved by testing theories against facts, the nature of which could be determined without presupposing the validity of any of the theoretical points at issue. One could show with 'theory-free' facts whether modern societies were consensual, or were converging, and so on. Furthermore, while sociologists disagreed about certain issues, the idea that society was a *system* – and thus an 'object-out-there' to be studied – was taken for granted.

Most sociologists agreed that while sociological generalisations could not (some said ever) reach the precision and universality of the natural sciences, none the less our accumulation of sociological knowledge (expressed in generalisations whose logical form *approximated* those in the natural sciences) was a genuine aspiration. The accepted differences between the methods of the natural and social sciences were either marginal or manageable; the great debates of the past on these issues had been resolved once and for all.

Nevertheless, it was precisely this bedrock of assumptions, upon which the debates of the 1950s and early 1960s depended for their overall theoretical unity, that gave way, as apparently resolved methodological debates reappeared once more in the late 1960s and the 1970s. Pioneering texts such as those of Winch, Garfinkel and Cicourel[1] raised once again the issue of whether sociologists should be concerned with *interpreting* social activity, rather than with subordinating it to behavioural laws, as in the natural sciences. The 'new' philosophies of science – particularly the issues raised by Kuhn's *Structure of Scientific Revolutions*[2] – penetrated sociology, and led to a questioning of whether theories could be constructed and tested against facts in the 'theory-neutral' way that so many sociologists took for granted.

Meanwhile, the peaceful, and technologically inspired progress which structural functionalism viewed as the characteristic feature of Western and, indeed, potentially all societies, was exposed as a 'myth' in the context of such events as the Vietnam war, the inner-city riots in the USA, and world-wide economic recession, in the 1970s. In the train of world events, Marxism was revitalised (as well as undergoing internal fragmentation), and it both fed off, and contributed to, the 'new directions' in sociological theory which have proliferated ever since. Consequently, sociologists now find themselves in a position in which one of the things they do agree about is that fragmentation is a major characteristic of their discipline.

Our response to this situation is to provide a text that seeks to achieve four main ends. First of all, to show how 'theory' or 'theorising' enters into *any* sociological analysis of particular social relations, and thus, by implication, to indicate the importance of a familiarity with theoretical debates in sociology to anyone with an interest in understanding the specifics of their social world. Indeed, as will be shown below, the most concrete social observation cannot help but draw on, and presuppose, a whole corpus of theorising; every sociological observer is a sociological theorist.

Second, to provide a systematic classification or 'conceptual map' of the debates in theoretical sociology. By this we mean that the proliferation of theoretical schools or 'paradigms' in sociology is, and has been, an *orderly* one; there are crucial questions and issues to which all competing theories attend, and thus presuppose. This underlying unity in the sociological enterprise can be reconstructed, and, as a result, competing theoretical traditions can be compared with each other systematically.

Third, we suggest that clarification of the debates in theoretical sociology also involves considering how the competing claims to validity made by different theoretical traditions may be assessed. In particular, we argue that there are reasonable grounds for accepting or rejecting different theoretical traditions or aspects of them. Theoretical disputants not only share a concern over a network of issues which provide the basis for a dialogue between them, but theoretical preferences are not, and need not be, arbitrary and/or emotionally grounded, as many have now come to think.

Fourth, and on the basis of the previous arguments, we indicate the directions theoretical sociology ought to pursue as a corrective to the sources of fragmentation identified above.

The remainder of this chapter will be given over to an outline of our arguments bearing on the first two tasks, which we go on to elaborate in Chapters 2–5. The third and fourth points are developed in the concluding chapter as a way of drawing out the implications of the preceding discussion.

Theorising and sociological analysis

In rejecting the possibility that a systematic body of theory might, some day, emerge from a long-term accumulation of empirically based specialist studies, we wish to argue that any analysis of social relations involves an albeit implicit commitment to some such over-arching body of theory in the first place. This involves the contention that any sociological analysis is implicated in a stratified form of theorising. Take the example of religion as a sociological phenomenon; specifically, the effects of religious beliefs have a social activity.

Any analysis of religion presupposes a definition of religion as a type of belief system and social activity, and therefore a view of the nature of society, of which religion is one aspect, together with an understanding of how knowledge of religion and its effects may be produced. Surely, one might argue, such definitional issues, if resolved at the outset, determine the nature of what will be discovered during the empirical investigation, in which case it is preferable to defer them to the end of the analysis, when one will have sufficient evidence on which to make a decision about what religion and its social effects are.

However, such an argument is untenable, as gathering evidence on religion presupposes that one already 'knows' what religion is, even if this simply involves accepting commonsense interpretations of religion current in the wider society. In fact, Weber's implicit definition of religion – a belief in the supernatural realm – reflected the commonsense idea of religion held in Western societies, itself deriving from the dualism between 'this worldly' phenomena and 'other worldly' phenomena recognised by the Judeo-Christian tradition.

To define religion sociologically, as a set of beliefs and associated forms of conduct, is to presuppose both the nature of social action and the most appropriate processes whereby knowledge about it is to be gained. For example, Weber's view of religion brings into play his argument that human conduct, while subject to external, material constraints, and rooted in material needs (for food, shelter, etc.) is essentially meaningful.

Human activity involves consciousness. To be human is not merely to adjust to nature but to plan one's activities in order to realise ideals in conditions of material scarcity. However, consciousness, mediated by language, allows human beings to distance themselves from their immediate surroundings and requires that they interpret their place in the world; they must confront the problem of the meaning of their existence. These questions of ultimate meaning confront human beings, as language users, in ways that distinguish them from other animal species.

While Weber can countenance secularisation, i.e. the waning of a belief in the 'supernatural world', his conceptualisation of social action buttresses the argument that the religious need for meaning persists in a secular world. The celebration of science and technology in modern industrial society has failed to convert human actors to an acceptance of 'this worldly' materialism. The 'religious need', and thus the problem of ultimate meaning, lurks as a constant anxiety in the most affluent of societies.

Weber's substantive interpretation of religion is also informed by his conception of how sociological analysis (of religion or of anything else in the social world) should operate. For Weber, the unit of analysis in sociology was the *individual actor* – 'the sole carrier of meaningful conduct'. By this he meant that social groups and whole societies were to be understood as complex aggregations of individual courses of action, *typified* by the observer for the purpose of comparative and historical analysis. This is why Weber's point of departure for his sociology of religion was the *individual's* confrontation with the problems of ultimate meaning.

However, this point of departure is not demanded by the facts. On the contrary, it is a product of a specific model of how knowledge is constituted in the social sciences. Weber took the view that the concepts of the social sciences *imposed* an order on the infinite complexity of the observer's experience, i.e. what can be observed. This order reflected the interests of the observer (what was of significance as a problem), and in addition the degree to which sociological abstraction was geared to grasping the peculiarities of individual or generic events. For example, one might be concerned with the details of Calvinist theology or a generalised comparison of Western asceticism and varieties of Eastern mysticism. For Weber both are forms of abstraction, as even the most concrete of investigations cannot hope to exhaust all the details of a phenomenon. Neither abstractions are to be regarded as penetrating the 'reality' of the social; they are simply heuristic devices necessary to the task of indicating the extent to which concrete reality departs from the idealised conceptualisations of the observer. Thus Weber's analysis of Calvinism does not reveal the 'essence' of the meaning of Calvinism, but simply focuses on certain exaggerated aspects which can be used to show how some religious beliefs were more like Calvinism than some other belief system (Lutheranism for example) which could also be 'idealised' for the purposes of comparative analysis.

A number of implications follow from Weber's arguments. The unit of analysis in Weber's sociology must be the individual actor, and society should be regarded as an emergent aggregation of types of individual conduct. This follows from his conceptualisation of how sociological analysis should proceed; namely, by abstracting from the particulars of the observer's experience of the world. Concepts are hypothetical, heuristic devices for ordering experience and preparing data for causal analysis; not descriptions of reality as such.

Furthermore, Weber faced the difficulty of studying the meanings that actors give to their conduct with a method that requires that its subject-matter be observable. To this end, Weber suggests that interpretations of the meaning of conduct can only be validated by recourse to statements about behaviour. For example, if it is argued that 'inner psychic loneliness' was the effect of a belief in the tenets of Calvinism, and that such belief had the consequence of rationalising practical (and particularly economic) conduct in a this-worldly direction, we can only know that this is probably the case (and not a figment of our imagination) by tabulating the empirical frequency of association (and likely causal relation) between these two observable states of affairs – belief in Calvinism, and rational economic conduct. Such a conclusion may be strengthened by observing how opposed or different beliefs have different economic effects: for example, Eastern mysticism and withdrawal from ascetic this-worldly oriented economic conduct.

Finally (and notwithstanding certain equivocations in Weber's position), he countenances the idea that conflicting interpretations of events (and meanings) can be resolved by theory-neutral data, with the proviso that an exhaustive account of any historical event can never be provided. These problems of theorising are implicated in Weber's approach to religion, yet are not demanded by any supposedly theory-neutral data on religion; in which case it is hardly surprising that quite different styles of theorising can be drawn on to produce a contrasting analysis of the same social phenomenon. Durkheim is a case in point.

In contradistinction to Weber's analysis of religion, Durkheim's approach takes as its point of departure the idea that religion is a social fact – a collective reality quite distinct from, and not to be identified with, an aggregation of individual resolutions of the socio-psychological problems of ultimate meaning.

As with Weber, Durkheim's analysis brings into play a whole train of sociological theorising. Again two issues become central: the nature of social action, and the processes whereby knowledge of its structure is to be achieved. Like Weber, Durkheim argues that human activity involves the use of cultural symbols, and that action is not reducible to material conditions. Social rules and conventions, reproduced through language, distinguish the social from the natural world. It should be stressed, however, that Durkheim did not agree with Weber that this incongruence between the natural and social worlds entailed a radical distinction between the methods of the natural and social sciences.

Durkheim understands sociology as possessing far more penetrative or explanatory power than Weber was prepared to accept. This is evident in Durkheim's definition of religion. His distinction between the sacred and profane (as opposed to Weber's conventional distinction between 'this world' and 'other world') indicates a number of his intentions. Durkheim regards religion (beliefs and practices relating to sacred things) as a *universal* feature of social life; one that changes its contents but never disappears. For example, society may not be characterised by God as a supernatural being, but the belief in sacred values cannot be eliminated – thus the role he ascribed to nationalism and moral individualism in tapping 'religiosity' in modern industrial societies. Durkheim's view of the universality of religion is more consistent with his own (high) estimation of the explanatory power of sociology, than Weber's more tentative approach. Weber eschewed any hopes for universal laws or statements about social life. Yet this view (even if correct) is difficult to regard as consistent with his analysis of the problems of ultimate meaning, which it seems *all* human actors have to face.

Durkheim's view of the universality of religion is rooted in his argument that such beliefs enable individuals to represent to themselves their own social structures and natural environment, while celebrating their dependence on society. Religion is simply a form of collective knowledge of society and nature, and a moral celebration of its facilitation of interaction. The belief in the soul, for example, is not an 'ignorant myth', but a recognition and celebration of the fact that society or collective life transcends the finite life of the individual and gives the latter meaning.

Durkheim rejects both the view that the constituent element of sociological analysis is the individual actor, and the associated argument that society is a complex matrix of interaction between actors. Rather, he argues that the conditions of interaction are social facts, collective representations or social currents. As a result, religion is viewed as an expression of *society's* consciousness of itself and its surroundings – precisely the sort of view that Weber sought to eliminate from sociological analysis. Similarly, suicide is for Durkheim not a project of an actor under various constraining normative and material conditions (as it would be for Weber), but an example of a social current, say egoism or anomie. The notion of anomie does not refer to an observer's heuristic device which summarises a number of discrete individual cases. For Durkheim, society and group life cannot be broken down into individual, component courses of action without losing the *raison d'être* of sociology as a discipline.

Durkheim defends the priority of society as the object of sociology by a (not unambiguous) argument which gives sociology the means of penetrating social reality in ways quite alien to the views to which Weber subscribed. Durkheim (contrary to his own explicit views which required sociological analysis to be free of all preconceptions and to start from 'facts') approached religion and other social phenomena with a theoretical model of the nature of society, its conditions of existence and historical development, which, as we shall see, was not directly induced from observation. For example, his definition of religion has, in contrast to Weber's, an explicit universal referent. While interested in the conditions and consequences of particular religions, Durkheim was especially concerned with the universal social significance of religion in ways quite alien to Weber's concerns. Durkheim's rational-deductive approach to theorising about religion is evident in more than his definition. His choice of a single case-study approach, i.e. an analysis of Arunta totemism, indicates that this religion is regarded as having universal significance. Arunta totemism is taken to be *the* most elementary religious form, and through its study one may elucidate the common, underlying structural and functional elements characterising all religions, namely their cognitive mediation of the sacred and profane dualism, and the organisation of celebratory ritual practices.

Durkheim, in contrast to Weber (and in contrast with his own emphasis on comparative, historical sociology), uses the case study to illustrate a universal deductive theory. In adopting a comparative, historical approach, Weber never countenanced the prospect of anything other than tentative probabilistic generalisations about the relations between religious belief and economic conduct, social class and religious affiliation, and so on. His model of how social scientific knowledge was generated dictated these modest aims.

A number of implications flow from this brief exposition of certain aspects of Weber and Durkheim's approaches to religion. First of all, the sociological analysis of religion cannot help but bring into play a whole body of theorising about the nature of society and social action, and how sociological knowledge may be generated. The most anti-theoretical observer is, in fact, involved in complex forms of theorising. Thus, even to recommend simple data collection on religion (or anything else) is to theorise the social world as an aggregation of particular items of behaviour which are amenable to such forms of investigation. As we shall see, the argument that the social world is a set of observable facts whose interrelationships and regularities can be studied through observation, is itself a theoretical postulate, and one that is not self-evident.

Furthermore, the forms of theorising involved in any concrete analysis of social action – including those used by Weber and Durkheim – are, despite their differences, not of such an order as to make a comparative evaluation of them an impossibility. These points underpin our central argument, and require some elaboration here.

While it is true that sociological theorising is, at present, characterised by its diversity, we will argue that an underlying order can, nevertheless, be detected; it has a *structure*. This structure is not the outcome of a consensus among sociologists about what the nature of social reality is; or about the ways in which our knowledge of the social is constituted. Rather, this underlying order derives from the fact that all sociologists have to pose certain fundamental questions, the answers to which are a precondition for any sociological investigation. There are, in our view, two such questions, which cannot be avoided, and all sociological knowledge at least assumes an answer to each. The questions are: what is the nature of social reality?; and how can we best obtain knowledge of it? These questions are unavoidable for any sociologist, because a refusal to countenance them itself constitutes a particular resolution of the problems they involve. For example, to argue such questions are 'irrelevant', because 'social reality' is 'self-evident', is itself a particular kind of answer involving a theoretical perspective. It should be pointed out that we are not suggesting that sociologists consciously and deliberately think about these questions before conducting their particular investigations or analyses, although some do. Nor are we suggesting that sociologists *should* always do so. It is not even necessary that completely satisfactory answers to these questions should be arrived at before the work of sociological analysis commences. Rather, we are suggesting that whenever and wherever sociological analysis is carried out, some kind of answer to both questions is implied: the investigation of social relations logically entails such 'theorising' whether it is recognised by the investigators or not. If it is the case, then, that sociology cannot be carried out except in terms of certain arguments, beliefs, or assumptions about what it *is* that is being studied, and how it is we can obtain valid knowledge about it, then it follows that these questions and the answers to them provide us with a basis or framework, in terms of which we can understand or 'make sense of' any particular sociological enterprise. We will now consider the answers that sociologists have given to each of these questions; looking first at the problem of social reality.

The nature of social reality: material or ideal?

Answers to the question about the nature of social reality have always fundamentally hinged on an assessment of two aspects of social life: its existence as a set of material phenomena, or its existence as a set of ideas that human beings have about the world they live in. This dualism is not so much an observable state of affairs as a characteristic of *all* attempts to theorise what sort of 'object' social reality is. These two possibilities – materialism and idealism – constitute the alternative resolutions of the question: what is the nature of social reality?

Those who stress the material character of social reality consider that human activity is best understood as behaviour taking place within constraining material conditions. The phenomena of nature determine the limits of our potentialities as human beings, whether those limits are climate, gravity, or our physical bodies. However, social phenomena themselves are also regarded as essentially material and constraining; whether they be forms of social organisation, productive systems, means of violence, cultural artifacts, etc. If we are to explain the major processes of social life we must, therefore, stress the fact of their materiality.

Such an answer is also often associated with what is called the doctrine of naturalism: that there is, by implication, little difference between human behaviour and the behaviour of animals or even inanimate objects. That human beings are 'purposive' and 'thinking' creates no serious obstacle to the application of the methods and techniques of the natural sciences to the subject-matter of the social sciences. Both the natural and social worlds are equally material entities and processes, external to the human observer whose 'connections' with these worlds are established through the material conditions of his or her nervous system. The sciences, natural and social, are, then, characterised by unity.

From the point of view of the alternative answer to our question – idealism – the above resolution of the problem completely misses the significance and peculiarity of human activity: the fact that human beings uniquely use complex systems of linguistic signs and cultural symbols to indicate to themselves and to others what they intend and mean to do. Such a viewpoint suggests that human activity is not behaviour (an adaptation to material conditions), but an expression of the meaning that humans give (via language) to their conduct. Social action is always, therefore, a process of endowing a situation with meaning, and it is those meanings, ideas, symbols, etc. that are the 'stuff' of the social world.

It is argued that such activities as worship, or suicide, are not simply a set of discrete behaviours taking place under certain material conditions (like birds migrating with the change of season). Going to church, kneeling, jumping off a tall building or under a moving train, are actions that cannot be understood except in a context of social rules and cultural meanings which can be deciphered by a human observer only by using his or her own interpretative skills. In the social sciences, then, we are forced to 'interpret the meaning' of social events. We have to use interpretative terms such as 'desire', 'love', 'good', etc., which are either inapplicable, or used in quite different ways in the natural sciences.

In the natural world, it is assumed that inanimate objects do not think about the meaning of their activities – human beings do. The objects of natural science obey laws, while human beings comply with cultural rules. Rules, in this sense, are again not applicable to the natural world. When you *comply* with the laws of the state, there is no equivalence to the way in which a stone *complies* with the laws of gravity when it has been thrown into the air. This is not to suggest that you are free to disobey state law, while the stone cannot disobey gravity. It means you can *think* about whether to obey the state or not, and that in so doing you *interpret* what the law of the state is, and what the likely future consequence of such action might be. This imaginative interpretation of a future state of affairs is a crucial element in present action. Any attempt to explain human action in terms of existing material conditions loses sight of the ability of a human being to act in terms of interpretations that do not even relate to a material present or past.

These, then, are the two solutions to the question, what is social reality? The solutions, materialism and idealism, are both exhaustive and mutually exclusive. As a result of all specific resolutions to the problem of the nature of social reality can be expressed in their terms, including those that seek to transcend or synthesise them. As we proceed, these rather simplified outlines will be developed further. For the moment, we have merely sketched out one dimension of the underlying structure of theory: the duality, materialism and idealism.

Getting to know social reality: nominal or real?

In sociological analysis two clear alternative solutions to the problem of how we can know social reality may be found. The first solution takes the view that the concepts we use to describe and explain the world – concepts such as religion, or bureaucracy, or social class – are merely convenient *names* which we coin in order to summarise the *particular* things that make up the social world. The reality of the social world (whether it be material or ideal) is that it is made up of unique, particular events and things. From this point of view the reality of a university, for example, is all the particular actors and activities that make it up at a particular time. Nevertheless, by using the generalising term 'university' we accept that it is convenient to generalise or summarise all these unique elements; that is to say, it remains possible to generalise about all these unique interactions which constitute a university, or a social class. In getting to know social reality, then, there is nothing wrong in using such general terms, as long as we do not mistake these general terms (names) for reality itself, which remains a conjunction of particular events. This basic approach to the problem of knowing is generally referred to as *nominalism*, and the mistake of attributing reality to our general concepts is referred to as *reification*. This error of reification arises when, for example, we refer to social classes as 'acting in their own interests'. Social classes cannot have interests, because social class is merely a name we give to a complex of particular social interactions; nor can they act, because only individuals are capable of action. To attribute such capacities to social classes, the state, or even society, is to commit the sin of reification.

Of course the language of sociology is full of general, collective and structural terms, but these must be recognised for what they are

– conceptual 'flags of convenience'. Thus, nominalism is not merely a rejection of any attempt to suggest that collectivities can act, but also involves the rejection of any 'misplaced' attempt to refer to realities that are 'other than', or 'go beyond' the particulars of our social experience. When Weber refers to the 'religion of China', therefore, he is merely summarising the 'typical' ways in which problems of ultimate meaning are resolved by a number of individuals located in a particular territory. The 'unity' and 'generality' implied by the phrase 'the religion of China' is a result of Weber's conceptual activities. For the purposes of gaining knowledge he writes 'as though' such a unity existed. Nominalism is a way of overcoming the impossibility of *knowing* social reality in all its particulars.

An alternative solution to that of nominalism is a position that claims that the significance of scientific concepts lies in their capacity to 'reveal' a social reality that is not immediately accessible to observation. Far from merely summarising observed particulars, such concepts actually penetrate to a reality that underlies and *explains* the particular events. For example, Marx argued that if social structures were 'given' to experience in this way, there would be no need for science at all.

This solution is referred to as *realism*. As we argued above, Durkheim's interest in the Arunta clans was not in describing their particular religious beliefs and activities, which might be added to and compared with similar analyses of other societies. Rather, the analyses of Arunta practices were taken by Durkheim to illustrate the 'elementary forms' of all religion, as the universal or general structures that characterise societies in general.

The answers to our two questions have now generated the basis for a fourfold classification of sociological theorising. These may be diagrammatically expressed (see Figure 1).

This fourfold classification, we will argue, provides a basis for analysing the structure of theoretical sociology. The elements of the classification are in no sense novel, they have often been used in other attempts to make sense of the disputes in sociology.[3] The duality, materialism/idealism, was used by Talcott Parsons as the organising theme in his attempt to reconstruct social theory in his book *The Structure of Social Action*.[4] Many of the Marxist critiques of academic sociology also take this duality as central to their project: in rejecting all forms of idealism. Also, the debates over

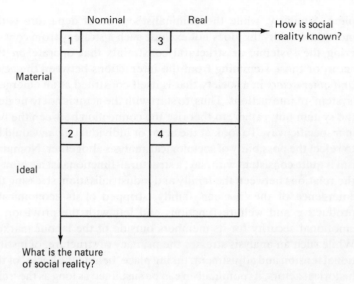

Fig. 1

whether the methods of the natural sciences can be applied to social science or not, have revolved around the issue of whether actors' interpretations (ideas) of the material conditions of their actions are to be given primacy in social reality. The present text goes beyond such a specification of the central issues in sociology by systematically linking these alternative solutions to the further problem of how such realities can be known.

This latter question and its alternative solutions – nominalism and realism – is a rather less familiar focus for debate in sociology. In so far as it has emerged as an issue of contention and debate, it has often done so as an *aspect* of yet other questions in dispute. For example, the long-term debate over the primacy of system/society/structure as against the actor/individual, incorporates certain elements of issues we have referred to in our distinction between nominalism and realism, but they are by no means identical. Realism does, as we have seen, regard the object of sociology to be 'social facts' or 'structures' of relations which are, as Durkheim argued, *sui generis* and not reducible to their particular or individual elements. Realism does in this way have an affinity with a position that stresses the primacy of structure, but this affinity is not complete. Similarly, while the nominalist's point of departure is the individual actor, this does not exclude such a strategy from considering the systemic or structural constraints that operate *on* the actor, or those stemming from the interactions between the actor *and other actors* in a society that is itself construed as an emergent 'system' of interactions. Thus, to start with the actor is not to neglect the system but, rather, to theorise the connection between the two in a specific way. To look at the actor or individual *alone* would be to reject the possibility of sociological analysis altogether. Nominalism is quite consistent with, say, a structural-functionalist account of the relations between the family and industrialisation, stressing the emergence of the 'nuclear' family, stripped of its economically productive and welfare functions and left with the provision of emotional security for its members outside of the labour market. While such an analysis stresses the primacy of structure, of institutional tension and adjustment, taking place 'behind the backs' of the historical actors, its nominalism can be sustained as long as the 'rule' that such structural constraints should not be reified, is observed. These constraints can, in the end, only be identified as particular, concrete events and actions with concrete effects on particular families. The functionalist account merely hypothesises a generalisation about the impact of factory production in a market economy on families. If shown to be correct, such a generalisation remains a summary of particular events.

The structure of theorising: four strategies

The diagram set out above outlines the two sets of contrasting answers to the two questions that, we have argued, must be confronted as a logical precondition of sociological analysis of the social world. We will now develop our argument by suggesting that the various combinations of solutions to the questions generate four broad strategies of sociological theorising. These strategies and their interrelations provide the basis for understanding different and competing theoretical projects in the social sciences; indeed, we suggest all such projects may be understood in this way, including our own. Our analysis presupposes a commitment to the realist position, that underlying structures are the objects of sociological enquiry; a claim that requires justification. In successive chapters we shall illustrate the usefulness of our schema for making sense of theoretical debates in sociology, and in the conclusion we will address the question of the grounds on which one strategy rather than another should be preferred. We can identify the four strategies, initially, by filling in the four boxes of Figure 2.

At this point we will briefly consider the main characteristics of each of these strategies which will be subject to detailed consideration in Chapters 2–5.

(1) *Empiricism.* This strategy combines the materialist and nominalist solutions, and, as such, entails the view that human activity is best understood as observable behaviour taking place in observable material circumstances: of the environment and the organism. Knowledge is obtained through systematic observation (sensory experience); by means of experimental or comparative analysis. In empiricism, to 'observe' is to attend to the contents of our sensory experience, understood variously as facts, sense data, or sense impressions. Generally speaking, empiricist observation means to view the world as directly reflected in the senses of the observer. The form that such knowledge typically takes is probabilistic generalisations about relations between observables. It

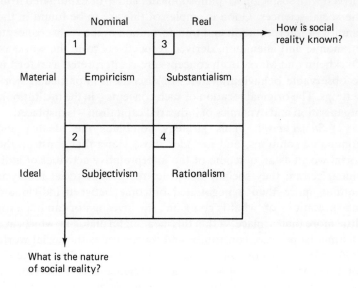

Fig. 2

entails a painstaking accumulation of the facts of repeated observations. For example, the incidence of strikes may be related successively to size of industry, type of technology, level of innovation, characteristics of the labour force, local political culture, managerial practices, level of trade-union membership, general level of economic activity, etc. This list of possible and significant factors is, by definition, open-ended and the results of investigation are always tentative. The 'patchwork' view of the social world which is the outcome of such a process of knowledge construction is the product of the assumption that society is a flux of particular events with no underlying order of reality. As a result, empiricism can do no more than summarise what has been observed. Its generalisations cannot go beyond observation except as hypothetical statements, which means that its 'laws' are nothing more than empirical generalisations. Moreover, a further distinguishing feature of empiricism is the energy it devotes to ensuring that all the concepts used in descriptions and explanations are defined in terms of observables. The language of theoretical sociology is understood as a convenient 'shorthand' for the organisation and summary of observations. Concepts that cannot be reduced in this way are viewed with suspicion as 'philosophical', and to be expurgated from the social sciences. Good examples of this are to be found in the empiricist interpretation and transformation of the realist concepts of anomie and alienation, derived respectively from the works of Durkheim and Marx. Both concepts are reinterpreted as referring to observable behavioural states of discontent in particular work settings. The original location of such concepts – in the institutional organisation and dynamics of industrial capitalism – is displaced.

(2) *Subjectivism.* This strategy combines the idealist and nominalist solutions, and includes those views that construe the social world as an outcome of the interpretative activities of individual actors; they socially construct reality. As social reality is nothing more than a negotiated outcome between individuals' interpretations of 'what is going on', the investigator can hope for little more than a 'place' within this meaningful dialogue, which, as a continuous process, constitutes and reconstitutes the social world from moment to moment. The social investigator is also engaged in interpreting 'what is going on'. Social science is not, therefore, a special or privileged account of social activities; it should merely seek to replicate what actors' interpretations of social reality are. To determine what strikes are, or what a particular strike is, is not a

meaningful project within this strategy unless it is considered in terms of how actors interpretatively constitute such phenomena. Contrary to empiricism, such social events cannot be factually described, free of subjective interpretation. A strike is not, therefore, an item of behaviour that can in some *unproblematic* way be statistically related to some other fact or facts. Whatever strikes are, is to be discovered in the accounts and interpretations made of them by actors in the social world: the accounts of the strikers themselves, the managers, the public, etc. A strike is not a 'thing', independent of varying interpretations; it *is* those interpretations.

(3) *Substantialism.* This is a strategy that combines the materialist and realist solutions, and accordingly the social world is conceived of as an objective material structure of relations. This structure is not accessible to direct observation. In fact, what *can* be observed must, in turn, be explained by that underlying structure of material relations. For example, strikes, as one aspect of a whole range of industrial conflicts, might be explained in terms of a theory of the capitalist mode of production, which identifies the dominant form of productive relations as antagonistic and exploitative: a result of the process of surplus-value appropriation. The structure of productive relations provides the context in which the general potential for strikes in the society is rooted, and in terms of which variations in their incidence, due to such factors as technology, size, etc., make sense.

(4) *Rationalism.* This strategy arises out of a combination of the idealist and realist solutions. Such a strategy understands society as an objective and constraining structure of ideas. Such ideas or meanings are not the attributes of individuals, as is the case with subjectivism; they are beyond any *one* individual consciousness. They establish a framework of limits and possibilities for individual actors' meaningful activities.

Such a strategy might lead to the analysis of strikes as contradictions and/or breakdowns in objective moral codes which define the rights and responsibilities of occupational groups laterally and vertically related in the social division of labour. As a result, struggles over the distribution of income for a 'rightful' share become inevitable. Such cultural meanings or codes are again not directly accessible to observation, but, as with the substantialist strategy, need to be delineated by theoretical concepts, which connect them with those aspects of our direct experience of the world that are puzzling and require some explanation.

Strategies and projects: some problems and objectives

The response to our claim that the four strategies outlined constitute an exhaustive classification of the ways of theorising to be found in sociology, might well be, first, that such an approach oversimplifies the complexity and variation that actually exist in the discipline. Second, and related to the first issue, it could be argued that only a very naïve approach would suggest that the perspectives of individual sociologists, or schools of sociology, were characterised by such 'extreme' resolutions of the problems of the nature of social reality and the genesis of sociological knowledge. Third, there is no doubt that some critics would claim that certain of the strategies we present are not even valid approaches to the construction of a social science, and on that basis should be eliminated altogether from our consideration.

Let us first address the problem of complexity and oversimplification. The fact that we have presented these strategies diagrammatically as four 'boxes' should not be taken to mean that we regard them as four clear-cut, exclusive positions into which we can 'fit' (perhaps with a little pushing) all practising sociologists. We have chosen the term 'strategy' carefully in order to refer to an active, constructive process of theorising in which the alternative resolutions constitute a *field of tensions* rather than established, unmoving positions. Thus, theorising in sociology tends not to be the sole product of one or other of the boxes – empiricism, subjectivism, substantialism, or rationalism – but the product of the field of tensions that operates across the axes of our diagram. The strategies should not, and in fact cannot, be considered fruitfully in isolation one from the other.

While, as we will show, particular theorists or schools of sociology may favour one or other of the strategic resolutions, they do so only on the basis of coping in one sense or another with the issues posed by one or more of the alternative strategies. Each of the strategies is then a dialogue, a mediative process which attempts to cope with the persistent sociological paradoxes that are generated by the alternative solutions: between fact and theory, freedom and determinism, structure and action, meaning and conditions, and so on. Each body of theory that we will consider in the following chapters is, then, a more or less complex attempt to mediate between competing claims, but from the point of view of a *strategic bias*. Our diagram establishes what is being mediated or argued about and provides a means of judging how relatively successful such attempts are at resolving the dilemmas of sociology.

In short, we have no wish to reduce the complexity of sociology to the confines of four strategies. Rather, we argue that the process of diversification has its own structure, including a structure of tensions. We can reproduce the diagram now in a way that illustrates the points made (see Figure 3).

The arrows represent the field of tensions and their associated dilemmas. These tensions are, we will argue, generated by the recognition that alternative strategies make valid claims which need to be taken into account, as well as the fact that each strategy is confronted by its own internal problems which undermine its capacity to construct a stable position in its own terms. There are, then, both pulls and pushes in the interrelations between the strategies, which result in particular theorists 'drifting' from one to another. The strategies are characterised by family relationships of both opposition and affinity; they each share one set of resolutions with an alternative strategy, yet are opposed on other grounds. We will be considering these matters in some detail in the following

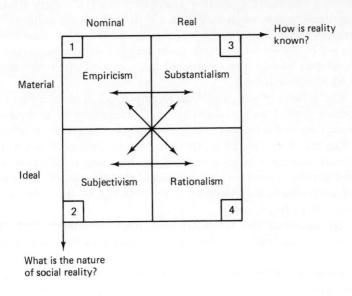

Fig. 3

chapters, but let us briefly illustrate this point about affinity and opposition.

Empiricism, for example, shares with substantialism a commitment to a material world external to, and constraining of, consciousness. Where it parts company with substantialism is in claiming that knowledge of the material world is obtained through observation or sensory experience. Here we can immediately identify a source of *internal* problems which arise out of the contradiction inherent in the statement that knowledge is the product of experience; a claim that cannot be justified through experience – the source of all knowledge. More important, empiricism's claim to produce knowledge of the material world begins to look rather weak, when it is suggested that its generalisations are not about that reality at all but are at best 'fleeting glimpses', conceptually ordered into statements about regularity, with little predictive power. In practice, many who would claim an empiricist pedigree, 'drift' into a substantialism with the claim that their concepts actually do 'grasp' reality; that social class is not a concept, it is a real thing 'out there'. A further source of incoherence within empiricism is the assumption that it is possible, through observation, to record 'neutral' facts. Such a project requires a language for describing such facts that is theory-neutral, a requirement that often results in a drift towards the subjectivist strategy and its concern with language as an interpretative medium. As will be shown in Chapter 2, the strategy of empiricism has often developed into this three-cornered confrontation with substantialism and subjectivism.

The affinity of substantialism to empiricism is balanced by the former sharing with rationalism the commitment to go beyond sense data or the facts in order to identify unobservable structures which are crucial to the explanation of the experienced world. To engage in such a task, substantialism must adopt the rationalist position that knowledge is constructed through theory, while retaining the view that knowledge nevertheless grasps the reality of an external, material reality.

To complete the symmetry and interconnectedness of the strategies, rationalism shares with subjectivism the view that human activity is a symbolic phenomenon. In order to escape from the implications of the view that social reality is entirely made up of personal interpretations or a 'multiplicity of private worlds' – so denying the possibility of sociology – subjectivists have been forced to countenance the idea that while it is individuals who symbolically construct the social, they do so *inter*-subjectively (in relationship to others). Once they admit the existence of 'shared rules', unifying individual subjectivities, subjectivists embark on a path that leads to the rationalist claim that such cultural rules are objective realities actually constraining, and explaining, the interpretative activities of individuals.

The main lines of affinity that can be identified among the strategies of sociological theorising suggest that the alternative approaches tend to cluster around the axis of subjectivism-empiricism-substantialism, on the one hand, and subjectivism-rationalism-substantialism on the other. However, there are also persistent oppositions around which debates have also clustered, namely those arising between empiricism and rationalism, and subjectivism and substantialism. That is, the details of the debates and issues in sociological theorising have typically clustered around the exploration of shared tensions and maximum contradiction. Thus, while empiricism is opposed to all other strategies, it is most opposed to rationalism, and the recent dominance of empiricism in sociology has led to the virtual elimination of rationalist concerns as inadmissible to science. The crucial point to emphasise is that the strategies we identify are not *isolated* resolutions of the fundamental problems of sociological theorising. They are systematically related one to another, thus making the strategic processes of theory much more complex than might have appeared from our initial presentation of the types.

There is a second source of complexity which is of great significance for our argument, and it bears upon the distinction we make between a *theoretical strategy* and a *theoretical project*. The term 'project' is used to indicate that particular sociologists or schools of sociology, in coming to terms with the problems posed by conflicting and affined strategies, construct distinctive projects which incorporate not only their strategic resolutions but their methodological rules, research programmes, substantive analyses, social concerns, etc.

The project is not, therefore, simply reducible to its dominant strategy. In fact, its interest and significance reside in the novelty and fruitfulness of its particular resolutions. The significance of the concept 'project' is that we are not suggesting that sociological theorising is a constant, unchanging process of repetition of the four strategies. The fact that the strategies of project construction remain the same, does not mean that there is 'nothing new under the sun', or that no progress can be achieved in the development of social science.

Marx, for example, rejected Hegelian social theory on grounds of its idealism, from a substantialist point of view. But as we will see in Chapter 4, this did not involve him in merely repeating in a mechanical, 'all of a piece' fashion, the materialism of earlier substantialists such as Feuerbach. He also rejected Feurbach's 'passive' materialism (the notion that human beings adapt to their material environment) while attempting to integrate into his own materialism the 'active' side of idealism, as he called it: the view that men actively construct their own history. Also, while Marx accepted the 'active side' of idealism, he rejected the Hegelian view of society *as a subject* with the powers to act, by drawing upon existing strands of empiricism to argue that it was 'real concrete men' who made history, not an idea. Marx's substantialist strategy was implied in the view that these 'real' men were implicated in structures of material relations (forces and relations of production) whose dynamics set the conditions under which men could or could not make history. The result was that the materialism of Marx was quite unlike previous statements of the materialist view; the project resolution of the strategic problems confronted was both unique and novel.

The two sources of complexity we have identified – relating to strategies and projects – provide a basis for recognising both the diversity and the potentialities for innovation in sociological theorising, while retaining a view of it as a structured process in terms of which such diversity and innovation can be made to make sense.

The third potential objection to our scheme, that certain of the strategies we identify cannot be considered as valid approaches to the construction of social *science*, is itself a view that arises out of the strategic oppositions we have outlined. The rejection of rationalist concerns by social scientists imbued with empiricist assumptions, is a case in point. For example, it is the common fate of rationalists to be branded as 'unscientific', or 'metaphysical', on the grounds that they do not generate testable hypotheses; that is, testable through exposure to empirical facts. The strength of this argument lies in the degree to which the 'commonsense' view of science stresses its grounding in empirical facts. The rationalist strategy, in seeking parallels between the logic of theory and the logic of the social world, stands out against such common cultural beliefs about the nature of science or valid knowledge. The role that rationalism has played, and continues to play, in the development of social theory and 'science' cannot be wished away, however. Nor can we simply ignore the critique of empiricism which is generated within such a strategy. It is our argument, then, that an understanding of the structure of theoretical sociology must give due weight to each of the strategic-projects identified. We will come to the problem of evaluation; of judging the relative adequacy of the strategies and their various projects in our final chapter.

Our project is, then, to provide the student of sociology with a means of coming to terms with the often conflicting perspectives current in sociology, in such a way as to indicate the underlying conditions of unity as well as diversity. Our goal is not to further fuel philosophical and theoretical debate, but to map out the grounds on which choices have been made in social theory; the strategies of research that have been adopted, and the dilemmas that these have generated. It is only through 'making sense' of our heritage – its conditions of unity and diversity – that fruitful new beginnings are possible. Also, we have already argued, through the example of the study of religion, that the particular study of social relations necessarily depends on an explicit or implicit set of assumptions about the nature of social reality and how we can know it. Thus, in bringing into the foreground systematic consideration of the structure of possibilities available to the sociologist we are not merely raising abstract questions for their own sake, but are hoping to clarify the conditions under which the various and particular studies of religion have been and may be carried out.

In attempting to map the conditions of unity in what appears to some as a fatally fragmented, if not chaotic, discipline, we have not sought to 'pull sociology together' from the point of view of one strategy that we prefer. In the chapters that follow we have made the attempt to allow each strategy to 'speak for itself' but not to the exclusion of other points of view, for it is our argument that in seeking to solve identical problems each sociologist must confront, or 'speak to' the alternative options available, even if only to reject them. This does not mean that all sociologists who are engaged in the construction of, say, a subjectivist project, will develop an explicit critique of empiricism or substantialism. Rather, in constructing such a project choices are made which silently exclude alternative resolutions of the issues confronted. Just as in personal interaction, the silences in social analysis are as important in understanding the communication as is the written or spoken word.

This last point brings us to a consideration of our own project or 'bias'. For while we are attempting to allow the various strategies to speak for themselves we cannot, equally, avoid engaging in the process we are describing. That is to say, we are constructing a project ourselves from the point of view of a particular strategy. The outline of our strategy already exists. We have, for example, referred to the 'underlying unity' of the sociological enterprise which 'can be reconstructed'; we have, in the paragraph above, suggested that 'silences' in theory are as important as what is said (i.e. the observables do not tell all). The more clues of this kind we accumulate, the more it is clear that our own choices constitute a *realist* rather than a nominalist location; to speak of an 'underlying structure of unity' or 'silence' predisposes us towards a resolution of the problems confronted which exclude certain major assumptions of the empiricist strategy, and, as we shall see, this also constitutes a rejection of certain subjectivist resolutions. The point we wish to make here is that we are as much constrained by the structure of choices as are the theorists we now go on to consider. In the following chapters, 2 to 5, we set out in more detail the characteristics of the four strategies, and their tensions, and present in some detail the major sociological projects that have been constructed from the point of view of each. We will show how these theoretical projects have attempted to deal with the dilemmas generated by the strategy adopted – by seeking answers from one or other of the alternatives.

2

Empiricism

As with other sociological perspectives considered in this book, the analysis of empiricism takes as a central theme the problem, 'What is social structure?' We have already indicated that this theme can be broken down into two interrelated questions: what is the nature of social reality?; and, how can we know it?

As should be clear from the introductory chapter, sociological answers to these questions cannot help but draw and contribute to arguments that have philosophical implications. Unfortunately, these arguments have all too often become the specialised preserve of philosophers rather than being directly confronted by sociologists. Moreover the degree to which this has been so has been reinforced by the dominance of empiricism in social scientific thinking. As we shall see, empiricism in social science has been marked by an 'anti-philosophical' attitude, which has had the effect of imposing a particular set of hidden assumptions, on sociological theorising. One consequence of this rejection of 'philosophical' issues is that we are forced to go to the empiricist philosophers of science in order to find a discussion of the assumptions underlying the empiricist strategy in sociology.[1] Such philosophy of science is of particular importance for us, as it is there that *positivism* has been most fully developed and refined; that is, the doctrine that the methods of the natural sciences can be transferred, with only minor if any modification, to the social sciences.[2]

The strategy and tensions of empiricism

Our consideration of the empiricist strategy starts with a paradox: namely, that while the solutions to the dilemmas of knowledge are, like those of any other strategy, infused with philosophically relevant arguments, the distinguishing feature of empiricism is its attempt to eradicate all 'philosophical' concerns from sociology (and the sciences generally). Such concerns are either denigrated as 'metaphysical' or are made acceptable by their transformation into technical, 'methodological' problems; a specialist concern of specialist methodologists. As we shall see, the paradox leads to a rejection of 'philosophy' that is just as 'philosophical' or 'metaphysical' as those strategies that are rejected.[3]

At the core of the empiricist strategy is a view of reality as constituted by material things. Knowledge of such reality is seen to be rooted in the sensory experiences that mediate the relations between nervous system and events in the physical world. For the empiricist, then, experience is sensorily based, and knowledge remains tied to these foundations. The concepts and generalisations of science are, therefore, merely shorthand summaries of particular, albeit repeated, observations; that is to say, such statements are *nominal*. Reference to any reality beyond particular observations always involves, for the empiricist, a confusion between general concepts and particular realities; it is a confusion that, it is claimed, characterises all forms of objectivism in the rationalist and substantialist traditions. Empiricism also departs from subjectivist assumptions (see Chapter 3) in suggesting that scientific observations of social reality can be expressed in an objective language; that is, a language that reflects the real world. The two elements of the empiricist strategy constitutes its commitment to *materialism* and *nominalism*.

Classical empiricism (often referred to as 'vulgar' by contemporary social scientists) regards knowledge as the product of observations; often referred to as the process of induction. In modern forms of empiricism this view has to some extent been supplanted, or at least complemented by 'deductivism'. Deductivist strategies suggest that knowledge results from the imaginative insights of the observer controlled by rigorous empirical test. These views constitute only a modification of classical empiricism, as the principles of nominalism and materialism are still adhered to. The imaginative insight must be presented in a logically consistent and empirically testable form: i.e. hypotheses that state what observable events would verify or refute them. Induction and deductivism have, then, constituted the main foundations of empiricism in sociological thinking, ranging from what, on the one hand, has been called 'abstracted empiricism', to holistic functionalism on the other.[4] The strategic assumptions which maintain the basic conditions of empiricism are both dogmatic and essentially unstable, leading to the creation of a proliferating field of tensions within the tradition.

At the centre of empiricism is the view that experience provides the sole and secure source of knowledge. This assumption both eliminates from science all philosophical questions concerning how it is we know reality, and at the same time is itself a debatable philosophical assertion.[5] In empiricism, therefore, science and metaphysics are both connected and *dis*connected. As we have argued, metaphysics are allowed into science in accordance with the rules of empiricism; that is, in a hypothetical testable form; yet once allowed in, such imaginative insights open up empiricism to questions that undermine a strategy based entirely on experience as the sole source of knowledge. As a result, the empiricist strategy is always vulnerable to criticism directed from the alternative strategies, a process that has been particularly marked in sociology during the last decade or so, undermining the pre-eminent position of empiricism in the discipline.[6]

The tensions in empiricism stem from the central part played by experience in the strategy. Two main issues arise, and involve two senses of the term 'objectivity'. First, if concepts are 'shorthand' summaries of experience, then in what sense may we say that concepts refer to entities beyond any particular experience? Projects within empiricism equivocate on this issue because their commitment to the existence of an objective material world, external to the human subject, is undercut by the view that knowledge of the world is confined to what is available in experience. This results in difficulties in sustaining coherent distinctions and connections between experiences, events that are being experienced, and the causal mechanisms that produce such events. Indeed, empiricism's initial commitment to an external objective world (and thus its association with the central concerns of *substantialism* – see Chapter 4) has been whittled away during its historical development from the sixteenth to the twentieth century.[7] The commitment has remained, but not the means necessary to sustain it. As a result, points of contact with the subjectivist strategy have been strengthened.

Second, empiricism suggests that the objectivity or truth of theories is secured through testing them and their competitors against experiences that are themselves theory-neutral and are not, therefore, matters of individual and/or 'uncontrollable' interpretations. Yet as subjectivists have argued, the possibility of describing experience in language that is theory-neutral is itself a matter of dispute in the philosophy of science. Consequently, many empiricists have been forced to accept the idea that reality is never confronted *directly*, but only through agreed conventions as to what reality is taken to be for the purpose of a particular experimental test.[8]

However, empiricist projects in sociological theorising have only fairly recently begun to come to terms with such tensions inherent in the development of their strategy.

Empiricism and positivism

Of central and particular significance for the development of empiricism in sociological theory have been the attempts to transfer natural scientific principles to the study of social reality. This 'positivistic' attitude involves two sets of contentious issues: first, the assertion that the empiricist interpretation of scientific knowledge – namely the construction of laws based on experience – provides an adequate account of the natural sciences; and second, whether natural scientific procedures are in any sense directly applicable to the problem of studying social reality.

Let us clarify what is meant by the term 'positivism'. Positivism is most frequently used to refer to the extension of empiricist models of natural science to the field of human action, by arguing for either a methodological or substantive unity of the two. The claim for methodological unity leads to behaviourism, while the latter implies reductionist explanations, i.e. the explanation of human action in terms of either 'heredity' or 'environment'.

Positivism in sociology is particularly associated with the behaviourist approach to social action. The claim that, unlike natural events, human action is meaningful both to the participants and the observer is rejected by behaviourists, as a ground for radically distinguishing between the natural and social sciences, on the basis of method, for they believe that the 'mental' or 'psychic' components of human action should be translated into behavioural statements; that all the scientific observer can know of human action is the actual behaviour that takes place, and that observable behaviour is as amenable to study by scientific method as any 'objective' natural phenomenon. While the behavioural approach in the social sciences need not necessarily involve the reduction of social action to physical or biological conditions, it is consistent with the view that the methods of all sciences are basically the same, allowing for variations in experimental potential and degree of precision, etc.

The impact of behaviourism in the social sciences is well illustrated by the work of Skinner.[9] His approach rests on the idea that in the scientific analysis of human behaviour all reference to unobservable entities and processes such as mind, motive and imagination, must be eliminated. Such entities are not 'publicly observable'. Indeed, for science, they do not exist. All that can be publicly observed is the behaviour of the human organism under varying conditions or stimuli. The methods used to study human behaviour are, therefore, logically similar to those of the natural sciences.

Skinner goes further in suggesting that the behaviour of all living species may be understood in terms of the same basic primary laws. These may be derived from the experimental study of rats, pigeons, and other relatively simple organisms, and applied to the (only apparently) more complex human activities, such as religious worship, language, human aggression, etc.

The search for such laws of behaviour involves determining the experimental conditions under which particular types of behaviour occur. The model of explanation employed is one of an atomistic chain of stimuli and responses through time, aided by the concept of 'reinforcement'. It has been found that a rat will emit an 'operant response' – for example, press a bar – when such behaviour is rewarded (i.e. reinforced) by a food pellet. Indeed, the bar will continue to be pressed even when such behaviour is no longer immediately rewarded by food pellets, especially when pressing the bar has been so rewarded only occasionally and not at every instance. The rat will try again because the intermittent patterns of reward suggest the 'next time' may well be the *one* producing a reward. (The application of this to 'compulsive' gambling on a fruit machine is fairly obvious.) The strength of the conditioned response (i.e. its persistence after rewards cease) can be measured precisely.

However, the problems of tautology in this scheme seem inescapable. Thus, it is argued, the bar is pressed when no food is presented because such behaviour has been 'reinforced'; yet the opposite

behaviour can be similarly explained by the argument that reinforcement has faded. As we are not told what reinforcement is in
terms other than the pattern of behaviour it produces, the persua-
siveness of the argument rests solely on the *predictive* value of such
experimental techniques.[10] Indeed, rather like shock therapy, such
explanations are supported by the view that they 'work' – i.e.
behaviour can be controlled and calculated – rather than by any
argument as to why they work. The 'strength' of a conditioned
response is thus defined in terms of the persistence of behaviour,
rather than of processes such as 'motive' or 'drive'.

However, of greatest importance in applying such methods to the
social sciences – the application of Skinnerian methods to human
behaviour – is the difficulty entailed in controlling the environment
of a human subject. The experimental method developed in the
study of animals assumes that to control the material environment is
to control the stimuli producing behavioural responses. The major
criticism of Skinnerian technique is that because human subjects are
capable of reflection, of reflecting upon past events and future
possibilities, the material conditions of action in specific experimental conditions do not exhaust the stimuli that may be present for any
particular actor who has the capacity to think beyond the immediate
situation. In short, the explanation of human action must take into
account an interpretative process which is not directly accessible to
such controlled observation.

Abstracted and systematic empiricism: a sociological project

The most evident empiricist project in the social sciences has been
variously termed 'abstracted', 'systematic' empiricism, or simply
'empirical' research; all these terms indicate a stress on observation
in the genesis of knowledge about the social world. Its 'systematic'
character arises from its dependence on statistical techniques in the
search for determinate knowledge. The adjective 'abstracted' was
applied to empiricism by C. Wright Mills in order to focus on what
he saw as the indeterminacy of empiricist knowledge – its atomistic
and trivialising character. However, despite its reliance on observation, empiricism *is* a form of theorising in sociology.[11]

The central features of this project in empiricism are defined by
the way in which the relations between 'theory' and 'data' are

viewed in the research process. The crucial point here is that theoretical concepts are always observationally defined, and theoretical statements of laws or generalisations refer to repeatedly experienced or observed regularities in the 'real' world. For example, class is defined in terms of indices such as income level, or patterns of consumption, attitudes, etc. C. Wright Mills has pointed to some of the important consequences of this view, two of which are of especial significance and involve the issue of 'determinacy'. When the abstracted empiricist refers to some social whole, like an organisation, he does so in terms that are empirical, descriptive statements – what are often referred to as 'variables'. An industrial organisation, then, will be defined in terms of such variables as size, location, product, form of authority structure or management structure, technology, strike rate, etc. Observed variations in these empirical variables provide the framework of the analysis. For example, management structures may vary in accordance with types of technology, or size may be observed to be related to strike rate. Thus, the various factors are observed, measured and correlated, and it is the level of significance of the correlation that provides the explanatory outcome. It is Wright Mills's view that the reduction of such a social entity as an organisation to a set of empirical variables violates its reality as part of a social whole with determinate relations of power and social class, knowledge of which is essential if we are to understand organisational structure. It is an approach to knowledge that is confined to producing indeterminate and descriptive knowledge of social relations.

The indeterminacy of such knowledge is obvious once we realise that any list of variables that is used to describe an organisation can always be added to. It is always possible to 'discover' in the empirical world yet another factor that would 'bear investigation' and may prove to be significantly correlated; for example, we could decide to investigate the types of connection between the industrial organisation and its external environment, such as the relations of its directors to other companies, its market competitors, the community in which it is located, the relations of its workforce to that community, its international relations – the list is unending. It is this characteristic of abstracted empiricism that expresses its commitment to an atomistic model of the social structure. Social reality is construed as an infinite complex of causal relations between events. This view is associated with the more or less explicit argument that sociological theorising will only attain scientificity after a long accumulation of detailed empirical studies, and after the conversion of the 'totalistic' schemes of speculative philosophy into lists of manageable variables. This model of scientific progress and the indeterminate relations between variables indicates the concept of structure that is being employed. Society is an 'emerging' patchwork of relations between variables that science can only ever approximate, albeit more and more closely.

Mills points out that such a project is in strong contrast to one that begins with some determinate model of structure which itself defines the significance of the variables to be examined. He also suggests that no matter how much cumulative observation takes place, as a result of abstracted empiricism the net result will still be an indeterminate patchwork of 'milieus' rather than a determinate model of social structure. The distinction between structure and milieu is useful for our purposes. For example, no matter how many studies of industrial disputes we carry out over time in the same industry or different industries, using such variables as those out-lined above as well as pay, local labour markets, particular conditions of work, etc., we will not arrive at a theory of the capital–labour relation and the significance it gives to the variables in our analysis. Similarly, all the studies of the variables connected with suicides could not cumulatively lead us to the conclusions arrived at in Durkheim's theory of anomie which is rooted in his view of the division of labour in modern society (see Chapter 5). The only 'totality' that will be arrived at is that already presupposed – an open-ended set of variables.

The indeterminacy of this view of sociological theorising is most clearly expressed in its conceptions of causal explanation, and scientific laws and concepts. Systematic empiricism attempts to arrive at its own version of determinacy through a process of systematic observation of a 'sample population' (usually on the basis of questionnaires or responses to structured interview schedules), the resultant data being subjected to techniques of classification, scaling, tabulation, cross-tabulation, and finally tech-niques for determining the statistical significance of the relations so observed. This latter operation serves to underpin any 'causal' explanation that might be tentatively proposed.

The choice of which empirical relations are to be investigated is determined by the traditions and conventions in a particular field of enquiry such as industrial sociology, race relations, stratification etc.; and/or by recourse to 'general sociological theories' which are interpreted as consisting of broad empirical generalisations record-ing past observations of recurrently related events, such as the connection between relative deprivation and delinquency, class location and educational achievement, etc. Once a theory is selected its concepts must be operationalised or observationally defined. For example, Blauner, in his study of alienation in industri-al society, first has to make clear what Marx's 'metaphysical' concept 'means' if it is to refer to events that can be systematically observed and measured.[12] In the event, Blauner concludes that alienation at work refers to four different things: the inability of workers to control the work process; the inability of the worker to develop a sense of purpose in the production process; the failure to become involved in work as a mode of self-expression; an inability to belong to a community. Each of these elements of alienation is then related to measureable behaviour, such as recorded attitudes on the part of the workers in different types of industry. Thus operationalisation involves defining what 'facts' a concept refers to and showing what is involved in observing such facts. This process of operationalisation most clearly reveals the basic tension in empiri-cism which recurs in all of its attempts to provide a model of sociological explanation. The tension arises out of the simultaneous commitment to the existence of objective material reality, and to a method (experience) of knowing that reality which cannot satisfac-torily sustain such a commitment.

The whole point of selecting variables for analysis is to prepare a research area for causal imputation, and it is in the attribution of causes that systematic empiricism encounters serious difficulties, stemming from its simultaneous commitment to the objective social world on the one hand and its stress on the experimental basis of knowledge on the other. In fact, the attempt to overcome the resultant problems has led to a methodological shift, from the search for 'causes' to the measurement of 'correlations', and from a concern with determination to the imputation of 'probability'.

The conditions and consequences of this methodological shift have been detailed by David and Judith Willer, who argue that the origins of systematic empiricism may be found, in large part, in the writings of J. S. Mill.[13] Mill argued that the complexity of the world, or the fact that laws intermeshed in such a way as to make any given object of investigation a complex one, forced the researcher to engage in the methods of similarity and difference, in order to establish which events preceded or succeeded others in time, and thus to formulate causal relations. Later empiricists have rejected this argument, stressing that the complexity of the relations between social variables renders Mill's hope of establishing 'what causes what' in some deterministic way a forlorn one. Rather, they have opted for a position that stresses the 'probabilistic' and tentative nature of social laws or generalisations. They have also objected to Mill's notion that causal relations exist in reality independently of the observer, imposing their reality upon him. They argue that causal relations or 'laws' are the product of the observer's construction on experience: causal imputation is, therefore, a mental operation and is *not given* to experience. This reassertion of the primacy of the observer's calculations, along with the argument concerning complexity, combine to produce a reluctance to refer to causal relations at all. Rather, analysis is dominated by methods fashioned to produce correlations of low and high probability. Claims are neither made for the finality of causal relations nor for their simplicity. The simple claim that a causal relation exists between class position and voting behaviour (for example, working-class people vote for the Labour Party) gives way to a more complex view, that class position is not the only variable involved in patterning voting behaviour; that along with variables such as residence, occupation, local political culture, etc., class position is a variable factor.

Systematic empiricism, then, emphasises its concern for correlations between observables. It seeks a diluted form of causality, namely, an 'acceptable' level of *significance* in the correlation. Also, given that such correlations are products of mental operations rather than an inherent feature of the world, their only necessity derives from the expectation, or *prediction* that they are relations that will recur in the future.

The search for significance in empiricism has the effect, argues C. Wright Mills, of subordinating substantive theory to methodological techniques in the formulation of explanations. Mills argues that the overriding concern for measurement ensures that abstracted empiricism concerns itself only with those aspects of reality that can be processed as observables, and to which correlation tests can be applied. Mills concludes that the actual task of 'finding out' requires little or no imagination; only the mechanical application of statistical techniques. For example, the analysis of suicide and its 'causes' ceases to exist as a significant theoretical problem for the abstracted empiricist. Suicide is merely to be related to a number of factors – religious affiliation, marital status, residence, income, occupation, sex, age, etc. – the list has no logical limits – in order to determine whether the correlation between suicide (the dependent variable) and a selection of these factors (independent variables) are significant or spurious. In this way the analyst will be testing what is called the 'null hypothesis'. That is, the observer starts with the assumption that phenomena are unrelated: that social reality is a set of random, atomistic events. The test of correlation disconfirms the null hypothesis, showing, for example, that suicide is related to marital status at a given level of significance. That is, the relationship cannot be explained by chance. The higher the level of significance the less likely is it a chance correlation.[14]

However, as the Willers argue, the negative conclusion, that the relationship between suicide and marital status is unlikely to be due to chance, does not allow us to make a positive statement that marital status is more significant than any other factor. In order to reach such a conclusion the observer would have to consider *all* other possible variables. The problem always remains that possibly significant variables remain unconsidered.

The rejection of the 'null hypothesis' is typically used as the ground for accepting the 'positive', if provisional, validity of the relationship between social phenomena such as suicide and marital status. Yet the possibility of so doing ultimately depends on some *ad hoc* appeal to, or unstated acceptance of, theoretical ideas which eliminate certain variables from consideration while including others. What, for example, would be the relationship between suicide rate and dream patterns, suicide and participation in sport, suicide and diet. The empiricist methodology has no means of rationally rejecting these factors from consideration, argue the Willers.

The consequences of such limitations on empiricist knowledge is that it is characterised by a high degree of indeterminacy in its attempts to specify the conditions under which social events occur. A further expression of this indeterminacy arises from the fact that knowledge based on experience of the past – i.e. correlations drawn from observations carried out yesterday – has no necessary predictive value. We may *expect* the future to be like the past, but we do so on pragmatic, not rational or scientific grounds. The problem is one of what is sometimes called 'partial vision'. Because human observers are restricted in time and space they cannot know, on the basis of present experience – empirically – what the future holds or what pertains in another place. Only an omniscient god could predict on such a basis. Therefore, argue the Willers, the only basis on which men can *know* the future is on the basis of logic; of rational laws, not empirical generalisations from experience.

The empiricist strategy, then, provides no means of knowing whether our correlations have significance in 'populations' we have not observed, until such time as we repeat the observational research design. It is often argued that the limitation on empiricist knowledge in the social sciences is a result of the ethical restrictions on experimental control. However, if we were to organise research design in such a way that, instead of seeking statistical correlations between an arbitrarily finite number of variables, we *deliberately* manipulate variables in experimental conditions, in the search for significance, as Skinner does, then the problem of determinacy still remains. This is for two main reasons. First, the experiment cannot rationally resolve the question of which variables to exclude from the manipulation, and thus we have no means of knowing whether what it finds 'matches' with what goes on in the 'real' world. Second, participants in such experiments are, despite all their best efforts, never representative, and thus again no grounds are provided for expecting a match between experiment and social world.[15]

The Willers have pinpointed a paradox here. Without the experiment, one is able to get 'closer' to social reality but with no precision; with the experiment, one gains in precision but the scope of knowledge is confined to reporting what one has observed so that extrapolations have little rational basis. Only future observations will prove 'decisive', and they too will take the form of all empiricist knowledge – a description of the immediate past with no grounds for generalisation except on pragmatic grounds.

Hypothetico-deductivism

This recurrent problem of indeterminacy has given rise to an alternative project within the empiricist strategy; a project that specifically rejects the atheoretical stance of 'abstracted' empiricism by attempting to marry the empiricist focus on observation and experience to the requirements of deductive reasoning – a marriage of methodologies known as hypothetico–deductivism. As a tactic within empiricism, it has sought to make rationalist and substantialist theory available to the empiricist analyst in a form that is acceptable to empiricist rules of method. That is to say, it attempts to import the determinacy of deductive reasoning (which depends on the assumption of unvarying, universal relations) into a knowledge system founded on experience (that is open-ended and hypothetical).[16]

Let us consider the implications of this alternative project for the explanation (once again) of suicide rates. Let us begin with a generalisation in the form: 'suicide is significantly related to the extremes of social integration'; i.e. a high level of social integration leads to relatively high rates of suicide (altruistic suicide), and a low level of social integration leads to relatively high rates (egoistic suicide). Hypothetico-deductive procedures suggest that it is possible to derive or deduce from *law-like* statements such as these a whole range of empirical applications, such as: the married person is less likely to commit suicide than the unmarried; self-employed authors are more likely to be characterised by a high suicide rate than members of the priesthood; etc.

The problem of explaining the level of suicide would then be solved as follows. Statements such as 'suicide is significantly related to extremes of social integration' would not only be capable of being broken down (or operationalised) into a large number of 'more concrete', empirical statements, but itself would be derived from a more abstract, more universal statement, such as Durkheim's 'society is a moral order'. In this way each single statement about an event in the empirical world is 'secured' through the possibility of deducing it from some more general statement which is itself deducible from a universal statement or 'law'.

Thus, the suicide rate is not only the outcome of observed regularities at a particular time and place, it is also *necessitated* by deductive logic – the application of laws to empirical situations. The empirical confirmation is a conclusion we would have expected as a necessary implication of the structure of our theoretical propositions. The possibility of securing any empirical observation such as the rate of suicide also requires a series of linked generalisations and deductions. For example, as well as the sociological series relating to society as a moral order and the consequences of its levels of integration, the explanation of suicide also requires socio-psychological generalisations of a kind that would explain not the overall social rate but why certain individuals rather than others within a social category – for example, the unmarried – commit suicide.[17] Despite the contributions of hypothetico-deductivism, this project within the empiricist strategy does not resolve the problem of indeterminacy.

This is because the laws that are invoked in hypothetico-deductive explanations are not statements of necessity but empirical statements. Laws are regarded as tentative statements about what probably will be observed, on the basis of past observations which have confirmed or not confirmed those statements. Suicides, and statements about the conditions under which they take place, are observables. The apparent 'necessity' of hypothetico-deductive explanations, as illustrated in the example of suicide indicated above, derives from the use of formal logic in theory construction rather than a theory of the social totality in terms of which suicide rates make sense. Thus, for example, we may 'explain' the high suicide rate of self-employed artists in urban contexts by deducing this generalisation from a higher-order statement – low social integration is related to high suicide rates. This deduction is a matter of logical necessity, as the statement that low social integration relates to high suicide rates is a generalisation referring to a whole range of observables, of which self-employed artists and other marginal groups are merely examples. Such groups have to have high suicide rates because they are grouped by definition under a high-level empirical generalisation. Yet we have no systematic grounds for accounting for this generalisation in the first place. Indeed hypothetico-deductivism in social theory has been associated with a rejection of all 'holistic' (i.e. substantialist and rationalist) thinking in the social sciences. Patchwork knowledge remains the limited goal of what is actually a restatement of empiricist theorising.

Empiricist tensions

A central theme of this book is that none of the four theoretical strategies identified can be considered in isolation, but rather each must be considered as a set of strategic solutions which determine its relative place in a field of tensions. In initially considering the nature of 'abstracted' or 'systematic' empiricism as a project in sociology we have already identified central tensions in the strategy as a whole which establish the potentiality within empiricism for a drift toward the three alternative strategies.

The principal tension in the empiricist strategy is that if the source of knowledge about social reality is the sense data of experience, any possibility of generating a systematic body of theory about the structure of societies is precluded. The commitment to experience undercuts empiricism's goal of grasping the objective conditions of action; empiricism states a goal that cannot be known. In 'abstracted' empiricism this leads to the generation of an open-ended, indeterminate patchwork of empirical generalisations vainly seeking the status of determinate scientific laws. It is a patchwork in the sense that its open-endedness permits the coexistence of quite disparate and often contradictory bodies of theory within the discipline, providing the resources for piecemeal hypothesising about events. Hypothetico-deductivism does little to displace this patchwork effect; indeed it identifies this practice with the maturation of science and the displacement of 'philosophical' holism in social theory.

The commitment to sense data as the means of validating statements about reality is not only self-contradictory but also creates a second set of problems associated with the impossibility of approaching that reality other than by means of concepts. The empiricist test of a theory assumes some means of describing reality via a theory-neutral observation language. The possibility of so describing such 'neutral facts' as a means of adjudicating between competing theories is an extremely persistent idea in sociology despite the well-rehearsed difficulties that have been shown to attend such an activity. However, even if we accept the possibility of theory-neutral data, empiricism fails in its attempt to use them to describe the objective social world. Empiricism has to admit that concepts cannot be literal representations of the real world – the language we use to describe the objective world is, of course, not the same thing as that reality – they are merely useful ways of organising observations. The concept of class does not, then, represent some *real* condition of men, it is merely a way of organising observations about inequalities, which, for the moment, has some 'pay off'. Such conceptual maps may be ideal-typical in nature; that is to say, they focus on some distinctive feature/s of these observations and represent them in their 'pure', logically consistent form. The 'real' is therefore always an approximation, known by showing how far sets of ideal types depart from what is subsequently observed. Thus even ideal-type methodology presupposes neutral observation languages, while demonstrating that empiricism's goal of describing the objective social world remains an illusion.

Indeed, empiricism's concern to generate knowledge from experience creates a third set of problems; namely the question of whether social structure may be reduced to the activities of and relations between individuals. Empiricism in social theory is associated with what has come to be termed 'methodological individualism'; or the ambiguous principle that social structure possesses 'emergent' properties. Social science uses generic, 'type' concepts to refer to patterns of social action, like church, state, economy, etc. However, these terms are not to be construed as referring to collective actors or to structural mechanisms beyond observation. On the contrary, they are analytical devices for the convenient presentation, and summary, of particular empirical events, i.e. specific, albeit repeated, events. In consequence, all statements about social structure may be translated into statements about typical actors and typical conditions. The ambiguity in this position lies in the problem of how to interpret the notion that in association human beings produce features of social life that are not present when actors are viewed separately – i.e. the problem of structure. The usual response is the concept of *emergence*, which recognises the new level of complexity that group interaction produces, but also suggests that these features of complexity are just as observable as those of individual behaviour. For example, while cashing a cheque presupposes a context of economic (and other) relations in terms of which it makes sense, that context is a complex of interactions which are just as observable as the act of cashing the cheque. Thus the attempt to recognise objective conditions of operation of individual actions is undercut by the empiricist principle of observability. This ensures that the concept of emergence becomes a *technical* device for organising complex relations between myriads of individual actors – denoted by concepts such as 'church' and 'state', rather than a full recognition of the pre-given totality of relations as construed in the rationalist and substantialist traditions. Moreover, methodological individualism may be further radicalised by taking the principle of observability to greater extremes; by reducing social structure to psychological mechanisms, as in Homans's exchange theory.[18] In consequence, empiricist sociology loses all reason for its existence, as social relations may be explained by examining the relations between individual behaviour and material conditions. 'Emergence' and psychological reductionism express the limited range of empiricist concepts of structure in sociological theorising.

Thus, the principle of observability not only renders incoherent empiricism's account of social structure, but is also associated with the denial or marginalising of meaning as a constitutive feature of social life. Empiricism appears to come to terms with 'meaning' as a crucial feature of social life only by dissolving it as a problem, rather than incorporating it into its analysis. On both counts the foundations of sociology as a discipline are undermined. This situation is only rectified to the extent to which dialogue is initiated with the other strategies of theorising.

The Parsonian project

The significance of Parsons for our discussion of empiricism lies in the fact that in the course of the construction of his theoretical project he confronts each of these tensions within empiricism. The solutions he seeks are at the same time attempts to sustain and save the empiricist strategy while recognising and attempting to define its relations with other strategies, particularly subjectivism and rationalism. Parsons is important in so far as he contributes to the clarification of the strategic tensions of empiricism as they express themselves in sociology. Second, like other major theorists he attempts to sustain empiricism through a possible synthesis with elements of the alternative strategies.

From the outset of his studies in the 1930s Parsons was concerned to construct the basis for a coherent and systematic theory of the *social*; a project that necessarily involved a strong attack upon abstracted empiricism. In so doing he hoped to synthesise certain disparate traditions of social theorising, so rejecting what he conceived to be one-sided or reductionist approaches to the specification and analysis of social structure.[19] Parsons was particularly critical of the atomistic, individualistic tendencies of empiricism, while maintaining the empiricist focus on material conditions, and the method of verification as *one* means of theory validation.

In order to demonstrate the convergence of what at first sight appears to be quite disparate forms of sociological theorising, Parsons produced a conceptual scheme in terms of which these theories could be seen as *elements* of a single structure – the structure of social action.[20] Parsons argues that any adequate theory of social action necessarily involves a common structure of conceptual elements; *all* analyses of action, stripped of their peculiar features use this structure, albeit in different ways, and with different emphases; it is a structure that cannot, as it were, be 'thought away'. The basic unit in this common structure is the *unit act*, which, broken down into its constituent elements, is seen to comprise:

1. an *actor*;
2. an *end goal or future state of affairs* toward which the actor *orients* his efforts;
3. the *situation* in which the actor is located, which may itself be subdivided into those elements (ideal or material) that the actor cannot change, but which none the less *condition* action, and those that the actor may use or manipulate as a *means* of realising his ends;
4. *norms* which provide the actor with a mechanism of selection in the orientation toward ends and make possible action as an *ordered* sequence.

According to Parsons this set of analytic elements provides the basic coinage of any theory of action.

Each of the writers considered by Parsons emphasises one element in this set rather than others, but moves to a more satisfactory, inclusive position. In his critique of existing theories of action, however, Parsons distinguishes between the positivistic and idealist forms. Parsons considers first the utilitarian theory of action which arose in the nineteenth century under the influence of the natural sciences. For the Utilitarian (such as Mill and Bentham) action was essentially the *isolated* activity of a *rational* being; the actor was a scientist *manqué* who used scientific method and calculation to relate the means and ends of action in terms of some calculus such as pleasure or pain.

This Utilitarian model of rationality found its classic expression in nineteenth-century political economy. The virtues of such a model lie in the precision and elegance that characterise its theoretical structure—features that offer the emergent discipline of economics both control over data and opportunities for the precise formulation of laws. Second, the focus on rationality was not, in Parsons' view, without a degree of empirical validity.

However there are two serious problems with utilitarian theory. First, its empirical validity is confined to certain types of social activity, most significantly to market-oriented activities. Second, the negative aspect of this limitation is that it fails to consider as significant for action (or at least considers it a marginal or residual problem) non-rational, emotional or value-oriented activities, involving sentiments and ethical positions which cannot be reduced to simple calculations of pleasure and pain. As a theory of action, then, it cannot sustain any claim to be universally relevant, or provide a basis for sociological analysis.

The crucial weakness of Utilitarianism for Parsons is that in focusing on the active choosing features of human social life, the theory cannot satisfactorily explain how it is that the rational calculations of a multiplicity of actors result in ordered social processes. In order to overcome this problem Utilitarians typically resort to unconvincing and metaphysical assumptions of order, such as an 'identity of interests' (illustrated by Smith's concept of the 'hidden hand' in the market), which simply beg the question; or explain social order by reference to hereditary states or adaptation to the physical environment. These attempts to explain social order as a biological condition or a 'natural' order of things Parsons rejects as a form of positivistic reductionism. The result of such reductionism, he argues, is to exclude the very thing that action theory purports to explain – human choice. If our social life is a condition of our human nature then our actions are in no sense the result of choice, they are determined by that human nature. It is also a theory that denigrates the role of values in social action.

While Parsons rejects such positivist theories of action he does not reject the positivist tradition that sought to found social science on the same bases as the natural sciences. What Parsons finds appealing in the radical positivist position, as exemplified in the works of the Social Darwinists as well as Herbert Spencer's evolutionism, are its presuppositions that the social and natural worlds are of such an order that it is both possible and desirable to achieve an objective, scientific body of laws about them. What he rejects in this positivistic tradition is its failure to acknowledge the part that values play in the construction of social order and, consequently, its failure to adequately theorise the conditions of human choice. According to Parsons, then, Utilitarianism is correct to emphasise choice in its model of rational action, but it fails to adequately theorise the conditions of social order; that is, it introduces metaphysical props and instabilities that transform the position into a brand of radical positivism. Radical positivism, while correct in predicating the possibility of a science of the social, undermines such a project by excluding both values and choice from its basic theoretical concerns. Positivistic social science sees man as a creature adapting to the conditions of heredity and environment, rather than as a creative being with the capacity of choice. This, then, is the dilemma that Parsons poses – a science of man in which man constructs his social order and yet is bound by its objective laws.

In contrast to these positivist traditions, idealism does focus on values in the structure of social action; or, as Parsons puts it, on categories that have a *subjective reference*. Actors have the capacity to reflexively take into account the intentions of others in their construction of courses of action. They possess the attribute of consciousness which does not characterise the objects and events studied by the natural sciences. Consequently, social action cannot be reduced to natural science categories. According to Parsons, there are two strands to the idealist tradition (which has its roots in German social thought). First, there are those Hegelian-influenced analyses which conceive of societies as 'meaningful wholes'. This involves arriving at an understanding of a particular social item such as political beliefs, or kinship patterns in terms of its *meaningful context*; a broader cultural pattern of which they are a part. Thus the emergence of the 'nuclear' family in the nineteenth century is understood as a reflection of the growing cultural significance of individualism. Explanation of social events is, in this view, very similar to understanding an aspect of a painting in terms of its place in the meaning of the painting as a whole; or, understanding the painting in terms of a wider tradition or 'meaning'. Second, Parsons considers subjectivist forms of social theory which focus on individual meanings as constitutive of social life.

As with the Positivist traditions, Parsons is both attracted and repelled by the contribution of idealism. First, he applauds the insistence that values are the decisive ingredient of social action, determining how it is that the choices made by actors result in social order rather than random or chaotic events. On the other hand, Parsons recognises the shortcomings of idealism in so far as it is prone to exclude material conditions of action from its analysis, regarding the social as the pure expression or realisation of ideas and value patterns. Not only does idealism tend to ignore the material conditions of action, it also undermines precisely that aspect of the positivist tradition that Parsons is so attached to – the possibility and necessity of a generalised and objective science of the social.

It is a characteristic of both strands in the idealist tradition (see the detailed discussion in Chapters 3 and 5) that they seek to draw a radical distinction between the methodologies of the natural and social sciences. In particular, it is argued, we must recognise the extreme limitations that the subject-matter of the social 'sciences' place on any attempt to generalise or construct laws. Rather, emphasis is placed on the uniqueness of cultural totalities, and of historical events, together with (especially in the Subjectivist tradition) an emphasis on subjective meaning and human will which are seen to pose insuperable obstacles to any generalised analytical theory.

However, Parsons identifies in Max Weber, whose work is in the German idealist tradition, a welcome critique of what he calls idealistic 'emanationism'. Weber's critique involves a focus on the *choosing actor* whose choices are not only guided by values but are constrained by material conditions. Also, Weber is significant for Parsons in his claim that 'generalised analytic theory' of the social world is possible despite the fact that it is a structure of meanings. In the end, however, Parsons regards Weber's position as suffering from the relativism that bedevils idealism. That is to say, Weber does not overcome the problem that a view of the social world as made up of cultural meanings must produce knowledge that is *interpretative* rather than objective in character. Weber's ideal types which are his means of overcoming the problem of the uniqueness of history cannot, Parsons argues, escape the relativity of the historical conditions in which they are developed. However, Parsons argues that this does not mean that all historical knowledge is relative to time and place. Rather, it means that while there are as many different views of an event and its causal antecedents as there are subjective points of view, each view is ultimately subject to the rigours of empirical verification. Thus, for Weber there always remains the link between experience and an objective reality which is the guiding principle of empiricism. Weber's position is one that Parsons is unable to accept because like abstracted empiricism it offers no theoretical determinacy – concepts and theories come and go as subjective points of view vary with time and space: the only constant is the test against reality.

Parsons argues that Weber's ideal types lose their relativism once they are seen in a context provided by the other three theorists, Pareto, Marshall and Durkheim. They then constitute a conceptual scheme which serves as the non-relative basis for social scientific investigation.

Thus, Parsons takes from idealism its stress on values in developing a theory of action which is capable of accounting for social order, but rejects its neglect of material conditions of action and its assertion that the fact that human interaction is meaningful renders an objective social science impossible.

The bulk of *The Structure of Social Action* is an exploration of the ways in which this relationship between values and conditions of action are confronted by Marshall, Pareto, Weber and Durkheim. In Marshall and Pareto, Parsons discovers two theorists who reject the residual status given to non-rational action in positivist action theory. Marshall, in his critique of utilitarianism, and Pareto, in his critique of positivist social science, both stressed the central significance of values in the structure of social action, and in particular rejected the one-sided emphasis on rationality in human action. In Durkheim, Parsons saw a writer whose early positivism was increasingly modified as he came to realise the significance of values in explaining the internalisation of social constraint. Meanwhile, Weber is shown to be of central significance in the Parsonian scheme of things, in so far as he is seen to confront the insights of idealism with the rigours of the positivist tradition; showing the necessary relationship between both *values* and *conditions* in the structure of action, while (at the same time) failing to adequately overcome the problem posed by the claim that the central significance of values in an action theory undermines any consequent claim that action theory can be the basis of a generalised, analytic social science.

From the convergent contributions of each of these writers Parsons distils the basis of his theory of action, which recognises the interdependence and irreducibility of three sets of action elements – the means and conditions of action (those elements in the situation that can be utilised by the actor, as against those that constrain his action); the element of choice in a means/end schema (that all action situations involve choices); and finally, the elements concerning ultimate values (that all action is goal-directed or purposeful).

Each of these elements are irreducible in the sense that they each have an independent effect upon action – one cannot explain the ends of action, i.e. men's goals, by reference to their conditions of action. The ends we pursue are not, for example, biologically determined. Nor does it follow that because we are all constrained by conditions we can do nothing to alter that we have no choice. Central to Parsons's whole project is the claim that actors have the capacity to choose while subject to constraints at the same time. It is the fact that actors have freedom of choice that is the distinguishing characteristic of the subject-matter of the social sciences. It is the fact that men are constrained that makes social science possible.

Each of these irreducible elements of action reflects a major emphasis of each of the traditions Parsons criticises – i.e. positivism, utilitarianism and idealism. Parsons, however, adds a further action element which cuts across all traditions – that of *effort*. It is, he claims, *effort* that binds together all the other elements of action. It is the actor's effort or energy input that is the source of action. Action is not the realisation of values or physical behaviour, because the values are realised and physical activity occurs only through the effort of actors. These convergent theorists have, Parsons argues, allowed him to synthesise the basis of a generalised sociological theory whose principal requirements are that:

1. a theory of action must be constructed in the action frame of reference: that is, human choices and subjective categories are not reducible to material conditions of action;

2. action is only realised through *choices* – the principle of voluntarism;

3. beliefs and material conditions are both independent of yet irreducible to each other;

4. core values are significant to the explanation of how social order between two or more actors is possible;
5. social action involving groups of actors exhibits emergent properties or levels of organisation that are not found at the level of dyadic interaction.

The interrelations between each of these five elements establishes for Parsons the basis of an analytical scheme for the analysis of all social phenomena. As such, it becomes *the* basis of an *objective* sociology. The substantive implications of his voluntaristic theory of action for sociology can only be specified, however, once Parsons has fully explored the implications of point five. The possibility of applying the theory of action to social relations involves the consideration of the emergent properties of aggregations of unit acts, or action systems. Thus, when an actor is considered as one of a number of actors in a complex *system* of action, the group rather than the actor becomes the central focus.[21] Parsons' concern, then, becomes how we move from a specification of the elements of a unit act to the analysis of a complex action system without losing or moving away from the action frame of reference. How do we conceive of social structure from the point of view of action?

This question touches on a number of tensions in the Parsonian project which may be alluded to here and discussed more fully in what follows. First, Parsons is attempting to construct a theory that focuses at one and the same time on the choosing yet constrained actor. Yet in order to account for social order in systems of unit acts he appeals to a common value system which provides the 'answers' to the actor's dilemmas in choosing courses of action in social situations. The choosing actor, therefore, implements existing common values rather than subjectively constructing them; that is, constituting an agency of their transformation. In what sense does such a schema allow for choice, or voluntarism?

Second, if value elements are *decisive* both in the structure of social action and in the processes of social change, what becomes of Parsons's initial opposition to any attempt to give exclusive weight to any of the interdependent elements in the action schema?

Third, how is Parsons to reconcile his commitment to the action frame of reference with his concern to analyse the dynamics of systems of action, including those of whole societies? Even if Parsons can successfully integrate choice and constraint into his theory, how can he analyse societies from the subjective point of view? To the extent that he is successful, the objective properties of social systems surely become nothing more than the emergent properties of courses of action pursued by individual or group actors: the central focus of empiricist sociological theorising. Remaining within the action frame of reference must result in a failure to take into account the rationalist and substantialist theme that social structures involve supra-individual, institutional relations which can in no way be grasped adequately within that perspective. For example, the relationship between the nuclear family and industrial-capitalist economic relations is not a relation between 'choosing yet constrained *actors*', but rather an interdependency between institutions. The interesting point about Parsons is his awareness of these problems. He wishes to overcome them by accommodating the insights of strategies opposed to empiricism; a project that must, inevitably, reveal these instabilities.

Action and system

The shift in Parsons's work from the central concern with action to a focus on systems – that is, the attempt to show the applicability of his theory of action to systems of interrelated acts – involves a whole series of related conceptual and theoretical transformations. For example, the analogy between social science and physics in the early work gives way to the more conventional analogy between biology and sociology, centring on the concept of system. There is a move from the focus on action *processes* (i.e. the analytically separate elements of actions are bound together through an actor's expenditure of effort over time) to *structure*, whereby the frame of reference for sociology is seen to be the elements of action systems structured as patterns of cultural meaning or values. It is this distinction, between process and structure, that provides the foundations for Parsons's structural–functional analysis of social systems and out of which arise the respective schemes of *pattern variables* and *functional prerequisites*.[22]

In developing the structural analysis of action, Parsons distinguishes between two aspects of the action situation: the nature of the objects in the environment facing the actor, and the orientation of the actor to those objects. Both these sets involve the *relationship* of the actor to elements of the action situation, i.e. the subjective referent is included within the basic conceptualisation of structure. The first set of what Parsons calls the pattern variables involves the way in which the actor may regard objects in the social environment – in terms of such characteristics as universalism or particularism or quality and performance. The distinction between universalism and particularism refers to the possibility that an actor may regard an object in terms of criteria that relate it to a 'whole class of objects' or in terms of its 'own peculiar characteristic'. To illustrate this distinction we can contrast the relationship that exists between a shopkeeper and a customer, on the one hand, and a mother and child on the other. A mother will respond to a whole range of unique qualities characterising the child, while the shopkeeper is concerned with only very general characteristics of the customer. Second, an actor may regard an object in terms of its efforts or what it has the capacity to achieve, as against the characteristics it has, independently of such effects or achievements. A contrasting example here would be the employer who recruits labour on the basis of sex or skin colour rather than on the basis of proven capacity, such as that measured by educational qualification.

The second set of structural distinctions outlined by Parsons concerns the attitude an actor has toward an object that is already classified according to the two contrasting sets of qualities discussed above. According to this second set of variables an actor may relate to an object (person or thing) in an emotional way (i.e. affective) or in a self-controlled (affectively neutral) manner. For example, marriage may be entered into as a result of an emotional commitment to another person – what one often refers to as love – or as a result of a contract in which family property is consolidated, or for status reasons. Finally, the actor may relate to objects in a *diffuse* manner, involving a relationship of many strands and dimensions. For example, the mother–child relationship referred to above is likely to be very *diffuse* – mother relating to the child in many ways. On the other hand, the shopkeeper relates to the customer in a highly *specific* manner – it is a single-stranded market relationship. Thus the mother–child relationship is characterised by its *particularism*, and *qualitative* nature; by its *diffuseness* and *affectiveness*. On the other hand, the shopkeeper–customer relationship can best be analysed according to the alternative set of pattern variables: its *universalism* and *performance* and its *specificity* and *affective-neutrality*. The pattern variables arise out of the structure of the unit act: they are the choices available to actors in all situations. At the same time, Parsons argues, they describe elements of all social structures in so far as social structure is made up of actors' past choices which have become stabilised and patterned. Also, once such choices have become stabilised as an action system, a fifth variable, or possibility, arises: that is the possibility of an actor pursuing his own interests (self-orientation) or the wider goals of the collectivity of which he is a part (collectivity-orientation). Parsons suggests, for example, that the social roles of the professional and the businessman vary only in so far as the professional is expected to take the collectivity into account in his work whereas the businessman is expected to pursue his self-interest.

The pattern variables, then, describe patterns of action that endure over time – they are the structural emergents of action. However, in developing his theory of the social system Parsons has to answer a further question. How is it that the processes of action occur so as to produce such structural patterns? In other words, why does action take on *systemic* properties? The simple answer is that human action always involves a relationship with *another*; that action is, therefore, necessarily reciprocal. This reciprocal interaction between Ego (the actor) and Alter (the other) has the characteristics of a system in equilibrium or balance. The relationship between Alter and Ego is one of *double-contingency*, that is, each actor takes into account the other when engaging in action. There is a mutuality which is a condition of action. The contents of such a relation are the expectations that Ego and Alter have of one another; they are, then, the values that are analysable in terms of the pattern variables. Such relations become enduring elements of structure once the choices entered into by the reciprocating actors are stabilised as definite of social roles and institutions, and are internalised by individuals so providing the motivation necessary for the maintenance of institutions such as the family. It is this stabilised pattern of normatively defined relations that is the basis of the emergent social system, which, once in being, has its own *functional requirements*: that is, needs that must be secured if it is to be maintained. Thus, while it is Parsons's view that all sciences use the concept of system, it is only in those sciences concerned with 'living systems' such as biology and sociology that the form of explanation necessary for analysis is functionalist. That is to say, it is in the life sciences that we need to explain why certain patterns of activity persist on the basis of their contribution to the system as a whole. Such functional analysis requires that we know what the needs of a biological organism or a social system are.

Just as in his discussion of structure or the pattern variables Parsons proceeded by cross-classifying two sets of distinction, so in his analysis of functional needs or prerequisites Parsons begins by distinguishing between the 'needs' of a system that arise out of its *internal* and *external* relations and those that arise out of the problems of *means* as against the problems of *ends* or *goals* (the means–end schema which provided the simple action frame re-emerges in the definition of system). The distinctions generate four system requirements or prerequisites: adaptation (external: means), goal attainment (external:ends), pattern-maintenance/ tension management (also known as latency) (internal:means), and integration (internal:ends). These requirements form the basis of Parsons' famous AGIL schema.

Briefly, adaptation involves the need for a system to adjust to its environment, obtaining resources necessary for its own functioning, while providing resources for external systems. All social systems face environmental exigencies, whether they be small groups such as families, social organisations such as business enterprises, or whole societies. In the case of whole societies it is the economic institutions and organisations that fulfil central adaptive functions by converting raw materials into consumable products. Goal Attainment is a peculiar feature of living systems as against inanimate systems, and involves those complex sub-systems of activity associated with defining and executing goals. In the case of whole societies, such functions are carried out by and through major political institutions and organisations such as parliamentary government. Action systems may also be analysed in terms of the need to secure adequately motivated actors (pattern-maintenance), a function performed for whole societies and groups by the family. Finally the maintenance of a system requires the solution of problems relating to internal solidarity and organisation if action in the pursuit of goals or adaptation is to prove successful. The example of religion is interesting here in so far as it may function toward integration or operate as a condition of division.

Thus all social systems may be analysed in such terms, while each sub-system such as the adaptive sub-system may itself be further analysed in terms of the AGIL schema. Thus, the economy may be analysed by identifying *its* adaptive, goal-attaining, integration and pattern-maintaining elements. Such a sub-dividing process of analysis may be taken as far as one's interest directs – a fact that has led to a characterisation of Parsonian analysis as being comprised of an infinite number of fourfold boxes. The flexibility of the AGIL schema is further illustrated by the use that Parsons makes of it in classifying the four systems that are emergent from the elements of the action unit. As well as the emergence of the *social system* of roles which secures the integration of action, there is the *biological system* which serves as the adaptive focus between human life and its external environment; the *personality system* functions as the generator of goal attainment, while the *cultural system* provides value commitments and, therefore, pattern-maintenance.

Thus, through the reinterpretation of the unit act as the condition for emergent systems of action analysable in terms of the pattern variables and the AGIL schema, Parsons establishes structural-functionalism as the theoretical basis of sociology. Parsons' project in achieving this end was to realise his critique of vulgar empiricism ('letting the facts speak for themselves'), and idealism. However, it is in the attempt to link action and system, in the attempt to view all system elements as emergent from complex chains of action units, that the tensions in Parsons's project begin to emerge and the attempt to save empiricism from its vulgar expression breaks down.

Emergent tensions in the Parsonian project

The first of the problems that emerges as Parsons moves from action to system is that the two elements of his system analysis – the pattern variables and the AGIL schema – do not match. For while pattern variables express a choice available to the actor in any situation, the functional prerequisites of action systems dictate that only certain types of action-orientation will successfully meet these system exigencies. For example, Parsons argues that in the adaptive sphere, action-orientations will tend towards the universalistic and specific. In short, the *choice* which is essential for Parsons's voluntarism is curtailed. There is, as one commentator pointed out, a contradiction between the 'variables' which are conceptualised from the standpoint of the actor facing the system, and the AGIL schema in which the reverse is true.[23] The question arises, is it possible to derive from those elements entailed in action, the elements necessary for the analysis of social systems? Parsons's attempt to see the relationship of system-environment as, in principle, derivable from the actor–situation relationship, is, in the end, misconceived. One unacceptable consequence is that the system, with its goals and motivations, is treated by Parsons as though it was an actor. Society becomes equated with an actor. In fact, the only properties enjoyed by a social system which are not present in the unit act are the mechanisms securing social solidarity or integration. According to Parsons the only difference between an actor in his situation and a society in its environment is that a society requires some means of holding itself together: namely, value integration.

A further, and contradictory, consequence of Parsons's inability to match the pattern variable analysis to that of systems analysis is that he is constantly forced into analyses that reduce social system processes to complicated sequences of unit acts (with the emergent problem of securing consistency or consensus). Alternatively, the analysis is posed at the system level; that is, as a set of interrelated constraints between subsystems – a form of analysis that singularly fails even to pose the problem in an actor-relevant fashion. The action/system divide forces the analysis to swing violently from one position to the other. It is interesting to note that both are positions that Parsons rejected in *The Structure of Social Action*.

During his later work, *Societies: Evolutionary and Comparative Perspectives*,[24] Parsons makes what is, in the light of SSA, a startling admission. 'I am', he admits, 'a cultural determinist not a social determinist.'[25] Let us look at what he means by this, and why he, as the theorist of voluntarism, was finally driven to make such an admission.

You will remember from our discussion of the unit act that action is always oriented towards ends. While it is the case that, according to Parsons, actors make choices between alternatives (normative selection), these ends or values exist as part of the situation. The question arises, then, where do these values come from? Parsons's answer emerges as he develops his systems theory. First, as we have seen, each element in the action unit becomes the basis of a system: the physiological processes are the elements of the biological system; psychological processes relate to the personality system; actors' orientations and choices become the elements of the social system; while ends or values make up the content of the cultural system. Each system involves a relatively autonomous set of processes bearing upon action, and each is the focus of a different science of man. Each of these systems also bears a special relationship to the AGIL schema. That is to say, the organism is the primarily adaptive system, while the personality generates goals, the social system comprises the integrative processes, and the cultural system is the source of latency and pattern-maintenance. The significant point for us is that Parsons regard values as emanating not from social processes but from the cultural system.

A further relevant development in Parsons's attempt to overcome the twin evils of materialism and idealism, was his attempt to rank these systems within a cybernetic hierarchy. Such a ranking is based on levels of energy input and information control. Thus, at the bottom of the hierarchy is the biological system which is high in energy input to the action system and low in information. The balance of such inputs systematically changes as we proceed up the hierarchy of personality and social systems, reaching a reverse situation with the cultural system which is regarded as low in energy and high in information (see Figure 4).[26]

The implications of such an analysis of the sub-systems of action are great. Through such a schema Parsons suggests that while action takes place under constraints imposed by the material conditions of the organism and its environment, specific actors' orientations are *directed* by the value system. For example, while all human beings need to eat in order to survive, cultural values operate as a system of control which dictates what is eaten, how it is eaten, with whom, and at what times. In Parsonian systems analysis, then, cultural determinism is secured through the operation of such values in social

High information/Low energy	SUB-SYSTEMS OF ACTION	FUNCTIONAL PRIMACY
	Cultural system	Latency
CYBERNETIC HIERARCHY	Social system	Integration
	Personality system	Goal attainment
	Biological system	Adaptation
Low information/High energy		

Fig. 4

roles and through their internalisation by the actor as need-dispositions. Elements in action that are high in energy and low in information are controlled (determined) by elements that are low in energy and high in information. In effect, one of the foundations of Parsons's voluntarism, the 'will' or 'energy' of the actor, is subordinated to the controlling function of culture. These values have a source outside the social, yet secure the possibility of social integration. Parsons arrives at a position in which, as he asserts, he has become a cultural determinist. The question remains, however, what is the source of these external values?

Parsons agrees with Durkheim that social order is secured by common values and, like Durkheim, he rejects any suggestion that the origins of these values may be found in the particular relations between men – they can be explained neither as 'representative' of society nor 'replications' of society's social arrangements. To view cultural values as having their origins in society would contravene the notion that systems are autonomous yet interdependent. While certain elements of culture are, according to Parsons, socially determined ideologies, the 'directive' values of religion have their source elsewhere. But what does *external* mean in this context?[27]

First, Parsons clearly refers to the source of such values as 'unknowable', and therefore commits himself to the view that they are essentially religious categories – 'ultimate reality', or to put it another way, they are God-given. Second, on occasion he appears to accept Weber's position that values derive from the inspirational qualities of actors; they have their source in charismatic leaders. However, this is a position that cannot coexist with the Durkheimean commitment to a prior common value system. Whatever their origins (and it is clear that Parsons has here moved into an idealist position), whether values *persist* depends upon the degree to which they facilitate adaptation and goal attainment. This functional explanation of why values survive is fundamental to Parsons's analysis of the nature and conditions of social change in society: his 'social evolutionism'.

It is only in his later work that Parsons systematically concerns himself with the problem of change *of* systems as against processes of change *within* systems, and his point of explanatory focus is derived from the problematic relations between the pattern variables and functional prerequisites we have already identified. It will be recalled that Parsons creates problems for his own voluntarism by arguing that the behavioural responses were 'called forth' by functional exigencies. In his analysis of social change, however, he converts this 'problem' into a virtue by arguing that not all such behaviour copes with the functional problems in the same way, and that some responses are more successful than others. In one stroke, then, he recognises historical diversity and accounts for evolutionary development.

Parsons suggests that societies may be placed on an evolutionary scale according to the extent to which they have developed 'generalised adaptive capacities'.[28] The most developed society is the one that is capable of adapting to its problems best. The elements that create this capacity and developmental potential are categorised by Parsons under the master concepts, differentiation and integration, in good Durkheimean fashion. It is these concepts that allow Parsons to describe the process of evolutionary advance of the social system as developments in specialisation and co-ordination of functional tasks. The adaptive capacity of a social system, Parsons argues, is the extent to which a social system can generate specialised and co-ordinative mechanisms to cope with functional problems.

A good example of this point is provided by Smelser's application of the Parsonian schema to the relationships between industrialisation and the family structure.[29] Smelser argues that the development of modern industry poses a challenge to the pre-industrial family structure and its performance of a number of functions; it is simultaneously a co-operative *productive* unit, and an agent of education, socialisation and child-rearing. Modern industry creates strains for the family system in that factory production undermines both the family productive unit and the ability of parents to maintain regular discipline over their children. Locating men, women and children in factories outside of the home undermines the whole basis of the pre-industrial family. As a result there are symptoms of unease, protest and social disorder. However, so Smelser argues, such problems were resolved to the extent that the function of the family became more specialised, with other institutions taking over some of its traditional activities. At the same time, this specialisation of activities encouraged mechanisms of co-ordination, with the result that the same functions continued to be performed but in different institutional locations from before. The family lost its responsibility for the production of goods and for the education and training of its children; these became the responsibility of the newly differentiated institutions of the factory and the school and the co-ordinative activities of the legislative state. The family continued to perform latency functions, and to provide through socialisation the motivation for its members to join the labour market.

Parsons set himself the problem of explaining how simple societies 'break through' to successive stages in the evolutionary process.[30] First, he argued, all *human* societies share certain structured features which give them greater adaptive capacities for controlling their environments than are enjoyed by animal societies or other living systems. These are technology, kinship, religion and language. Each performs a primary role in relation to functional requirements – that is, technology fulfils major adaptation functions; kinship meets latency or pattern maintenance requirements; religion provides the basis for society's cultural goals, whilst language secures the conditions for social integration. By virtue of these *universal* features all human societies are more differentiated than other living systems. That is to say, they have specialised mechanisms such as tools and language which render them more effective in the solution of their problems. The evolutionary development of human societies also involves a radical, historical change in the *balance* or interdependence of the four systems: the biological, personality, social, and cultural systems. Culture, for example, comes to supplant biology as the major adaptive mechanism in such action systems. This is because the evolution of human societies has involved the increasing capacity of culture to operate as a 'collective memory' and knowledge store, allowing for increasingly wide sets of alternatives in their response to functional problems. Thus, science and technology supplant instinct as a structural principle in human societies.

While all human societies have greater adaptive capacity than all other living systems, some human societies have evolved further than others, through the creation of structural innovations of such adaptive significance that Parsons calls them 'evolutionary universals'. The universals represent a functional schema which Parsons derives from combining of Durkheim and Weber's accounts of Western development. Six evolutionary universals are of particular importance. The first is the emergence of a system of cultural legitimacy which goes beyond the integrative capacity of kinship ties. Such mechanisms for generalised political unity include nation-states. Second, a 'well-marked system of social stratification' is a condition for such political developments, enhancing the system's capacity for central decision-making and co-ordination of tasks and, therefore, goal attainments.

The third of these universals is the differentiation of the economy, and in particular the establishment of markets and money as a medium of exchange, so facilitating the mobilisation of resources in the flexible solution of functional problems. One implication of this view is that the capitalist system is more adaptive than any socialist competitor.

Fourth, Parsons reasserts Weber's claims for the greater efficiency of bureaucratic organisation in complex decision-making. Again, echoing Weber, Parsons includes among his universals a universalistic legal code, facilitating the operation and extension of market mechanisms and bureaucracy. Such a code also facilitates flexible responses through the application of abstract rules, so enhancing the rationality of action.

Finally, Parsons includes institutions of political democracy and elective leadership as providing the conditions under which disparate groups may be successfully integrated into a single normative order, such that talent may flow to its most effective organisational location.

By delimiting these universals of structure Parsons is concerned to provide a basis for setting out the main stages of social development by indicating those features that facilitate the 'advance' of human societies. It is, then, the 'universal' function that these cultural features perform in relation to system needs – in particular their adaptive potential – that determines their high survival value. By adopting this functionalist approach to social change Parsons effectively by-passes a central problem for such explanation: what are the *origins* of these cultural patterns which have such adaptive potential? We return to the same problem that we encountered when discussing the dominance of culture in Parsons's systems theory: are they self-determining (Durkheim) or the product of personal inspiration (Weber)? Parsons's answer goes no further than suggesting that because of their functional significance such cultural items are likely to be 'hit upon' by various societies in varying historical circumstances. It is arguments like this that give functionalism a bad name! For what is suggested is that the functional effects of a cultural item like 'democracy' can explain its causal origins; it is a teleological argument.[31] In any event the process of 'hitting upon' remains extremely vague. From the outset, Parsons always tried to counter *reductionism* in sociological theorising, and emphasised the interdependence between the structural elements of action, and later, between the systems comprising the cybernetic hierarchy. While this involves the attempt to transcend the dualism between materialism and idealism, Parsons at the same time wishes to resolve the dilemma between actor and system. He is thus grappling with all four points of tension in empiricism's relation with the other strategies. Both these attempts at synthesis are fused in his 'cultural determinism', in that the directive, 'controlling' character of cultural values is coupled with the argument that the content of actors' orientations is *given* to them by the cultural system.

Yet, as we have seen, the relations between the social and cultural system are conceptualised in an equivocal manner. As is the case with all other system–environment relations, this particular one alternates between a relation between cultural and social institutions, on the one hand, and an actor drawing on cultural resources to confront the meaning of 'ultimate reality', on the other. For all the influence of Durkheim on Parsons, Weber's influence is, in the end, crucial. Indeed it is this that helps to explain why the source of cultural innovations remains obscure, and why Parsons's evolutionism is of a qualified form. As Weber argued in his theory of charisma, sociological theory cannot 'explain' the unique, novel inspirations of an individual as he reacts to and transforms his cultural heritage. This is one reason why Parsons must agree with Weber that it is wrong to suggest a *necessary* direction or 'logic' in social evolution, even though the former's moves towards rationalism and systems theory suggest just such an argument.

Tensions in the Parsonian project and the critical response

It is clear from *Structure of Social Action* onwards that Parsons, while adopting an empiricist strategy, is concerned to resolve the problems of empiricism by confronting and learning from alternative theoretical strategies. However, the synthesis in terms of which Parsons constructs his own project is characterised by an emergent field of tensions which, in the end, undermines the value of his contribution.

As we have already shown, systems theory, constructed on the basis of the biological analogy, in combination with the cybernetic hierarchy, pushes the Parsonian project in the direction of the speculative idealists that he had rejected in *SSA*, revealing a cultural determination in 'the last instance'. The whole direction of the Parsonian attempt to reconstruct empiricism has a number of equally important parallels with the Althusserian reconstruction of Marx. In Parsons, the crucial directive features of social structure (i.e what causes it to change in certain directions) remain obscure except as a general and ambiguous problem of the relations between cultural innovation (idealism) and adaptive effectiveness (materialism). Ironically, the incoherence at the core of Parsons's theory is the old chestnut of the ideal–material duality – in short, the dualism that exists in all empiricist locations remains unresolved.

While Parsons's conception of the social drifts uneasily into the rationalist tradition, his understanding of the processes by which knowledge of the social is attained remains more securely within the parameters of the empiricist strategy. In continuing to argue that sociological knowledge has advanced through conceptual innovation (i.e. cultural innovation) and successively closer approximations to the 'real', Parsons indicates a continued commitment to the view that different theories may be judged according to whether they adequately grasp the facts. As we have argued, such a commitment presupposes the existence of theory-neutral observation language; an assumption that the subjectivist strategy has done so much to erode.

The critical reactions to Parsons's work in Europe and the United States have involved a major attack on precisely those features of his 'system' that indicate his 'drift' from empiricism – that is, Parsons' search for determinacy in sociological theory. The functional prerequisites combined with the cybernetic hierarchy, which insists on the controlling and, thereby, determining role of culture, are the elements through which Parsons imposes a theoretical determinacy on functionalism. The critique of Parsons that was most influential in returning functional analysis securely to the empiricist fold appeared in the writings of Robert K. Merton.

Parsons attempted to establish as a basis for sociological enquiry a set of axioms and necessary relations establishing the parameters of what society is, and can be, in its various forms. In this he established as a problem the question of how the social is to be demarcated from the objects of other sciences. For Parsons the point of science was to establish a determinate system of theory in terms of which any empirical generalisation could be placed and made theoretically sensible – for example, understood in terms of A,G,I or L. These latter are the basic terms of the theory, and their interrelations are known not because we have observed them, but because they 'make sense' and are more coherent than other, prior theories (as we have seen, Parsons does want to argue that they make sense because they adequately grasp the 'real').

Merton's critique argues that a general theory in sociology, in terms of which all 'lower' level generalisations may be understood or derived, while a laudable project, is one that emerges from the cumulative research process rather than through conceptually establishing necessary relations at the outset.[32] Indeed those who argue otherwise support the construction of philosophical systems rather than science. Also, those who take as their model of science the rigour and grandeur of physics fail to realise that between physics and sociology stand 'billions of man-hours of sustained, disciplined and cumulative research'.[33] Thus a great mass of observation is required before the successful development of great and scientific systems of thought are possible. Merton thus warns against premature and speculative theory building; defensible theories are those that relate to particular, substantive areas of sociology such as deviant behaviour, social perception, reference groups, behaviour, etc.

By advocating 'middle range theory', Merton wishes to distance himself from both global theory and empirical generalisations; the latter being characteristic of the 'abstracted empiricism' discussed earlier. He clearly distinguishes between scientific theory and such empirical generalisation. Theory only begins, he argues, when the 'bearing of such uniformities on a set of interrelated propositions is tentatively established'.[34] Further, a scientific law is a statement of invariance derived from a theory, and in terms of which empirical uniformities, such as rates of suicide, make sense. Indeed, Merton uses Durkheim's *Suicide* (and Weber's *Protestant Ethic*) as examples of such middle-range theorising.

While Merton argues that grand theorising, of the kind Parsons engages in, is unscientific because we are not in a position to know *what* limits exist on *what* classes of social activity, it is Parsons's belief that no scientific practice can occur until we specify, theoretically, what these parameters or limits are. The pattern variables and functional prerequisites were constructed precisely to carry out this theoretical task.

Merton's response is an ambiguous, and in the end, contradictory one. He reiterates that scientific laws rest on many years of disciplined observation, gradually accumulating as a series of overlapping hypotheses about substantive areas of social life and standing the tests of time and falsifications.

Nevertheless he concedes that while valid general theory lies at the 'end of the research road', some provisional 'orienting framework' is necessary in the constructive middle-range theories. Merton is aware, then, that theories of the middle range presuppose more general categories and statements. He is able to conclude that, in so far as Parsons admits that his own theoretical framework is not a finished product, but is emergent out of 'islands' of theoretical knowledge (Merton's substantive areas) to form a 'continental land mass' (Merton's general theory), then there is little difference between Parsons and himself.

Merton's claim that the differences are in the end those of emphasis fails to make a stand on the issue of determinacy. For Parsons, such 'islands of theoretical knowledge' merge to form a system of determinate theoretical statements. In Merton's view these islands of 'middle-range' theory comprise (in principle) limitless series of testable hypotheses about different classes of behaviour. It is Parsons's view that the practice of research requires general answers to such questions as: What is society?; What are its conditions of existence? Parsons presents this in his combination of action framework and functional schema.

The equivalent of a general orienting framework in Merton's work is his codification of functional analysis, which effectively removes from functionalism the determinacy that Parsons is at pains to ensure, so condemning middle-range theorising to an endless accumulation of testable hypotheses. According to Merton, middle-range theory construction is to be guided by an orienting framework, or paradigm, of functional analysis. Yet such a framework, on Merton's own admission, is *not* a theory. Merton's sociology always remains at the level of open-ended hypotheses; a further example of what the Willers call 'systematic empiricism'.

Merton suggests that the paradigm of functional analysis provides a basis for cumulative research and cross-reference between various theories of the middle range. The presentation of the paradigm, however, indicates that the guidelines on which middle-range theories are supposed to operate are so broad as to be meaningless.

Merton identifies three central features of functional analysis which in his view require modification in the light of empirical evidence. These are the postulates of functional unity, universal functionalism, and functional indispensability. Each of these ideas invokes the notion of *system functioning*. As a form of explanation developed in biology, functionalism assesses the role of organic processes in so far as they contribute to the maintenance of the organism as a whole. The form of functionalism that is applicable in sociology, according to Merton, is a theoretically much-weakened version, being the process of establishing the consequences of cultural items for the broader structures in which they are implicated. The strong version of functionalism, adopted by the early social anthropologists, which was committed to a view of what the needs of an ongoing society were, and how mechanisms for the realisation of such conditions operated, is, in Merton, diluted into vague descriptive statements. Merton achieves this transformation by converting functional *theory* into a set of procedures or *techniques* of investigation for the establishment of middle-range theory. It is the common empiricist process of replacing theory with method, significance with rigour.

Merton objects to the view that functionalism should involve showing how an institutionalised feature of society contributes to the maintenance of the *whole* system, on the grounds that this idea is more applicable to some societies than others. If, for example, we argue that religion integrates society, this is less likely in highly complex systems in which the integrative effects of religion may be confined to the internal relations of sub-groups whose conflictual relations may elicit system disintegration. Thus Merton argues the item in question may have diverse consequences, both functional and dysfunctional, for individuals, for sub-groups, and for the more inclusive areas of social structure or culture.

> Whether cultural items do uniformly fulfil functions for the society viewed as a system and for all members of the society is presumably an empirical question of fact rather than an axiom ... The unity of society cannot be usefully posited in advance of observation. It is a question of fact not a matter of opinion.[35]

Two points may be emphasised here. First, Merton offers no clue as to what is meant by the social system or society, nor are we offered any idea of its *vital* processes or conditions of existence. Because of this silence, function and dysfunction are rendered *vague* concepts loosely referring to consequences for adaptation and/or equilibrium – terms that are given no theoretical content or meaning. Second, given the slippage of the concept function – it now means consequences for 'equilibrium' – Merton suggests that items may be functional, dysfunctional or non-functional (i.e. irrelevant) for *different* aspects of the social structure. Answers to the questions, 'for what are items functional and dysfunctional?', and 'why are they functional or dysfunctional?', can only be arrived at through observation.

Merton turns next to the idea of universal functionalism, or the notion that any institutionalised social behaviour, if it persists, must be performing some function. He suggests that the same item may be functional, dysfunctional or non-functional for different aspects of the social structure. Thus not every item has 'positive' consequences for the system. Again, 'positive' is devoid of any meaning here, as no theory of system requirements is put forward: function here means *consequence*. Additional *ad hoc* assumptions are also introduced. Thus Merton introduces the assumption that persistent cultural items have a net balance of functional consequences either for the society considered as a unit, or for sub-groups sufficiently powerful to retain these forms intact by means of direct coercion or indirect persuasion. Again positive and negative consequences are matters for observation, as no theory is presented that will give theoretic pertinence to what one will observe. On the contrary, what is offered is a number of 'tips' that will help the observer observe the seamless web of social life; that is, be aware that some items disrupt some aspects of social life but have the reverse effect on others – precisely how is a matter for observation.

Finally, Merton turns to the idea of 'indispensability', or the suggestion that either a particular structure is vital to the meeting of one or other functional requirements of a social system, or that certain functions have to be performed (by a range of structures). For example, either the 'family' is essential for social reproduction, or reproduction is essential for society and may be realised by a variety of structures including the 'family' or 'communes', etc. Leaving aside the important question of what the functional needs or prerequisites of social systems are, Merton argues that the same prerequisites may be met by *alternative* structures, though the range of alternatives will be limited in a given case by structural constraints.

Thus, for example, if it is admitted that societies require a value system for their integration, this may be realised by quite different values, in different periods of history, and in different types of society. The problem with this suggestion is that no indication is given as to the range of equivalents in different types of society; again it is purely a matter of empirical investigation. Of central significance is Merton's avoidance of the issue of system needs: what are the requirements and/or conditions of existence of society? When he does face the issue – the lynchpin of any functional analysis worth the name – Merton admits that it 'remains one of the cloudiest and empirically most debatable concepts in functional theory', and there it is left.[36]

What Merton means by function, then, are the consequences that specific elements of culture or structure may have for various group interests or wants (to be empirically determined), or disruptive effects on some system or system part (not defined). By replacing the theoretical commitments of earlier functional analysis with a series of claims suggesting that societies are empirically variable, Merton dissolves its theoretical pertinence, blunts its theoretical cutting edge. Symbolising the emptiness of what remains, is his assertion that when dysfunctions outweigh functions there will be pressure for system change. As Merton provides no means of weighing anything, what is offered is an empty formula of a commonsensical kind.

As a result of his codification of functional analysis, Merton endows middle-range theory construction with a set of sensitising techniques of social investigation, but with nothing in the way of ideas as to what society and its conditions of existence are. Such a position involves a contradiction: middle-range theory is guided by an idea of *system* and of scientific theory whose very indeterminacy ensures that society will be understood as a never-ending seamless web of open-ended relations between endless 'items' of culture. In Merton's critique of Parsons, empiricism returns with a vengeance, and the old empiricist idea that science involves the abandonment of *a priori* speculation reveals itself as a contradiction. Empiricism merely supplants one *a priori* with another, asserting it with at least equal dogmatism. In Merton we return full circle to the logic of systematic empiricism, reviewed earlier, and as a result he presents only the shell rather than the substance of functionalist theory which Parsons at least attempted to construct.

Conclusion

Merton's critique of Parsonian structural functionalism illustrates the tensions of empiricism in operation. Methodological techniques and piecemeal generalisations, set in a purely descriptive framework of concepts, are substituted for the necessary statements of relations which characterise scientific explanations.

The significance of Parsonian theory and the main reason for preferring it to Merton's 'codification', or the similar 'cleansing' operation performed by Kingsley Davis, lies in the former's attempt to give systematic answers to the questions of what society is, what are the possible forms it can take, and what are the mechanisms whereby society changes from one type to another. Merton's re-statement of what is in effect a quite vulgar empiricism involves the implication that all theoretical statements may be overturned by subsequent observations, and are revealed as simple summaries of what has been observed in the past. Davis illustrates further the difficulties in empiricism, and again, with Merton, he celebrates them as the virtues of a mature science!

Davis[37] argues that functionalism is synonymous with sociological analysis, in that any theorising of the social (except abstracted empiricism, the validity of which is dismissed) presupposes the method of showing how elements of social structure are interrelated, and the employment of the concept of system in spelling out such relations. Because functionalism addresses these tasks it cannot be viewed as a peculiar or 'special method in sociology and anthropology'.

Davis's argument is specious; his review of functionalism excludes all its distinctive and controversial features, particularly reference to system needs or requirements, and the primacy given – particularly in Parsonian sociology – to value elements in sociological explanations. Indeed, as we have seen, it is precisely these features that constitute functionalism as an advance on the limitations of empiricist description as celebrated by Merton and Davis. The latter do little other than to elaborate on common sense, and thus render science as unnecessary or irrelevant to our knowledge of the social. As Hempel and others have argued, unless system needs or requirements are specified clearly, and the problems of teleology avoided, functionalism is confined to obscurantism and/or vague description.[38]

While the projects constructed by Merton and Parsons depart from each other in regard to the levels of necessity and systemacity given to the statements derived from them, Parsons directly confronts the contributions of rationalism and substantialism in seeking to go beyond observation. Parsonian theory provides not 'conjectures' to be refuted by future observations, but systematic statements which are the conditions of any observation, and tell us what we cannot observe. As a result, a truly generalised body of theory becomes available, and renders illusory the idea that such knowledge will be the result of 'billions of man hours of observation'. Nevertheless, Parsons does not break completely with empiricism, and therefore both he and Merton provide different projects within the strategy of empiricism.

Merton's 'empty functionalism' and Parsonian theory both remain committed to the idea that theory may be validated by a reality that is independent of theory, and may be so described in theory-neutral observations. While this view is presented in a rather trite way in Merton's argument – it does not indicate any awareness of the importance of conventionalism in empiricism, as is evident in Popper's work from the outset – Parsons's position, not surprisingly, is more aware of the difficulties associated with it.[39] Parsons argues that the structure of social action, and later, the pattern variables and functional scheme, are not ideal types or useful fictions (subjectivism) nor generalisations from experience (empiricism). Furthermore, they are not to be understood as 'timeless essences', which make redundant any subsequent work of observation (as in some rationalist and substantialist speculations). Rather he suggests that while these concepts do represent universal, constant features of human action, the particular values or contents they have vary historically, and are problems of empirical research. In addition these schemes do not exhaust reality; they are analytical; other schemes used by other sciences – for example, economics and politics – are not precluded. Statements about such universals are a precondition of scientific observation. Without them one remains trapped in empiricist 'open-ended' description; without observation one remains committed to speculative philosophy.

But it is just this point about statements of universals that Merton and others have diluted and misrepresented. As a result they redirected sociological enquiry back into the paths of abstracted empiricism from which Parsons sought to depart in the first place.

Parsons's 'analytical realism' – the view that the universal elements grasp aspects of the real – also shows the extent to which the break with empiricism is never achieved. Parsons construes his own theory as one more step in the cumulative 'unpeeling' of the social world, so that as a result of generations of observation and conceptual innovations the social world is finally laid bare. The echo of empiricism's original claim that science elaborates on our common-sense experience of what is 'there' is unmistakable.

The popularity of Merton's codification of functional analysis expressed the possibility of a working relationship between abstracted empiricism and middle-range theory and the general condemnation of 'grand theory'. The Mertonian plea for islands of middle-range theory as stepping-stones to grand theory continues to provide what justification there is for the fragmentation of sociological analysis into various specialist areas, and the constitution of methodology as a theory-neutral area for the genesis of techniques of enquiry. The breakdown of empiricism is potentially camouflaged by giving its critics their own specialism, 'sociological theory', though this has not prevented all specialisms from becoming areas of theoretical dispute.

Merton's project has been given further philosophical support by those drawing on Popper's conception of science. The contributions of rationalism and substantialism are broken down into manageable hypotheses which are then subjected to piecemeal tests of refutation. Such contributions, once treated in this manner, lose their original global significance and are trivialised by being converted into tentative generalisations about interrelated variables, as in Dahrendorf's and Banks's tests of Marx,[40] and the numerous attempts to test Durkheim's theory of suicide.

In addition, empiricism's commitment to theory-neutral observation, while still of some significance, has been to a large (and belated) extent supplanted by more pragmatic, conventionalist arguments. Thus the validation of theory presupposes acceptance of other theories as background 'truths', a technique that is a matter of pragmatic agreement between observers. Empirical reality is therefore *never* confronted directly. This procedure is often reinforced by the traditional empiricist 'fall-back' argument that theories are valid not just because they reflect the real world, but also because they 'work', or predict events which then make them amenable to human control and manipulation. Such an argument, when allied with conventionalism, involves a break with empiricism, as it involves an arbitrary conception of truth and must shed doubt on any notion of knowledge as a cumulative process of development. This is exactly the point of dispute in the famous Popper–Kuhn debate.[41]

Indeed, these points illustrate the re-emergence of one of the central tensions within empiricism; the attempt to base knowledge on experience establishes a contact with subjectivism in *its* collapsing of the distinctions between experience, events, and structural mechanisms. Empiricism's acceptance of conventionalist arguments has played no small part in the general ascendancy of subjectivism in sociological enquiry, and it is to this strategy of theorising that we now turn.

3
Subjectivism

This chapter examines subjectivism as a strategy in social theory. However, subjectivism should be viewed in terms of a dialogue with the competing strategies, discussed in other chapters. This is because a number of strategic tensions arise out of subjectivism's resolution of the problems of the nature of social reality and the way we acquire knowledge about it, which force it to confront these other strategies of theorising. The strategy of subjectivism together with its tensions will be outlined briefly before examining in detail a number of attempts to construct theoretical projects which have been inspired by subjectivist arguments.

While subjectivism shares with empiricism the view that knowledge is founded in human experience of the world, as a strategy it departs from empiricism in claiming that the defining characteristic of human experience is that it is a constructive, interpretative process, which constructs the *known* world. What the world is for a human being is not a set of material conditions which *cause* the behaviour of a biological organism. Rather, human behaviour depends upon how individuals interpret the conditions in which they find themselves. Hunger, pain and anger in the human world cannot be described without investigating how individuals use language and symbols to construct what such states *mean for them*. For it is only by understanding the individual experience of subjective interpretation that we will understand why human beings behave in the way they do; why, for instance, thresholds of pain, attitudes to death, and so on, differ so markedly from person to person, and from culture to culture.

Human beings 'act' rather than behave because, unlike objects such as machines, they can use their capacities to symbolise –

perfected by the acquisition of language – to construct plans in their imagination and use them as a basis to select a course of action. In addition, this symbolic capacity allows human beings to monitor their activities – to change their minds and to alter their plans in ways that physical objects and machines simply cannot do. Moreover, no other animal appears to have developed such a level of symbolic communication as would allow this pattern of specifically human 'reaction' to the world. Consciousness and 'reflexivity' – the capacity to reflect upon what one is doing at the same time as doing it, knowing that one could do something else but *choosing* not to – separates the human actor from the machine and other objects in the natural world.

'Society', then, is not a set of natural conditions as a result of which observed patterns of behaviour occur, but is a complex of socially constructed meanings. It is comprised of the ideas and interpretations that human actors hold about it. To discover these meanings requires an investigation of individuals' subjective interpretations. Yet, as we shall see, this task is not as easy as it might seem, and attempts to carry it out reveal two crucial tensions in the subjectivist strategy which may be outlined briefly here.

If human actors construct the meaning of the social world, are we free to construct any meanings we desire in any way we choose, or is it the case that we only construct meanings by following a set of shared rules or procedures? The answer to this question is crucial for the strategy of subjectivism. For if we admit the notion of shared rules – the idea that the meaning of the social world is structured in such a way as to limit the free creativity of subjective interpretation – then we move towards the strategy of rationalism, according to which just such a pre-existing structure of rules provides the basis for subjective interpretations rather than being an emergent outcome of them.

If, on the other hand, we avoid this drift to rationalism, then we face the difficult task of grasping the meaning of individuals' subjective experience without imposing our own interpretations on it. For example, if 'suicide' is a meaning, socially constructed in part by the victim, how can we ensure that we accurately describe his or her motives rather than our own interpretations? The inherent weakness and tension in this second version of the subjectivist strategy is that it is finally forced into the sterility of the claim that all knowledge is locked in the head of each individual – we can know nothing outside *ourselves* (i.e. solipsism). All subjectivist sociologies are, therefore, driven into a compromise position, between the *rule-governed* and *creative* interpretative process. Theoretical projects constructed from the point of view of a subjectivist strategy involve, then, a set of theoretical tensions which straddle these alternative solutions and constitute drifts towards rationalism, on the one hand, and solipsism (the denial of sociology), on the other.[1]

The second major theoretical issue arises from the view that human life is situated within a symbolic context. The issue is that of the relationship between 'subject' and 'object'. Subjectivist sociologies stress that human action flows from subjective intentions and that social structure is, therefore, a subjectively based accomplishment. The social order is not a pre-given material structure, nor a determining normative system of rules. It is, rather, a continually emerging texture of meanings produced by individual human actors. However, the fact that both participants in, and professional observers of, the social world find it necessary or convenient to treat it as though it were a pre-given order 'out there', involves the fallacy of treating a subjective product as an objective thing (i.e. reification), so masking the *real* source of the social order – ourselves (this argument is relevant to the Marxist concept, 'alienation' – see Chapter 4). Nevertheless, each subjectivist project is faced with the problem of identifying the sphere of objective reality, once it is accepted that reality is made up of more than subjects, that some*thing* exists outside the minds that know it.

An influential point at which to begin a discussion of the subject/object relationship is in the work of the phenomenologist Edmund Husserl, whose critique of reified thinking in science has provided a fertile source of ideas for the construction of subjectivist projects in social science.

Objectivity and subjectivity

Husserl's phenomenology should be seen in the context of the massive expansion of applied and pure science that accompanied the development of industrial capitalism in the nineteenth century.[2] In particular, it involved a rejection of the dominant positivistic view of the nature and function of science, which regarded as relatively unproblematic the extension of scientific method to the explanation of human action. For our purposes positivism may be understood as an intellectual and political tradition which has sought to ground all sciences in empiricist foundations: to denigrate other types of knowledge that could not be assimilated to this form (for example, religion and metaphysics), and to ensure that policy-making by the state was guided by scientific experts from which it was hoped peace, prosperity and social progress would flow. Positivism stressed the methodological similarities between the 'natural' and 'human' sciences, claiming that human action could be viewed as *objective* events, subject to the same or similar laws that had been discovered in the physical sciences. These laws were founded on sense data as a result of confirmatory or negative test. This positivist philosophy of science divorced scientific practice from ethics and political value judgements, which were regarded as statements of an essentially non-empirical kind, and thus matters of subjective and arbitrary opinion rather than objective science.

Husserl's critique of positivism developed in his later works suggests that such views unconsciously distort and undermine the proper function of the sciences in the modern world. The resultant 'crisis of the sciences' has, according to Husserl, two related aspects. First, the conception of science as value-neutral is unconscious of the human purposes to which science is put, and so abandons the proper ethical subordination of science to human reason. Second, the positivist or objectivist conceptions of the nature of reality and of scientific method are guilty of the fundamental error of confusing their conceptions or ideas of reality with reality itself. For example, those who use the concept 'social class' in order to make sense of their world, mistakenly believe that the concept 'social class' is part of a concrete reality. This is the sin of reification or, in Whitehead's words, 'misplaced concreteness'.[3] In order to avoid this error Husserl's phenomenology changes the question that science poses. Rather than asking what reality *is*, phenomenology poses the questions: how does reality come to be constituted by mental operations as a known object?; how do we go about constructing our ideas of what reality is? The first question, 'what is reality?', involves a logical nonsense, claims Husserl. It assumes that we can *know* about the existence of a material reality in advance of *thinking* about it. For example, the theory of evolution explains the emergence of 'consciousness' as an outcome of material changes, but we can only *know* this to be the case through the constitutive operations of consciousness. That is, we can only know of a world of non-consciousness (i.e. non-human) *through* consciousness. Without consciousness there can be no known world. Thus, argues Husserl, statements about objective external reality can never escape the confines of human consciousness. The central implication of phenomenology is, then, that the acts of knowing *and* the objects that are known are products of human consciousness. They are both, therefore, products of human intentionality.

That supposedly objective structures are in fact the product of the constituting operations of active human subjects, is the main theme of subjectivist theory in the social sciences. In so far as the subjectivist strategy in sociology follows the Husserlian project it also involves an exercise in consciousness-raising and radical doubt with respect to the 'taken for granted' ways in which we look at the world and our place in it. In particular, there is the basis for a developed critique of conventional sociology which, by treating the social world as made up of objective phenomena, effectively abandons the central function of a possible sociology – that is, to reveal the subjective operations through which our understanding of the objective world is constructed. The phenomenological project also has the ethical function of returning to 'positivist humanity' the human capacities of reason and intentionality.

Husserl's phenomenology does not, however, involve a denial of a world prior to consciousness. Rather, it entails a suspension of belief in such pre-given objectivities, so that we may focus upon the way in which we come to know them, through our subjective activities – *nothing* can be assumed or taken for granted. In effect, Husserl conflates our original problems of knowledge. The distinction between the questions, 'What is the nature of reality?' and 'How do we know it?' is, for Husserl, an unreal distinction, because the way we know reality constitutes what it is. To follow Husserl's argument through, by outlining the methods that he adduced in order to reveal the essential subjectivity of the world, would take us too far from our primary task of considering the subjectivist strategy in sociology. Rather, we will now consider its various projects in sociology with the knowledge that various elements of the Husserlian project inform them. In particular, we turn to Max Weber, Schutz, and the ethnomethodologists.

The Weberian project

Elements of Husserlian phenomenology have come to influence sociology through a number of routes: directly, through the attempts of Schutz to apply phenomenology to the problems of the social sciences, and indirectly through the Husserlian influence on the Frankfurt School of critical theory and what have become known as the phenomenological marxists (see Chapter 4). Central to each of these projects has been the Husserlian contention that the sciences should be founded in the 'constitutive operations' of the subject, a strategy that would confront all forms of objectivism, reification and alienation in the social sciences.

Schutz embarked upon a phenomenological social science by way of a critique of what he regarded as the major attempt in classical theory to construct sociology from a subjectivist point of view: the methodological work of Max Weber. As in Schutz's own work (see pp. 94-100 below), Weber's subjectivism is characterised by two distinct but related ways of viewing the emergent properties of social structure. Weber accepts the subjectivist proposition that the subject-matter of social science is not given to the observer in any direct fashion, but results from the scientist's *interpretative selection*: that is, his own 'constitutive operations'. In addition, social phenomena are not themselves 'finished productions', objectively existing, but are in a continual process of being produced and reproduced by the interpretative activities of social actors. For Weber, then, structure is an emergent property; it emerges out of the doings of human subjects and the conceptualisations of professional observers.

Two sets of methodological distinctions are utilised by Weber in order to distinguish the social sciences from the natural sciences. First of all, he distinguished between the two on the basis of the different properties of their subject-matter: inanimate nature on the one hand, and mental and spiritual life on the other. The natural sciences may, in attempting to explain the relations between 'things', use theory and observation to generate *causal laws*, so calculating the regular occurrence of physical events. While Weber considers that causal laws are not, in principle, impossible in the social sciences, these sciences have what he regards as an additional advantage – that is, of being able to penetrate historical events through an *understanding* of their meaning; by discovering the human intentions lying behind such events. Weber's point is that social and historical events have 'authors' – intentional participants, who, because they are similar to ourselves, allow for the possibility of *understanding*. This procedure, which Weber refers to as *Verstehen*, is denied to us in our attempts to gain knowledge of the natural world.

The second distinction used by Weber, which does not entirely coincide with the natural/social distinction, is based, not on any inherent property of scientific objects, but on the type of abstraction or frame of reference that may be brought to bear on the phenomenal worlds of men and nature. In general, these frames of reference are of two kinds: the *individualising*, which involves a focus on the unique, concrete aspects of phenomena, or the *generalising*, which seeks to establish the regular law-like relationships between phenomena. That these two forms of abstraction are not meant by Weber to refer to the natural-science/social-science distinction is clear in so far as he considered psychology to be a generalising science. Nevertheless the cultural or social sciences are seen to be primarily the study of those unique processes through which social reality is constructed. There is no distinction in Weber, between individualising history and generalising sociology. They are part of the same intellectual project.

It is within these broad subjectivist parameters that Weber critically confronted a number of objectivist traditions in the German cultural sciences – particularly the substantialism of Marx and the rationalism of the Hegelian tradition. He constructed a project, however, poised precariously between subjectivism and empiricism, continually drifting in one or other of these directions.

The historical observer

For Weber all reality, including the social world, comprises an infinite flux of events over time and in space. It is a reality that defies any final, exhaustive description or summary, allowing only for incomplete and partial accounts which abstract from that reality in a number of different ways. All knowledge, he argues, involves both selection and abstraction even where the knowledge results from studies concerned with the details of concrete historical events. The form of abstraction that is used is not determined by the fact that the research is being carried out by a sociologist or historian or even physicist, but is determined by the nature of the research problem confronted. Thus, both 'generalising' and 'individualising' abstractions are used by all sciences. It is, then, the way in which these methods relate to one another rather than their distinctiveness that is important in understanding the scientific process. A significant aspect of this relationship as far as Weber's conception of sociology is concerned is the link between abstraction and values. For Weber rejects the empiricist assumption that generalisations about history refer to objective events that are reflected in the senses of detached observers. It is Weber's contention that the events about which we generalise are the product of value-selection by human beings. For example, the study of the history of a particular economic organisation or institution, such as production relations within the weaving industry, already presupposes such generalising concepts as *economic* and *industry* without which the study could not proceed. The possibility of abstracting such a particular process from the myriad events of history is a product of the selectivity of human beings who thereby endow their study with particular cultural significance. In short, it is a value-laden process. Social scientists, then, like all human subjects, endow events with meaning and it is only once they have generalised on such a basis that any causal analysis is possible. Causal statements in social science are, according to Weber, impossible without value orientations.

Weber does attempt, however, to maintain a distinction between value orientation, which involves determining the significance of historical events as worthy of study, and value judgements, which entail committing oneself to a positive or negative moral evaluation of the events themselves. Value orientation appears to operate at a number of levels, incorporating the values of a culture (what is deemed significant or otherwise), the values of a discipline such as sociology, and the values of the observer such as a sociologist.[4] The implications of this position include the view that what is conceived of as historical reality changes as a result of cultural change, and that the field of knowledge in social science changes with the historical process itself. Weber's position departs radically from the positivist view that social science is a linear, cumulative process. Far from value orientation creating a subjective barrier to the acquisition of valid historical knowledge, it is the indispensable means of acquiring any historical knowledge at all.

In committing himself to the view that our socio-historical knowledge is *created* by the social scientist in a cultural context of shifting values, Weber comes up against one of the major problems of the subjectivist strategy. What prevents the constitutive operations of subjectivity from merely inventing history? Surely, there is nothing to stop us making up nice *histories* which accord with our own values? It is at this point that the major tension in Weber's project arises. The constraints on story-telling are a set of procedures that Weber derives from a broadly empiricist strategy, and these lay the foundations of what emerges as an unstable synthesis of subjectivism and empiricism.

Let us briefly consider these procedures. It is through value orientation that the social scientist constitutes his object of study – he selectively detaches a set of events from the totality of history. In this process the scientist must further refine his concepts through abstraction; that is to say, certain distinguishing features of the phenomenon or set of events are selected as its most important characteristics from a particular point of view. It is this process of abstraction that involves the construction of an ideal type. The purpose of the ideal type is not to explain or even to describe social reality but to *prepare* abstracted historical individuals or configurations for causal explanation. They are 'conceptual utopias' through which we may analyse social reality by examining the precise extent to which reality approximates to or departs from their pure form. Thus, one can construct an ideal type of the protestant ethic by conceptually arranging certain traits actually found in an unclear, impure form in various protestant beliefs into a consistent ideal-construct which accentuates its essential tendencies. From that point on, historical research involves determining in each case the extent to which this ideal-construct approximates to or diverges from reality; to what extent are its features found in Calvinism, Methodism, etc.

However, while conceptual constructs in social science derive from subjective points of view,

> In the mode of their *use* ... the investigator is obviously bound by the norms of our thought just as much here as elsewhere. For scientific truth is precisely what is *valid* for all who seek the truth.[5]

What Weber has in mind here are the canons of logical consistency, care in the use of evidence, and publication of sources, which are the institutionalised bases of all scientific knowledge. At the same time, however, he suggests that without a prior value commitment the validity of the social science project cannot be defended. Thus, while we cannot sustain the empiricist belief that reality is reflected in our concepts, nevertheless an ideal type that is merely the 'creation of fantasy', remote from objective possibility, will be of little use in empirical research.

The ideal type is central to Weber's attempt at causal analysis. He poses the question: what mental operations do we perform when we argue that one event is causally more important than another in determining a particular historical outcome. Weber draws on the example of the battle of Marathon between the Greeks and Persians, suggesting that the significance of the battle lies in the contention that it probably was significant in dertermining the subsequent course of Western history.[6] He is careful to point out that this does not mean that Western history would have been totally different had the battle not occurred, but that it would have been significantly different. Again, 'significant' in this context means in relation to certain selected aspects (via abstraction) of particular cultural events. Thus Marathon was significant in relation to the causal origins of aspects of Hellenistic culture which characterise the political and other institutions of modern Western Europe. How the battle is causally imputed as a 'significant event' involves the creation of ideal-type courses of events through what Weber terms 'thought experiments'. In the case of Marathon, its causal significance derives from the probability that if the outcome of the battle had been a Persian victory, then our knowledge of the ways in which Persians acted in relation to other subjugated peoples would suggest that certain aspects of Hellenistic culture would have been weakened in ways that might well have affected the course of Western history 'significantly'. The general implication of this argument is that the estimation of causal significance rests upon the construction of ideal types of alternative possibilities or counter-factuals. This is the meaning of Weber's view that in respect of both the conceptualisation of events and their causal explanation we must create unreal events in order to study real ones.

An uneasy synthesis between subjectivism and empiricism emerges in Weber's work. This is the product of a form of analysis which although based on the constituting operations of subjectivity, achieves 'objectivity' as a result of the operation of the canons of scientific method rather than a direct confrontation with empirical reality. Weberian methodology never allows the observer to encounter the empirical world directly – the traditional hope of the empiricist. Rather it provides the observer with a means of estimating the extent to which his unreal idealisations have grasped aspects of events, through systematic historical research. The problem remains, however, that while Weber is aware that history is not comprised of pre-given data but is constituted by the historian, he sometimes does appear to countenance the possibility of directly confronting 'real events'.

Weber regards the relations between ideal types and concrete reality as including the possibility that items within an ideal type will reflect aspects of reality. For example, when studying belief systems such as Calvinism, in so far as various aspects of such beliefs are explicitly formulated by a religious thinker or organisation, they may be drawn on directly in forming ideal-typical constructs by the observer. Thus our *own* conceptual imaginations in forming ideal types are heightened to the extent to which the main principles of an ideology 'have either only very imperfectly or not at all been raised to the level of explicit consciousness, or at least not have taken the form of explicitly elaborated complexes of ideas'.[7]

The problems and strains that emerge in Weber's work as a result of this tension between the dual strategies of subjectivism and empiricism become the starting-point of the critique of Weber's project developed by the more thoroughgoing subjectivism of phenomenology. Weber's debts to empiricism are expressed in two aspects of his methodology. First, they are expressed in his argument that the procedures of scientific verification and the logic of historical explanation prevent a drift into subjectivist fantasy. Second, his nominalist position involves the claim that value-selection and abstraction create one-sided models of social events which can provide useful tools of analysis, but that these should not be mistaken for reality. This ideal-typical procedure can be applied to particular types of social relation, such as charismatic authority. It can be applied to holistic models of social structure, such as 'rational bourgeois capitalism', and it can even be applied to developmental schemes, such as the 'rationalisation of the West'. But in all cases he presents us with 'conceptual utopias' devised by the investigator for specific purposes. Such a procedure involves an absolute rejection of the view that these concepts refer to some underlying reality of history; thus it is a rejection of any Marxist developmentalism which conceives of real societies developing through feudalism, capitalism and socialism. There are no 'key factors' of history. In short, there is no way in which social reality could be deduced from the conceptual models we apply to it.

Subjectivity and social life

In Weber's methodology, then, social structure is always constituted through the ideal types of the historical observer. However, the raw materials of these types – historical events – are not equivalent to the events studied by the natural sciences; they are meaningful. They arise out of the courses of social action undertaken by individual human subjects. Weber's analysis of historical events as social actions, and of structures emerging from courses of action, provides a further context for his synthesis of the disparate sociological traditions of subjectivism and empiricism. Just as the historical observer engages in subjective selection from the events of history, so those events are made up of actors' interpretations and meanings. In the social sciences, therefore, the observer enters into a meaningful dialogue with the subject-matter itself. It is an interpretative process. However, Weber's debt to empiricism remains, in so far as his view of history as made up of meaningful acts is modified by the claim that such social acts take place under conditions of scarcity, and that interpretation of meaning cannot be dissociated from the empirical observation of human *behaviour*. Through such claims Weber distances himself from the pure subjectivism that was to be taken up by phenomenology.

Weberian interpretative sociology is, therefore, rooted not simply in the constitutive operations of the observer but in the relationship between these operations and the meaningful acts he is attempting to explain. The possibility of an 'objective' analysis of these subjective meanings lies in Weber's conception of the instrumental rationality of human action – its means–end character – which is present, he argues, in a heightened form in modern capitalist societies, dominated as they are by technical reason.[8] For Weber, the act of understanding action presupposes the investigator's ability to place meanings in context: that is, contexts that are sufficiently close to the observer's own way of thinking to make sense. It is in modern 'rational' societies, where instrumental action is transparent to the observer's understanding, that Weber's ideal types are of especial explanatory significance.

Crucial to the process of understanding is the fact that human action is motivated. Such motivations are potentially objects of self-consciousness – we are able to reflect on why we and others act in particular ways – and this consciousness provides a basis for the systematic analysis of action in the form of chains or interconnected systems of practical reasoning. Implicit in this concept of action is the actor's capacity to choose between various means in order to achieve given ends. It is this possibility of human choice that, for Weber, explains the basis of human 'free will', and explains why human action is never fully determined, and why history is an open-ended sequence of events – human behaviour is not reducible to the material conditions of action. However, far from such free-dom of action leading to the conclusion that human action is not amenable to the logic of scientific rationality or calculation, Weber claims the reverse is the case, for the motivated means–end charac-ter of action links it indissolubly with rationality and calculability. The very texture of our commonsense understanding of social relationships depends on the concept of rational action, which is, in turn, a condition of orderly social existence, including the planning of one's actions in relation to others.

The means–end character of action makes it susceptible to ideal-type analysis, argues Weber, and he distinguishes four basic types of action, although only two are clearly genuine examples of rationality as he understands the term.[9] First, *purposive rational action* involves the self-conscious assessment of the probable out-comes of a number of strategies available to the actor, in terms of some calculus of costs and benefits. Second, *value-rational action* involves the single-minded pursuit of a paramount goal no matter what the consequences for other goals, which are, therefore, margi-nal with respect to the organisation of an actor's resources. Both types are regarded as rational because they involve conscious planning of the use of resources in pursuit of ends. It must be remembered here that the availability of resources is important for Weber's analysis, for his interpretative sociology is firmly rooted in a context of the scarcity of material and cultural resources. Action is always conceived of, therefore, as occurring within variable resource contexts such as 'life-chances' in relation to a market, a context that informs his analysis of class action.

The other two types of action are marginal to the concept of rationality and are not, therefore, strictly speaking, types of action at all. Weber's type of *traditional action* refers to an unthinking obedience to the demands of custom or habit. It is marginal because its 'unthinkingness' renders it opaque to an observer who wishes to make it an object of his understanding. It is an orientation to social norms rather than a process of practical reasoning. Finally, *affectual action*, which is even more marginal to rationality, involves a behavioural response to emotive states. Such action can be simply illustrated by contrasting a 'blink' with a 'wink'. Depending on the social context, a wink may be part of a chain of purposive or value-rational actions; it may denote an informal understanding in the course of a business meeting or initiate a sexual encounter; whereas a blink does not involve such social significance, except where it is misinterpreted.

Concrete actions are constituted by complex combinations of these ideal types, and this confronts Weber with the problem of how we are to use the ideal type in the analysis of such reality. Part of this problem involves, for Weber, relating the 'direct' subjective meaning of action to a broader context of meaning. By 'direct understanding' Weber refers to the immediate comprehension of an action, such as understanding a grimace of pain, or understanding that the numerical calculation $2 \times 2 = 4$. Such meanings may be further understood by placing them in a broader context in which their performance makes sense. For example, the grimace of pain may be meaningful within the context of a legally regulated system of corporal punishment, while the numerical calculation may have significance within the context of capitalist accounting procedures such as double-entry book-keeping.

Weber's notion of direct understanding here, raises again the main tension in his work – the attempt to synthesise subjectivism and empiricism. Weber grapples with the difficult problem of how the meaning of an action can be grasped without at the same time understanding the context in which it *makes* sense. Weber's attempt to combine empiricist procedures with interpretative understanding in this case appears to lead to the empiricist conclusion that meaning can be *first* directly observed and then contextualised. As we shall see below, a fully subjectivist strategy would stand on the principle that all meaning is contextual and that any departure from such a principle involves a collapse into empiricist error.

A second problem relating to the use of the ideal types of action is how they can be used in the *explanation* of a course of action. In effect, how does Weber adjudicate between competing plausible accounts of the 'real' meaning of a course of action? While, for Weber, the reasons actors give for their actions are an important component of the causal analysis of such action, there is no principled reason why these actors' accounts should be preferred to those of the observer's interpretation. For just as Weber argues that inequalities in the distribution of means are a constraint upon the realisation of meaningful acts, so too does he emphasise that actors are often unaware of the 'real' reason for their actions. On the other hand, actions that appear to an observer to be identical may have quite different meanings from the point of view of the actors. Also, motives and meanings may be mixed complexly in respect of particular courses of action. How, then, can the observer be reasonably sure that his account is an adequate one?

Weber offers two related procedures: adequacy at the level of reasoning, and causal adequacy.[10] Given the constraints imposed by our own position in historical space and time, he suggests that we may grasp meaning adequately at the first level if we are able to reconstruct the *rules* of, or 'ways of going about', the activity that interests us. The construction of these rules will involve repeated recourse to examples in order to finally grasp a typical complex of meanings: i.e. we must repeatedly observe the rules in operation. The limitation on such a procedure is that certain 'rules' will escape us if they are beyond 'our habitual modes of thought and feeling'.

Causal adequacy refers to establishing the conditions under which a particular course of conduct or action will or will not actually take place. If we take the example of 'shooting in self-defence', using Weberian procedures, we would first develop a set of criteria or rules through a process of repeated observation, so generating a typical meaning complex of 'self defence'. The determination of causal adequacy would once again involve placing this ideal type within a broader context, say the political and military situation in Northern Ireland, and considering the conditions that led to the person with the gun using it under specified circumstances.

Of central interest here is that Weber comes to the conclusion that meaning and motive can only in the end be determined adequately by recourse to the empirical, 'objective' events which are its context; the meaning can be found in the field of response or behaviour. The whole interpretative superstructure is undercut by recourse to direct empirical observation of the facts, as the procedure that clinches the determination of adequacy. Indeed, some critics have suggested that Weber's methodological concern with meaning and motive is best thought of as rather an elaborate means of generating useful hypotheses from which the observer can derive probabilistic statements about behaviour which are then subject to empirical test.[11] Such interpretations of Weber have the paradoxical consequence of marginalising the whole concern with meaning; it is no longer a distinguishing feature of the subject-matter of social science. Weber invites such interpretation of his work by seeking to make the analysis of motive as 'objective' as possible. Nevertheless, as we have seen, his central concern with the subjective nature of the social world would lead him to reject such interpretations.

Weber's attempt to construct a theoretical project that integrates a subjectivist view of social reality with a methodology constituting that reality as the subject-matter of an 'objective' science, is in the end indecisive. His efforts to place meaningful action in a context that includes the material conditions of action, lead to a conception of causal adequacy that would be regarded as unexceptional as a statement of empiricist epistemology. The case for subjectivism is undermined by Weber himself.

This drift toward objectivism does not, however, lead Weber to subordinate the meaningful act to *material* conditions of life; a feature of Marxist analysis that he rejected. For Weber, meanings were never to be conceived of as disembodied 'cultural values' but were accounts embodied in practical material life. What Weber sought to eradicate was a materialism which reduced ideas and values to a reflection of the material conditions of social existence. In his sociology of religion, for example, he was at pains to stress the association between material conditions and religious attachment, while also stressing the contingent character of that relationship.[12] He posits a connection between 'this worldly' ascetic religious beliefs and the conditions of life of an emergent, urban bourgeoisie. Protestant beliefs, he argued, provided a meaningful framework which had an affinity with the material position of these proto-capitalist businessmen and manufacturers. However, not all such groups turn to such a form of religious belief as the appropriate symbolic expression of their material position; nor is it possible to deduce the existence of such beliefs from a knowledge of their material conditions. The affinity between beliefs and their material conditions is, therefore, in part, a *creative* process in which specific groups seek out meaningful explanations for their lives. The beliefs themselves are not spontaneously generated by the situation but have their own history of determinations, often arising in quite other contexts.

Weber, then, focusses on the interplay of meaning and conditions of action, and the concrete, contingent nature of that relation. In stressing that the properties of social structure are emergent out of concrete and contingent historical situations, Weber wishes to emphasise the creative aspect of human action. In this, Weber rejects any rationalist view of meaning as residing in 'mind' or 'culture' and expressing itself as a universal structure of rules. He would, therefore, reject the very possibility of completely describing the semantic structure of a language according to some analytical schema. The meaning-relations between words are not fixed by objective rules in some final way, but are the outcome of the genuinely creative activities of individuals in changing historical circumstances. Weber does not deny the structural properties of meaning; rather he suggests that these are emergent from the relations between actors in an historical process, which itself offers genuine opportunities for creative action.

Weber's attachment to such a view arises substantively in his work in the concept of charisma.[13] He defines charisma in terms of the way in which the personal qualities of an individual may be seen by others as in some way exceptional or even supernatural. Such qualities exist so long as the person concerned can sustain a belief in them among his followers. Weber argues that charisma can operate as a revolutionary force in human affairs, in so far as the charismatic individual is able to inspire his followers to break with established routines and in so doing found novel normative orders not on the basis of instrumental calculation but of moral inspiration. While suggesting that there are general preconditions for such charismatic eruptions, it follows that the emergence of a new normative order from such a source cannot be deduced from any structural theory of history or developmental scheme, neither of which can recognise the specific significance of a charismatic break with the past. In consequence such developmental schemes may only have a heuristic value for Weber, for history has no determinate structure other than that imposed on it by such schemes for the purposes of analysis. The concept of charisma is, then, a reminder that history is the contingent outcome of actors' interpretations and is not susceptible to explanation in terms of 'laws of development'.

Weber's analysis presents itself as a continuous attempt to establish an empirically contingent relationship between types of action, specified through a process of abstraction and selection, and actual, concrete courses of action. This process is clearly illustrated by his account of the relationship between class position and action.[14] The starting-point for Weber's analysis of class is the distribution of life-chances in the market. He employs the term 'class situation' as applying to the probability that a given state of (a) provision with goods, (b) external conditions of life, and (c) subjective satisfactions or frustrations, will be possessed by an individual or group. A class is, then, a group of persons whose shared life-chances cluster in terms of the differential distribution of chances or exploitable market chances, and on the basis of personal and social ties, over the course of several generations. Certain typical social actions may flow from such structural locations but these are contingent and not necessary effects – the actions of actual class actors are not predictable. As Weber argues:

> ... the concept of class interest is an ambiguous one as soon as one understands by it something other than the factual direction of interests following with a certain probability for a certain average of those people subjected to the class situation. The class situation and other circumstances remaining the same, the direction in which the individual worker, for instance, is likely to pursue his interests may vary widely ... The emergence of an association or even of more social action from a common class situation is by no means a universal phenomenon.[15]

Class situations are, then, positions upon which coherent class actions may be based, but the specific forms of these actions can in no way be deduced from a concept of class and its 'real interests' as is the case in some of the Marxist formulations to which Weber objected. The indeterminacy of the view that there are as many class situations as there are clusters of life-chances is reinforced by Weber's commitment to historical research founded in value orientations. The analyst may choose to focus on certain class situations and actions rather than others, because of their significance for a particular historical problem. Also, in an examination of the concepts of group, class, and interests, Weber rejects the 'misuse' of all collective concepts whereby the capacity to act is attributed to a collectivity. The individual, he argues, is the 'sole bearer of meaningful conduct'. The observer may legitimately focus on class interests only in so far as they are closely specified by the analytical constraints of a particular research problem, and only then if we remain aware of the great whirlpool of antagonistic and contradictory value relations which actually characterise concrete situations.

For Weber, social reality is 'doubly created' by the constructions of the historical observer's shifting value orientations and the meaningful acts of historical actors under conditions of scarcity. The nature of, and constraints on, social action can only be known from one-sided points of view. Such constraints (for example, the 'iron cage' of bureaucratised systems of domination in modern capitalism with its associated ethos of 'disenchantment' and instrumental rationality) relate to Weber's particular interpretation of history from the standpoint of the values of Western individualism, to which he subscribed and which he also regarded as under threat in the modern world.[16] For all Weber's emphasis on, and analysis of, objective institutional structures in his work, this objectivism – the tendency toward substantialism and rationalism – is undercut by his subjectivist understanding of the basis of social structure (rooted in social action) and sociological knowledge (value orientation and ideal types).

Indeed, Weber's historical sociology only escapes from the charge that it is no more than story-telling by subscribing to empiricist canons of proof and demonstration; in particular by drawing on John Stuart Mill's conception of causal explanation in science (as in the example of the battle of Marathon). Yet these canons are not seen as reflections of reality, but as values; a belief in which is a precondition for scientific work. A subjective and evaluative rather than a rational basis is given as a *raison d'être* for science. In addition Weber is not content with the empiricist concept of historical 'facts' – 'interpretation-free' data – yet we have seen he countenances such an idea in discussing how ideal types connect with reality, and more generally in his idea of 'direct understanding' of, for example, a grimace of pain.

Weber's subjectivism, the belief that social reality is the double creation of historical observer and actor, can and has been criticised from the point of view of the very subjectivist strategy in which his analysis is rooted. When Weber establishes his rules for the observer, and an analysis of social action that supposes that actors attach meaning to what they do, he takes for granted that the social world is *there* for both the observer and actor. He says little about how actors actually sustain the sense of an objective world 'out there'; what procedures they use. In addition, Weber presumes that the observer is outside such procedures, and can therefore devote his energies to constructing historical methodologies without enquiring how he *too*, along with everyone else, sustains a sense of that objective social world. It is Weber's failure to recognise the significance of such procedures for the construction of a subjectivist project that led to Schutz's critique of Weber; a critique that drew upon the arguments that Husserl had marshalled in rejecting all forms of objectivist social science.

Schutz: phenomenology, sociology and subjectivity

The significance of Schutz's critique of Weber lies in the fact that it identifies the central tension in Weber's project as arising out of his attempt to construct an observer's methodology for the objective analysis of subjective meaning. While applauding Weber in his effort to identify the source of emergent social structures in the subjective motives of individual actors, Schutz argues that Weber's project founders because he fails to understand the implications of the fact that the observer's categories are themselves a purely subjective construction.

Weber's methodology presupposes an *existing* complex of meaningful acts which constitute the social world and its roots in motivated action as 'out there' to be studied. For Schutz, then, Weber's *verstehen* methodology is not simply a technical method of sociological investigation. Rather, this process of understanding is the very fabric of social life; the process through which we all constitute the social world as a meaningful object. *Verstehen* is not a method of social science; it is what social science should be studying.

While rejecting Weber's drift toward objectivism, Schutz, in attempting to construct a fully subjectivist social science, does not follow Husserl into a consideration of the constitutive operations of a transcendental ego – a path which would lead away from social science as a possibility – but poses the question: What general processes must all empirical egos perform for the social world to be constituted as 'there'? The transcendental ego is replaced by the 'actor'.

Schutz's analysis is predicated on the view that the 'objectivity' of social structure is an emergent property of these constitutive subjective processes. Rather than following Weber in examining the material and cultural conditions under which concrete meanings are or are not realised in history, Schutz focuses his project on the problem of how human subjects use language and interpretative procedures in indicating to themselves that others exist; in accounting for the very existence of the social world. Social structure is not conceived of as an external constraint but as one of the ways in which we interpret our experience and then take it for granted.

In developing his argument Schutz distances himself further from Weber's 'objectivism'. First, he rejects Weber's distinction between meanings and the events to which they are attached. For Schutz, the meaning *is* the event, and action is a meaningful process. Schutz also rejects the simple notion of 'intended' meaning on which Weber bases his analysis of action. Meaning is a complex system located in a subject's consciousness of 'lived-time' as a 'being-in-the-world'. Meaning does not inhere in particular experiences or events, but in the succession of 'I' perspectives that we bring to bear on them. The meaning of our experience is, then, constituted by the reflective 'glances' we make at our flow of consciousness. It is this personal history of interpretative processes that gives meaning to present experience, and constitutes the subject's 'project'.[17]

When we act, argues Schutz, we project an imagined act into the future; we imagine the completion of our project before it takes place. This projection involves a complex process which is merely masked by Weber's notion of attaching meaning to behaviour. Meaningful action he distinguishes from behaviour by viewing it as an interpretative process. The experience of pain may be 'undergone', or 'felt', or 'fought'; it is not mere response but an interpretative response.

For Weber, the unity of an action is either obvious (direct understanding), or is given by taking into account the broader context; the meaning of action derives from the observer's analysis of the likely motives of an actor within certain historical circumstances. For Schutz, Weber merely assumes the context of meaning and imposes observer's categories on what is a completed series of subjective processes. Schutz wishes to eradicate from the analysis all references to 'conditions of action' and 'contexts of meaning' which are not themselves integrated into the process of interpretative, subjective experience. Such concepts operate to objectify what are the emergent properties of intentional acts. The idea of unconsciousness is also rejected as contradictory 'since in our view experience implies consciousness'.[18]

Schutz's starting-point, therefore, is the solitary ego's experience, and the description and explanation of action refers only to the conscious, attentive glances of the ego in its 'map-readings' of the past, present and future, as these are constituted not in some external, historical circumstance, but within the flow of subjective experience. The break with Weber's attempt to apply objectivist methodology to subjective experience is complete. However, in order to go beyond the solitary ego, and to construct a phenomenological project in social science, Schutz must take his analysis further. He must take account of inter-subjectivity – the existence of a social world – and he must do so without drifting into empiricism as, he argues, Weber does.

In order to achieve this goal he poses the question: what operations does this intentional ego have to perform in order to become aware that others, and wider social realities exist for it? This is not to be construed as a conventional sociological question in the form, 'how does the social world mould the personality of the individual?' Rather, it is a phenomenological question: what does consciousness (of the ego) have to do in order to ensure that the social world that we 'naturally' take to be there, can be constituted as an object?

Schutz enters into analysis of the social world through a primary assumption: that all egos constitute the social world in experience in similar ways. We can, he argues, deduce this to be the case from 'what we know to be the case' – i.e. inter-subjectivity is an experienced phenomenon. We consciously constitute the social world in similar ways because the social world is experienced as being made up of other consciousnesses.

Superimposed on the primary processes of subjective constitution are the products of this intersubjectivity, such as linguistic forms and expressions and 'typifications' or shared meanings, and it is these that allow us to constitute an objective world. The subjective roots of these typifications may be, for all practical purposes, ignored. Thus, objective meanings may be thought of as forms of linguistic usage and meanings that can be understood independently of particular subjective intentions. Their immediate roots lie in a way of life or language community in which such meanings make sense. While it may be shown that the game of cricket has its roots in subjective intentions, this has little relevance in the attempt to understand its meaning in England today. Nevertheless, Schutz would continue to stress the subjective status of such meanings in contrast to the Durkheimian concept of 'social facts' (see Chapter 5). The significance of objective meanings lies totally within the ego's attentiveness to present, past and future experiences. Such shared meanings constitute resources used creatively and attentively rather than constraining and often unacknowledged (unconscious) conditions of action.

According to Schutz, the transition from subjective experience to the constitution of the social world is facilitated by the 'we relation' or the direct experiential encounter with, and accounting for the existence of, another ego. This 'encounter of the second kind' is the prototype of all conceptualisations of social relations, generating the resources necessary for the ego's subjective constitution of the structure of the social world. The ego's constitution of the immediate presence of another (the 'thou' relationship) becomes a 'we' relationship in so far as there is generated a 'mutuality of recognition'. This mutuality or sharing of experience does not, he suggests, involve an identity of experience, but a co-ordination of experience:

the two positions are face-to-face, their streams of consciousness are synchronized and geared into each other, each immediately affects the other ... the two motives validating each other as objects of reciprocal attention.[19]

And again:

It is only from the face-to-face relationship, from the common lived experience in the *we* [relationship] that the intersubjective world can be constituted.[20]

It is at this point of his analysis that Schutz attempts to construct the basis of a subjectivist project in sociology. It is through this merging of individual consciousnesses that the social world comes into being. Social reality is conceived of as an inter-subjective construction, but the subject creates the 'other' and the social world as an object to himself. The objectivity of the social world is, therefore, a product of subjective experience, not an external, constraining reality. It is also at this point that the central tension in Schutz's analysis arises; for there is a crucial equivocation in his analysis of inter-subjectivity which stems from his attempt to synthesise Husserlian-inspired phenomenology and sociology.

In order to go beyond Husserl's principled phenomenological position that the consciousness of the ego is *all*, Schutz must posit the existence of other egos, but the 'other' has no existential status. That is to say, the other ego exists only in so far as it is constituted through ego's own consciousness. The attempt to move from subjective processes to the existence of an objective world on the basis of a presumed inter-subjectivity, collapses because the other does not actually exist; it is merely an outcome of ego's consciousness. This is the price of rejecting the notion that a material world external to consciousness can be known to exist, a price that Weber, for one, was not prepared to pay. Schutz's attempt to construct a subjectivist project in sociology collapses back into a purely phenomenological one. He attempts what Husserl rejected as an impossibility – to get outside of consciousness through the medium of consciousness.

The weakness of inter-subjectivity as a springboard into the social world is clearer as Schutz extends his analysis to ego's constitution of more distant 'others' in time and space – from 'we' to 'they'. Schutz describes this transition as a movement from the subjective meaning context to a series of 'highly complex and systematically interrelated *objective* meaning contexts'.[21] These typifications are social resources available to the subject in the 'map-reading' of its experience of the social world; the related-to world of contemporaries, predecessors, and future generations. While it might be argued that these typifications are necessarily external to the subject, Schutz argues that they are only meaningful in so far as they become part of the subjective processes; are reflected upon by individuals in terms of their projects and interests. Also, he argues that such resources are ideal types. Thus, ideal-typical construction is not, as Weber argued, a method of social science, but the very basis of all inter-subjective constitution of the social world.

Schutz's attempt to go beyond Weber by clarifying and elaborating on processes of subjectivity, as *the* strategic commitment of sociology, has the effect of imposing severe limits on the role of the observer. While Schutz is prepared to accept the detachment of the social scientist and agrees with Weber that sociology should be concerned with ideal-typical forms of action, he is not prepared to countenance that such constructs are merely part of the descriptive and explanatory tools of the observer – they are the tools of all actors in accounting for their worlds.

For Schutz, then, the observer loses his privileged position. The observer's 'right' to theorise unacknowledged conditions of action is eliminated, for the 'objective social order' is a subjective resource in the experience of *all* actors, and has no further explanatory significance. To use such typifications as an aid to explanation and call it science, as Weber does, is to assume a privileged position which has no foundation.

Social science cannot go beyond the world of common-sense because the sense of a world in common is all that exists, and it is this that is the subject-matter of sociology. The sociologist should be concerned with the ways that such shared meanings creatively constitute the social world, rather than positing social reality as an external, constraining reality which explains subjective responses. In Schutz's project, then, Weber's attempt to theorise about the material conditions under which concrete meanings are produced is displaced, leaving actors' accounts and subjective resources supreme as the constituents of the social.

Schutz's argument draws on Husserl's critique of objectivism, yet also departs from it significantly. Husserl argued that in order to discover the processes whereby we constitute the world as 'there', with all its objects, regularities, including ourselves as individuals with our psychological characteristics, we should engage in a 'phenomenological reduction'. This involves the process of suspending belief (not *denial*) in *all* aspects of the objective world; so revealing those primary subjective processes, through which we constitute our sense of the world, and which we quite unconsciously depend in our existence of social beings. For Husserl, our view of human action as flowing from individuals possessing psychological processes is not a 'fact' but an interpretation which we have posited and then taken for granted as 'real'.

Yet the intractable problem for Husserl was that even if this project was successful no one else could ever know of this success, because to communicate what one had found out about 'pure subjectivity' would involve using the very resources – language and concepts – that one had bracketed out in the first place! Phenomenological truths thus become rather like mystical experiences; the road to which can be pointed to, but the conclusions remain over the horizon. Pure subjectivity if discovered is *completely personal*.

This is why Schutz's analysis of subjectivity takes the ordinary, mundane ego as its point of departure. Rather than investigating how the social world emerges from *pure* subjectivity, by stripping the world away in a phenomenological reduction, Schutz takes the social world as his subject-matter and asks, via the attitude of regarding it as 'strange', how we constitute it. Yet, in the end, the purely personal subjective world in which Husserl is trapped absorbs Schutz's project also. The difference is that Husserl hints at a (albeit mystical) world of meaning beyond the mundane subject, while Schutz confines social science to replicating the personal constructs of the mundane ego.

Ethnomethodology: a phenomenological sociology?

Schutz's subjectivist critique of Weber's empiricist leanings is in many respects mirrored in contemporary 'phenomenological' sociology, particularly in 'ethnomethodological' writings. The latter term refers to a number of different sociological projects whose unity derives from their subjectivist critique of conventional sociological traditions. However, ethnomethodologists, as we shall see, have been forced to draw on some aspects of the traditions they criticise.

The unity of ethnomethodological writings deriving from a shared subjectivist strategy should not prevent us from noting important differences within them; nor should any continuity with Schutz prevent us from recognising that the ethnomethodological critique of sociology draws on intellectual currents other than phenomenology, including those arguments that have been directed at empiricist theories of language by British and American analytic philosophers.[22] This point need not detain us except to note that ethnomethodologists have rather more to say about language in the construction of the social world than had either Schutz or Weber. Indeed, as we shall see, for most ethnomethodologists, with one or two important exceptions, mind, consciousness and experience have often been equated with linguistic practices.

This diversity within ethnomethodological writings is to a large extent attributable to the difficulties (experienced by Weber and Schutz) involved in constructing a subjectivist sociology without coming to terms with one or more of the other strategies of sociological theorising. Put another way, if the social world is an outcome of subjective interpretations how does one avoid the conclusion that sociology is impossible because each actor lives within his own interpretative world? How is it possible to justify the problem of the need for an intersubjective approach and for a strategy that views the world of groups and institutions as simply a subjective construct? These problems which re-emerge in eth- nomethodological writings may be considered after we have iden- tified the sources of unity in ethnomethodology. As we have suggested, an important source of unity is the shared critique directed at 'conventional' sociology, combined with an emphasis on certain aspects of subjective perception largely ignored by sociolog- ists.

Despite their differences, the strategies of empiricism, rational- ism and substantialism take as their point of departure the view that the social world is a reality, external to any one consciousness, and as such is an object 'out there' to be studied. However, eth- nomethodologists, while agreeing that social science and everyday life operate on the basis of just such an assumption, none the less claim that it remains an *assumption*, an interpretation. Despite this, most sociologists concentrate on the description and analysis of 'social facts' – institutions, organisations – without examining the ways in which these emerge from the interpretative activities of individual actors. Take the example of bureaucracy and Bittner's discussion of it.[23] Conventional analysis of business bureaucracy as an objective structure of relations and its causal links with other organisations such as the state, he argues, ignores that which ethnomethodologists seek to make a problem: how actors interpret to themselves and others the sense that a bureaucracy exists as a social order. From this point of view, bureaucracy is not a 'thing' implicated in causal relations with other things, but a *process* of interpretation in which the meaning of a bureaucratic social order is constructed.

This issue is critical, for it is argued that the social world cannot first be studied as an object, to be supplemented after the event by an analysis of actor's subjective interpretations. Such a procedure cannot work because the sociologist is in no sense a privileged, detached observer capable of standing outside the social world, and objectively recording its 'facts' (although some ethnomethodologists, considered below, have claimed that something along these lines is possible). Technically speaking, this issue concerns what Sacks has referred to as a confusion between topic and resource in conventional sociological theorising. Sacks argues that sociologists inadvertently draw on commonsense assumptions about the nature of social reality, about its 'facticity' or orderliness, for example, when constructing models of its structure. As a result, commonsense assumptions masquerade as objective descriptions of the social world without ever themselves being subjected to analysis. Such assumptions are used as a resource and not treated as a topic in their own right; objective descriptions are convincing because both author and audience implicitly share assumptions about 'what we all know to be the case' about the social world.[24]

Douglas's critique of Durkheim's and other 'positivistic' applications of statistical methods to the social world is a further case in point.[25] Official statistics on suicides are constructed on the basis of assumptions about the meaning of death made by various recording agencies, rather than reflecting some objective reality, external to such interpretations. Cicourel argues a similar case in regard to crime statistics, making the additional point that statistical methodology uses interval scales which are assigned numerical values without ever showing that such sharp and orderly distinctions are actually characteristic of the everyday constructions of social life.[26] For example, analysis of public opinion is often presented in the following form: 20 per cent think Mrs Thatcher a very good Prime Minister, 40 per cent good, 25 per cent fairly good, etc. The result of such interval scales is that little attention is paid to the complexity and subtle shades of opinion and grading actually present in 'public opinion'. Rather, the supposedly neutral method of scaling is an observer's construct which involves a particular interpretation of social reality. Sociologists thus tend to mistake statistically reworked assumptions about the nature of reality for reality itself.

A persistent theme in ethnomethodological writings is what is referred to as the 'bracketing' of the objective social world; a process whereby our tacit assumptions about that world are put aside in order to focus on the processes whereby a sense of social order or structure is constructed by actors. This is not an argument about how actors come to internalise the objective social world through socialisation. Rather, it involves asking how actors construct the sense of an orderly world for themselves and others. Conventional socialisation theory presupposes what ethnomethodologists wish to make a 'topic' – the existence of social order. However, such a project presupposes the possibility of a bias-free account of the methods by which actors interpretatively account for their worlds; a view not without certain difficulties, as a number of ethnomethodologists themselves have recognised.

The ethnomethodological critique of objectivism and the idea that the observer has privileged access to the objective social world, independent of the processes through which actors constitute it, involves a model of the human actor which is quite distinct from that found in conventional sociology. The conception of the actor in conventional sociology is rejected as failing to view human beings as knowledgeable creators of the social world, who know a good deal about how the social world operates and their place within it. The central problem for most sociological analysis is the elucidation of *unacknowledged* conditions of action – conditions of which actors are quite unaware. 'Structural' explanations, rooted in such conditions, involve the use of laws, and a model of the actor as a bearer of structures, and therefore a predictable 'object'.

Ethnomethodologists tend to dispute this view, or in any event suggest that the orderliness of social life should be viewed rather differently. In particular, the argument that unacknowledged conditions of action (material or ideal) operate independently of the generation of meaning within particular situations, is criticised. Here ethnomethodologists ground the actors' subjective interpretations in an analysis of meaning and language which can be best elucidated through Garfinkel's influential idea of accounting, and the associated concept of indexicality.[27]

According to Garfinkel, actors or members make sense of the

world by rendering it accountable. Accounts are the methods actors use in producing a course of action or social event. Accounts are constituitive of the events they describe and explain. An event cannot be described independently of members' accounts, for any attempt to do so would merely generate an 'observers' accounting' based on often tacit commonsense knowledge. What is involved here is a rejection of the empiricist distinction between events, on the one hand, and our experiences, descriptions and explanations of them on the other. This conclusion is a result of the subjectivist principle that human experience is a process of interpretation rather than a sensory, material apprehension of the external physical world. While, as with rationalism, the social world is viewed as a cultural, linguistic universe, the idea of accounts is used to reject the idea that actors are the bearers of a code or meaning, the properties of which derive from a structure beyond the situated practices of particular actors' subjective interpretations. Before we discuss the implications of the situated accomplishment of 'social order' via Garfinkel's idea of indexicality, it is important to note that his emphasis on the linguistic properties of accounts has been criticised by other writers involved in similar projects. For example, while Cicourel is also interested in the production of a sense of order by actors in social life, he has emphasised that language is not the only medium through which such order is produced. Rather, he has drawn attention to our multi-media capacities, for example the use of visual and aural data outside linguistic practices.[28]

Returning to Garfinkel's ideas, actor's accounts are always generated in particular situations, and their meaning is a product of their occasioned use, rather than being a generalised expression of some dictionary meaning common to a community of language speakers. This is what Garfinkel means by indexicality.[29] Consider this item of dialogue: 'What is the matter?' – 'nothing'. This cannot be comprehended outside of the occasion in which it occurred – for example, an argument between lovers, business partners or actors on stage. It makes little sense to attempt to conceptualise some real underlying meaning of 'what is the matter?' – 'nothing', or of any other phrase, outside of the context of its use. Meaning is fixed in concrete situations and is not an expression of some objective semantic code. A dictionary, or theory of culture, is no substitute for the explication of meaning in its contextual use. The processes of the social world cannot be reduced to a thing external to, and

constraining of, the situated occasions in which it is made accountable. To objectify is to court reification.

There is a further aspect of indexicality that makes this conclusion
necessary. Accounts have to be analysed in context because they
index, hint at or presuppose knowledge and assumptions which on
that occasion remain tacit. 'What is the matter?' – 'nothing', may
relate to a long sequence of dialogue in which the word 'nothing' has
come to mean, 'what is wrong is so obvious that no more need be
said'. All dialogue, or accounting, has this property. No dialogue is
possible without a tacit 'taken-for-granted' background. Indeed,
ethnomethodological experiments have been conducted that show
that when such backgrounds are deliberately and persistently ques-
tioned, accounting, and thus a sense of social order, fragments. For
accounting to continue, actors have to accept that on certain issues
little or nothing needs to be said because 'everyone knows'. Any
everyday routine illustrates this. The occasioned nature of accounts
and their implication in tacit knowledge express the two related
aspects of their indexicality.

This reference to tacit knowledge hints at an important equivocation in ethnomethodological writings; the question of whether such
background knowledge or expectancies are unacknowledged conditions of action, in a 'conventional' sociological sense. However
most ethnomethodological writings stress that such tacit knowledge
is organised for occasioned use, rather than constituting the effects
of external social constraints on situational practices. Pollner's idea
of a 'corpus' of knowledge (rather like Schutz's stocks of knowledge) is thus intended to emphasise that tacit knowledge is ordered
and reordered anew with the ebb and flow of situations.[30] Their
'background' character does not mean that they are external to the
subjects' interpretations – that they are rooted in the wider society.
Rather, they are within the member's subjectivity drawn on as
resources though not always easily accessible to memory.

Ethnomethodological projects are not, then, as a number of
critics have argued, merely new ways of carrying on the 'old
practices' of symbolic interactionism.[31] This is so precisely because,
in the main, symbolic interactionism presupposes what the ethnomethodologists take to be at issue, namely the objective constraint of the social world, and is in effect, an empiricist-inspired
solution to what Garfinkel has regarded as the 'awesome problems'
that indexicality poses for the analysis of accounts. Before examin-

ing how such 'awesome' problems have or have not been resolved, symbolic interactionism may usefully be considered here in order to point out the distinctive character of ethnomethodological writings.

We should remain sceptical about the claimed similarity between ethnomethodological writings and the symbolic interactionism stemming from the writings of Mead, partly because so many interactionists have tended to complement rather than reject structural–functional theory in American sociology. Also, interactionism operates with a concept of the actor that is quite different to that found in most ethnomethodological writings. There are certain similarities that can be identified, such as Herbert Blumer's rejection of the view that actor's definitions of situations are a passive internalisation of cultural meanings through processes of primary and secondary socialisation.[32] However, the 'constraint' of culture is not rejected but qualified, a vital error from the standpoint of those like Pollner and Garfinkel who wish to stress the occasioned accomplishment of social order. Second, as Attewell has indicated, the writings of ethnomethodology which have addressed the complexities of *how* actors create a sense of social order were prefigured in Goffman's writings.[33] While recognising that there are certain affinities between some ethnomethodological writings and the less 'positivist' representations of symbolic interactionism, we would argue that the differences are far more significant. The point of departure for interactionism is the self as it emerges in society; society being viewed as a given, ongoing process of symbolic interaction.[34] The 'self' is not a thing but an internalised social process which allows the human organism to distance itself from immediate physical constraints, and to monitor its activities in accordance with plans. Such plans express the actor's identity, acquired and sustained in interaction. This capacity to reflect upon and monitor one's own activities involves being able to 'take the role of the other' – to see oneself as others do. Self-monitoring and the acquisition of identity are only possible through the social use of significant symbols, which, in the human species, are taken to the highest levels of flexibility and sophistication in language. Words express the meaning of oneself-in-the-world. One's identity, along with other objects, makes sense to others to the extent that such meanings are shared. Society is, then, made possible through the existence of universal symbols; symbols that mean the same thing to all concerned. Meaning is shared to the extent that human behavioural responses are similar, so facilitating co-operative interaction. The meaning is in the response. The actor does not respond to external material constraints but seeks to maintain his symbolic conception of the world, and his place in it, through interaction with others.

To be a 'good student' is to have that symbolic conception confirmed by behavioural signs from significant others: i.e. recognition. Such signs will include high essay marks from teachers and verbal assurances in tutorials but will probably exclude the opinions of unqualified persons. Three possible contingencies always arise: recognition and confirmation: rejection or negation; restructuring of the same identity. For example, a succession of poor essay marks may be understood as a sign of lack of intelligence, and may lead to a re-evaluation of one's self-estimation. The self as 'good student' may, however, be maintained by a restructuring of the sign/symbol relation; essay marks from teachers may be regarded as irrelevant, and other signs – the opinion of friends – substituted. The point is that the sign/symbol relation, mediating identity recognition by others, is crucial to the maintenance of self-identity.

For the symbolic interactionist, becoming a member of society means that in taking the role of the 'generalised other' one acquires access to universally shared symbols as well as those generated within particular interaction situations and one's own idiosyncratic interpretations. It is the assumption that such universal symbols exist as a cultural resource that denies the ethnomethodological claim that all meaning is indexical. In addition (though not all interactionists stress this as much as Mead did), being a member of society does not just involve the receipt of an identity, but involves acquiring the means of both changing it and contributing to social change. Maintaining one's self involves the capacity to choose, and no matter how much deliberation enters into activity, spontaneity is built into the 'performance'. For example, an interview, no matter how well planned, rarely goes exactly as intended.

Ethnomethodologists challenge the view of society as 'ongoing' as well as the symbolic interactionists' conception of meaning. Interactionists ask what are the processes that lead to the actor's acquisition of society. They regard role-playing as crucial in this. The actor is seen to negotiate the meaning of situations within the parameters of wider society. For ethnomethodological writers (as for Schutz) this presupposes what is to be explained. How does what the interactionist takes to be there ('society as symbolic interaction') come to be constituted as 'there' by actors, including the interactionist observer?[35]

In addition, ethnomethodologists argue that 'universal symbols' conceal a complexity of situationally specific meanings which are 'glossed over' by the observer. They are a myth. Moreover the suggestion that meaning lies in the response, presumes that 'accounts' and behavioural responses are distinct, with one defining the other. The meaning of the phrase 'intelligent student' cannot be derived from observations of behaviour, but can be analysed only in terms of actors' subjective interpretations. The analysis of behaviour cannot provide the foundation for shared meanings. Thus the basis of an ethnomethodological critique of symbolic interactionism is the *rapprochement* the latter makes with empiricism. Symbolic interactionism, for all its efforts to see things from the point of view of the actor, still maintains a view of the observer as privileged – as one who can explain the genesis of the self and the universal symbols that provide the conditions for the social construction of reality.

The implications of this critique of symbolic interactionism and the objections to, or departures from, conventional sociological theorising are profound. There can be no substitute for the situationally specific study of methods of accounting. There cannot be a study of social life 'in general' before, or as an aid to, a study of social life in its situated concrete manifestations. The indexicality of accounts renders any attempt to discuss meaning across time and space a mistaken distortion. Are presuppositionless descriptions of accounts possible? Can the commonsense assumptions of sociologists be bracketed successfully? Surely the results of such a project, even if successful, must produce a body of 'knowledge' that is as fleeting and ephemeral as the situations that are studied.

These problems cannot be discussed with reference to a unified body of theorising called ethnomethodology. For while we have identified a unity deriving from the critique of 'conventional' sociology and the focus on issues ignored by such conventional analyses, it is also true that once ethnomethodologists attempt to realise their intentions – to analyse how actors render the world orderly and accountable – a diversity of theoretical projects arises. This diversity can best be approached by returning to the idea of 'accounts', and in particular to the attendant problem of how it is possible to produce an accurate description of them. There have been a number of quite different responses to this issue.

Douglas, among others, has drawn attention to the ways in which commonsense assumptions are implicated in supposedly objective descriptions of social reality, suggesting that the analysis of such assumptions could be the foundation for genuinely objective knowledge about the attribution of meaning by actors.[36] He argues that while the empiricist claim to identify the real-world events of suicide and crime is, in the end, an illusion, we can none the less find out exactly how the meanings of crime and suicide are created, without objectifying them; so returning sociology to the real ground of social life. There are, however, serious objections to this line of argument. How is a true account of a member's accounting practices, and thus the 'real' situated meaning of suicide, to be constructed unless a second observer is present to question the tacit assumptions of the first, and a third to check on the second, and so on? The method of accounting thus involves an infinite regress and the true account remains an intractable problem. This must be so, given the rejection of any objectivist solution to the problem of meaning and conflicting accounts of meaning. The ethnomethodologists' account of meaning is just another account, rather than a privileged one. As a result, the attempts to recover the meaning of suicide, crime, illness and sexual identity, are of questionable validity, unless objectivist arguments are countenanced. Yet as we have seen, it was the rejection of such arguments that formed the theoretical point of departure for the ethnomethodological project. What is of interest is that Douglas, for one, appears to court the possibility of objective accounts of subjective meanings – for example, by careful observation, tape recordings and so on – all of which begs the question and leans on empiricist props.

Douglas draws on empiricism in order to avoid the conclusion that the 'real suicide rate' is simply an aggregation of individual judgements. There are two problems here. Douglas's critique of the way sociologists draw on commonsense assumptions in the construction of social theory suggests that careful observation can reveal the bias of such assumptions by way of a comparison with the observer's description of the 'real events' of suicide. Such a procedure presupposes that the observer does have privileged or 'bias-free' access to these events. Yet Douglas's view that the observer's description of events must be considered to be just another account, does not allow such a resolution of the problem. The distinction between interpretations of suicide and the observed 'real events' of suicide can only be secured within an empiricist strategy, and it is this incoherence in his argument that leads Douglas to veer between subjectivism and empiricism. At times 'real suicides' (empiricism) are possible, at other times they are simply interpretative outcomes. Furthermore, once we have eliminated the possibility of a comparison between accounts and 'real events', and in order to sustain the view that suicides are an aggregation of individual interpretations, Douglas must continue to lean on empiricist assumptions in order to show that it is possible to produce accurate accounts of other actors' accounts. If we admit with Douglas that the recovery of subjective meaning is always problematic, and that actors' accounts cannot be described via sensory experience, then surely we have no basis for accepting the observer's account as valid. Unless Douglas is prepared to accept a Weberian methodology, objective accounts are only possible in the natural sciences, while relativism appears to be a permanent state of affairs in the social sciences. In order to avoid such an outcome Douglas is forced to cover himself by calling upon the very empiricist assumptions that his original critique sets out to undermine – the emperor's clothes, however scanty, are all that is available to him.

However, ethnomethodological analysis of how members render the world accountable and orderly have not been confined to attempts at the recovery of meaning in the sense of specific, occasional bodies of commonsense knowledge. In face of the 'awesome problems of indexicality', some writers have focused on the *procedures* and *methods* of accounting rather than on the fleeting, substantive meanings that the former produce or organise. Here the argument is that if meaning is fixed in its occasioned use, and remains both ephemeral and opaque to any attempt to construct a true account, then the only elements of social life that are not occasioned and thus of generalised significance are the formal procedures through which accounting takes place. Not surprisingly, the similarity between this idea and Schutz's attempts to clarify the general conditions under which all actors produce the meaningful social world has not gone unnoticed. In addition the attendant indifference to substantive historical problems and the tendency to use examples as purely illustrative is particularly strong in ethnomethodological writings of this type.

Sacks, for example, is concerned with the sequencing of dialogue in recorded conversations.[37] The sequencing of what is said is important, rather than what is being talked about. Cicourel also focuses on interpretative procedures which he recognises as being trans-situational or generalised, drawn on by actors in the production of concrete meanings.[38] The significance of these writings is that the problems of indexicality are avoided rather than resolved. Substantive problems of meaning recede in the face of a concern with formal and general properties.

However, to countenance either the existence of trans-situational rules, or a generalised capacity of all actors to process meaning according to a formal code amenable to sociological analysis, involves a drift toward the central concerns of the strategy of rationalism. Rationalism, in suggesting that the operations of subjectivity presuppose a transcendent normative or cognitive structure, undercuts any attempt to sustain a project that makes 'structure' an emergent property of occasioned accounting practices. Rationalism and subjectivism are in an uneasy relation in Cicourel's work, and in Pollner's writings we are given little reason for accepting that the 'practices' that produce occasioned corpora (of commonsense knowledge) are invariant.

Other ethnomethodologists have eschewed such attempts to resolve the problems of subjectivism by recourse to the contributions of empiricism or rationalism. The works of Blum and McHugh are interesting because they repudiate all attempts to arrive at 'true' accounts of accounts, and reject the possibility of theorising their formal constituents and conditions of existence.[39] Rather, the difficulties of rendering objective accounts of accounts are transmuted into positive virtues, for in so doing the myths of 'truth' and 'objectivity' can be revealed for what they are – situationally specific conventions. To produce a successful account of members' accounts is to initiate a dialogue that only terminates when all of the participants concerned are agreed. Thus: I have 'understood' what you are doing/saying, and why, when you and I agree that I have. Implicit in such a resolution of the problem is that there is no reason to believe that what Blum and McHugh have to say has any validity or referent outside of their own agreements and perspectives. This is the closest that ethnomethodological writings have come to producing a purely subjectivist form of sociological theorising – one that reduces social structure to 'story-telling'. Most other eth-

nomethodologists have sought to temper the insights of subjectivism with quite opposed strategies in order to construct a project that
can do rather more than regard the world as a seamless web of
meaning. But for these writers – both those who, like Douglas, rely
on empiricism, or those like Cicourel who draw on rationalism – any
attempt to regard 'ethnomethodology' as a revolutionary break
with sociology must be regarded as mistaken. The developments in
ethnomethodological writings show that the only way out of the
problems of subjectivism is a *rapprochement* with those strategies
that the latter characterised as objectivist. Otherwise, any project to
recover meaning from an ever-changing-meaning context is to state
a problem in such a way as to admit of no principled solution.

Conclusion

The projects of Weber, Schutz, and recent ethnomethodological
writers, have each sought to resolve the tensions that characterise
the subjectivist strategy in social theory, and in so doing have been
forced to confront other strategies quite opposed to subjectivist
premises.

Weber's historical sociology of action is prevented from becoming a form of 'story-telling' only by ensuring that ideal types of
meaning obey the rigours of empirist scientific procedure; as a
result, Weber's analysis of meaning is translated into a form of
social behaviourism. Moreover, this step is taken because Weber
always regarded the human capacity to create meaning as situated
within historical conditions of material scarcity. From the outset,
Weber remained trapped within the strategic tensions posed by the
attempt to synthesise subjectivist and empiricist strategies in social
theory.

The significance of Schutz's critique of Weber is that these
tensions were avoided at the cost of constructing a project in which
it became impossible to regard the objective social world as anything other than a construct of individual consciousness. Schutz
attempted to present a generalised model of the properties of *all*
individual consciousnesses (analogous to Husserl's attempt to ex-
plicate the properties of the transcendental ego); but without
recourse to rationalist premises this project remained trapped
within individual consciousness. Indeed, such rationalist premises

were rejected as examples of those 'objectivist' errors that the subjectivist critique took as its point of departure.

Weber's unstable synthesis of empiricism and subjectivism, and Schutz's failure to resolve the problem of the relationship between subjective and objective meaning, provide the background to many of the issues raised in recent ethnomethodological writings. These have continued to confront the central problem – how to analyse subjective meaning and the nature of inter-subjectivity. The result of their work has been to show that any attempt to return the analysis of meaning to concrete situations can only be achieved by drawing on rationalist or empiricist premises as crucial props. Otherwise subjective meaning remains an elusive goal of a subjectivist sociology.

4

Substantialism

Unlike the strategies identified in the two preceding chapters, substantialism is, in the social sciences, inextricably linked with one name: that of Marx. While it would be mistaken to assume that Marx is alone in adopting such a strategy or that Marxism, in all its various forms, is always predominantly substantialist, it suits the purpose in this chapter to confine the discussion to Marx and Marxists. First, however, we must briefly indicate the ways in which the substantialist strategy confronts the dilemmas of social reality and how we know it.

As the term 'substantialism' suggests, this strategy conceives of social reality as fundamentally material in its constitution; it stresses the primacy of existence over consciousness. It lays stress on the ways in which the material conditions of social life – ranging from the physical nature of the human organism to material resources of power such as the techniques of warfare or the instruments of production – are fundamental to the explanation of social and psychological processes. It is argued, for example, that men as subjective, intentional beings are inconceivable except in relation to the material conditions of their physical make-up, and without the material conditions of brain and physiology which set them apart from other animals. The emphasis that archaeologists place on the skull capacity of prehistoric men as a rough measure of their location on the scale of humanity is an example of such materialist assumptions. Equally, the argument that microchip technology will 'revolutionise society' derives from an implicit or explicit material-ist theory which explains social behaviour in terms of technical conditions. In both cases human action and social relations are seen to be constrained by the 'facts' of an objective, material world.

As we shall see, a materialist position does not have to be quite as crudely deterministic as these examples suggest. An analogy that is often used in order to illustrate the complexities of a materialist position, is that of a book. A book, such as the one you are reading, is made up of a set of meanings, but at the same time has a physical existence: the materials of its production – ink, paper, binding, glue. The physical makeup of the book does not, however, *determine* the meaning. There are those meanings that the authors wish to convey and the meanings that the reader draws from it – and we all know they are not necessarily the same. It is because of the possibility that a variety of interpretations or readings are possible and also because meanings may themselves change over time – the variety of meanings we can derive from readings of Shakespeare in the twentieth century are quite different from those which were current in the seventeenth century – that subjectivists stress that the social world is made up of the meanings constructed by individuals rather than objective material conditions. The materialist counters such a claim by arguing that, in the case of the book, no meanings could exist except through its physical existence, and that despite changes in interpretation over time the material existence of the book or a Shakespearean manuscript remains a constraint upon the possibility of interpretation and a limitation upon change. In short, the materialist argues you cannot think yourself outside of and beyond the constraints of a material, objective reality.

Substantialism is not unique in stressing the primacy of the material world. As we have shown, it shares this particular resolution of the material/ideal dilemma with empiricism which also argues that the objects of the social sciences are external, material things. To put it another way, the empiricist argues that the phenomena of the social sciences are equivalent in their characteristics to those of the natural sciences and can be studied in much the same way. This equivalence between natural and social science was referred to by Comte as the unity of method, while philosophers of the social sciences refer to it as the doctrine of naturalism.

However, while the two positions accept that social reality has a material basis, they differ over the nature of that materiality; the empiricist strategy claiming that while reality is material it is made up of particular, individual, unique things. Thus, when we use a general term such as social class we are merely *labelling* a series of unique social events; giving them a general name. This is what is referred to as nominalism. A substantialist, on the other hand, would assert that social class was a *real* phenomenon; that reality is made up of general configurational wholes and not purely individual, unique things. In fact, substantialism, like rationalism (see Chapter 5) gives primacy in explanation to those general phenomena; the real structures which *underlie* and give rise to individual manifestations.

The term 'underlying' hints at a second difference between substantialism and empiricism: that is, in the answers they give to the question, how can we gain knowledge of this external, material reality? The empiricist argues that we know reality through our experience of it; that the aim of science is to explore systematically those 'things' and events of which an independently existing reality is composed, through the medium of the senses (which themselves have a material basis). For empiricism, then, it is not legitimate to regard anything as scientific knowledge that is not the result of observation or experience. Thus the material, external world is the source of what is known, and controlled observation or systematised experience are the means of obtaining knowledge. While substantialism accepts that the source of knowledge is a material, objective reality, it rejects the view that it is a reality *given to* experience. Science is not, for the substantialist, the mere accumulation of empirical facts. Science goes beyond the observation that things are related one to another in a regular fashion, for such knowledge merely *describes* an existing state of affairs, which must, in turn, be explained. Thus, the often repeated sociological observation that voting behaviour is related to status or class position must, in order to become part of scientific knowledge, be explained by some underlying causal mechanism which is not given to observation – it is a 'hidden' reality and it is the project of science to progressively reveal this reality which is not immediately accessible to common-sense. If the explanation of events was immediately apprehended through the senses, argues Marx, there would be no need of science. According to the substantialist position, then, the process of gaining knowledge, the activity of science, crucially involves the construction of theoretical knowledge about these underlying, hidden causes. Paradoxically, the material reality can only be known as the result of a theoretical process; by constructing ideas about it. Substantialist science is not founded on the accumulation of statements of observed relationships, but a body of theory that attempts to conceptualise the real, material structures that explain and maintain such regularities.

An example of such a substantialist strategy is Freudian psychoanalytic theory. In Freudian theory the observed regularities of individual behaviour are not taken at their face value, but are explained in terms of structures such as id, ego and super-ego and their emergent relations in the course of life-experiences. These structures and their relations are not only *not* given to observation but they are concealed by the very behaviours that they give rise to. That is to say, the observed behaviour Freud starts out to explain, such as the symptoms of hysteria, involve a 'repression' of their underlying conditions – they are hidden from the patient and the observer. These hidden structures are none the less real, and are rooted in the material conditions of the human organism, such as its sexuality.

The concept of repression in Freudian theory suggests a further dimension of the divergence between the empiricist and substantialist strategies which relates to the doctrine of naturalism or unity of method referred to above. Despite giving primacy to the material, objective character of social reality, substantialism does not accept the methodological equivalence of natural and social science, because the observed reality of the social world may be actively involved in obscuring or concealing (repressing) the underlying reality. A substantialist such as Marx would argue, for example, that the study of the labour market as a system of free contractual relations in which wages are a payment for work done and differential wages are in accordance with the supply of labour (i.e. prevalence of trained skills and inborn talents), is merely to observe the ideological forms which operate to conceal the real, exploitative relations of production (for an extension of this argument see p. 142). The role played by ideology in the social world ensures that the relationship between social science and its object of study is quite different from that characterising the natural sciences and their objects. The objects of the natural sciences are not active, conscious beings capable of representing themselves to themselves in ideological forms.

Fields of tension and theoretical project

In Chapter 1 we argued that we should not expect any school of sociology or even any sociological theorist to fit neatly into one of the four formal strategies outlined. In fact, there is a tendency for the more fruitful and creative sociologists to straddle at least two of the positions. In characterising substantialism as a strategy, therefore, we are merely clearing the ground in order to identify that *theoretical project* in sociology which is constructed from a broadly and predominantly substantialist strategy. The significance of substantialism once incorporated into a specific theoretical project is that it produces a characteristic pattern of tensions or problems which must be resolved.

The core tension of substantialism manifests itself as a problem of validation. How is it possible to determine the truth or certainty of a statement about social reality when observation as a means of validation is rejected? The problem of validation arises because substantialism posits the existence of a material, objective world out there which can be known only by the means of constructing it in theory. How can we know that the theoretical construct comprehends the 'hidden' reality? This is a tension inherent in substantialism and is bound to generate problems for any theoretical project constructed on the basis of substantialist strategy.

We have also argued that such core tensions underlie the way in which theoretical projects can be observed to drift from one strategic position to another. In the case of substantialism there is a tendency to drift toward a rationalist strategy because of the problems involved in satisfactorily linking the theoretical concept (the thought object) to empirical reality (the real object). Where the problem remains unsolved there is a tendency for the materialist view of reality to become increasingly subordinated to an idealist conception of knowledge; that is to say, the material world effectively exists only in our theories about it.

Finally, the construction of a theoretical project creates a series of subsidiary problems or tensions of its own making and we can only identify these by considering in detail a particular project. As we have already pointed out, in the case of substantialism the choice is not at all difficult, as Marxism is by far the most influential example in the social sciences. Marx is unique among the classical theorists in postulating that materialism is *the* scientific approach, while his trenchant critiques of humanist philosophy and subjectivism trumpet his belief in the primacy of the objective, real world as the source of knowledge. However, while we will argue that Marx, in his construction of a theoretical project, adopts a substantialist strategy more consistently than do other major theorists, his theoretical value lies in the extent to which he both recognised the dilemmas that such a strategy confronts and attacked the very bases on which such a strategy is founded – the material/ideal and subject/object dichotomies. The development of Marx's thought shows a progressive awareness of the problems that substantialism produces in dialogue with the alternative strategies of empiricism, subjectivism and rationalism. Marx's theoretical work can be viewed as a series of confrontations with these alternative strategies in which he attempts to take account of their force while, at the same time, developing a series of critiques of those projects constructed on such bases. That Marx's work is a series of such confrontations helps to account for the wide variety of competing schools which have developed under the broad umbrella of Marxism. Contemporary Marxism cannot even be identified with the theoretical strategy of substantialism – there are empiricist, subjectivist and rationalist Marxisms on offer, and each of these antagonistic schools seeks and finds authority for its project in the texts of Marx and Engels.

This phenomenon of the fragmentation of Marxism has often been used as a criticism of Marx, the suggestion being that any body of work that can generate such theoretical diversity must itself be fatally flawed and inconsistent. While not wishing to suggest that Marx is flawless or consistent, we would wish to turn this argument, in good Marxian fashion, on its head. The diversity of Marxism results from failure to come to terms with the fact that Marx's substantialism is an attempt to dialectically overcome the dichotomous structure of the material and ideal and the subject and object dilemmas, by taking account of the alternative strategies.

Marx's writings can be viewed as a progressive attempt to undermine such dichotomous relationships: between a knowing subject and known object; being and consciousness; rational and empirical knowledge. Even the foundations of the duality material/ideal are, paradoxically for a self-proclaimed materialist, rejected in their dichotomous formulations. The diversity of modern Marxism arises out of the retranslation of Marx back into the formal strategies that he attempted to overcome, in the construction of a unique theoretical project. It may be argued that this tendency of modern Marxists to retreat into the relative security of a formal theoretical strategy, merely underlines Marx's own failure to break out of what he regarded as the dualist trap, and that in his attempts to dissolve the

conceptual dualisms he merely slides from one incompatible position to another, creating, as Acton asserted, a 'philosophical
farrago'.[1] Whatever Marx's failures, however, this 'farrago' is largely one of our own mixing, for it has been the very traditions that
Marx rejected that have provided the strategies for the contemporary extensions of his work. It is by way of a reassertion of the
primacy of the subject that phenomenological Marxists have been
able to claim the 'younger' Marx as their own. It is through a
reaffirmation of the primacy of the object as the source of knowledge that empiricists have sought Marxian authority, while structuralists look to the methodology of *Capital* for signs that Marx has
finally eliminated the subject from his theory. Each school demands
its pound of intellectual flesh and in so doing implicitly denies the
continued vitality of Marx's own project, which is, in essence, the
denial of their premise, the dualistic foundations of knowledge.

How then was it possible for Marx to construct a theoretical
project which rejected the material/ideal dualism, yet remained
materialist? How has it proved possible for subjectivists to find a
theoretical pedigree in the writings of Marx, who stressed the
objectivity of a real social world? In order to address these problems
we will focus on four 'stages' in the development of the Marxian
theoretical project. Each of these stages constitutes a confrontation
with and critique of an alternative strategy. Each stage illuminates a
field of tension in the construction of the project and each provides
some justification for the construction of a post-Marxian school of
Marxist thought.

Much of the now-published writings of Marx were originally
notebooks and drafts, ground-clearing works which constantly
reconstructed his own project. Most of his work is polemical in the
sense that Marx is always engaged in a critique of existing theory as
a conscious method of illuminating both the novelty of his own
approach to the study of society and the nature of the emergent
capitalist society itself. It is through a 'critique of political economy',
of theorists such as Adam Smith and David Ricardo, that
Marx arrives at his own analysis of capitalist relations in the volumes
of *Capital*. Marx believed that it was an error to make hard and fast
distinctions between intellectual products such as the theory of
'political economy' and the social reality to which it referred; the
theory of 'political economy' was for Marx an element of that
reality, an aspect of the 'practices' through which men reproduced

those very relations in their ideological form. Thus, a critique of such ideological practices serves to illuminate the real social relations of capitalism. The critique was never conceived, then, as a purely intellectual exercise, but as a social and political activity. Marx's efforts to construct a theoretical project by adopting a substantialist strategy can be viewed, as we have said, as a series of such critical interventions, each attacking an alternative strategy of social theorising and each developing further Marx's own analysis of capitalist society and its historical forerunners. The four identifiable stages of Marx's construction of a theoretical project are:

Stage 1 The critique of idealism and the early development of a materialist alternative. The focus of the critique was Hegel and the 'young Hegelians' and a significant weapon in Marx's attack was the materialist philosophy of Ludwig Feuerbach. Here Marx confronts the *rationalist alternative* and in so doing provides a fruitful source for empiricist interpretations of his work. By adopting Feuerbachian materialism, however, Marx creates a tension in his own project as a result of the drift towards *empiricism*.

Stage 2 A rejection of Feuerbach's determinist materialism, which involves the attempt to dissolve the subject–object dichotomy through the concepts of praxis and historical materialism. It is from this stage of Marx's work that modern *subjectivist/phenomenological* interpretations of Marx find their major sustenance.

Stage 3 The critique of humanist socialists, which while directed against utopianism in political practice, had the effect of balancing the drift towards subjectivism through a reassertion of the commitment to science as the study of a real, objective world. Such writings again bring a positive response from Marx's *empiricist* interpreters.

Stage 4 Finally, the critique of political economy, which involves the attempt to eliminate any drift towards empiricism while leading to the attempt to confront and resolve the central tension in the substantialist strategy – i.e. the problems of validation, and the consequent drift toward rationalism. The return to Hegel as a basis for overcoming this central dilemma provides a foothold for the *rationalist* interpreters of Marx.[2]

Stage 1: the rejection of idealism

Materialism is central to Marxian theory not only because it is the pivot of his analysis of society but also because the way in which his understanding of materialism develops is illustrative of his attempt to resolve the dilemmas posed by the dualistic concepts of reality (ideal/material) and knowledge (subject/object). Thus, while Marx's materialism emerges initially as a counter to Hegelian idealism – a simple inversion which merely replaces the essentialism of the idea with that of matter – Marx quickly moved to a critique of the material/ideal duality itself, thereby reconstructing the very basis of what was conventionally understood by materialism. The explanatory significance of a material world is not secured through the philosophical assertion of its primacy but through its recasting in a social–relational, historical form and context.

Much of Marx's early writings are a dialogue with Hegel which while broadly accepting certain aspects of Hegel's method are increasingly critical of his idealism and philosophical abstraction. Thus, while Marx accepted Hegel's view of knowledge as a theoretical construction of reality rather than man's immediate experience of it (an impossibility under conditions of alienation), he was to reject Hegel's rationalism: the view that reality only existed in ideas – the idea constituted reality. According to Hegel, because we can only know those things that we are capable of thinking, then reality must be a thought creation. Moreover it is consciousness as manifested by the idea that unifies subject and object, so mediating the relationship. There can, then, be no external, separate, objective world that is not created by consciousness. The only way such an objective world can exist is through consciousness. To those of us steeped in the assumptions of positivist science Hegel's position appears to be an absurdity. However, it does address two problems that are central for sociology. First, it emphasises man's creative or constructivist capacities. It stresses that man is not a passive experiencer of an objective, conditioning reality but is an active being-in-the-world. For Marx, man's active being-in-the-world is primarily expressed through *labour*. That is to say, that social life is also acting *in* and *upon* nature. From the very beginning, then, Marx is clear that the creative aspect of man arises out of the relation to nature as well as the relations between people.

Second, Hegelian theory does attempt to eliminate an alternative absurdity, and that is the empiricist belief that knowledge has its source in an objective, external reality – that when we think we merely reflect the imposition of an external reality. Such a view not only reduces human beings to conditioned automata, switched on through the senses, but assumes that the thoughts in our heads are the same thing as the reality to which they refer.

For Marx, then, the constructivist and anti-empiricist elements in Hegel were attractive. It was the idealism to which they led that he rejected. A conventional way of characterising this relationship of attraction/rejection is the phrase 'Marx turned Hegel on his head'. This notion of inversion does in fact express Marx's early attempts simply to replace Hegelian idealism with a determinist materialism:

> For Hegel, the process of thinking, which he even transforms into an independent subject, under the name of 'the Idea' is the creator of the real world, and the real world is only the external appearance of the idea. With me the reverse is true: the ideal is nothing but the material world reflected in the mind of man, and translated into forms of thought.[3]

It is this inversion of Hegel that immediately finds a resonance in empiricist interpreters of Marx who wish to stress the material reality of an objective world and emphasise that the senses are the high road to knowledge. It is a position that Marx derived from his reading of Feuerbach, feeding his antipathy towards philosophies of the abstracted subject, the basis of religious and metaphysical reasoning.

Such materialism was essentially unacceptable to Marx, however. For while it emphasised the reality of the material world it undermined what Marx took to be Hegel's achievement – his emphasis on man's active, creative being-in-the-world. It was a materialism that ensured a drift towards empiricism, and an image of man as an object, conditioned by his material environment. It was a materialism necessarily in tension with his view of man as a creative being and his view of knowledge as constructivist. The significance of this tension for Marx's emerging theoretical project is best seen in relation to the central concept of his social analysis – alienation.

For the early Marx, the fact of man's alienation, both from nature and other men, was crucial to an understanding of his subjection and exploitation. It was indeed the process of alienation that robbed him of his creative capacity. Human beings through their social relations created social forms such as religion and the state, and these socially constructed forms then came to dominate them as an external objective force. People create God, yet God is conceived of as the creator of human kind. Human beings construct forms of the state, yet the state comes to rule over them. The concept of alienation as developed by Marx stresses the alienation of labour in the course of the development of capitalist relations, whereby the products of labour in the form of commodities exchanged on a market are divorced from and dominate the men and women who produce them. Alienation is, then, the process through which we become objects to ourselves, rather than the subject-creators of our own history. In this sense Feuerbachian materialism is merely another form of such alienation which reduces human beings to objects, and, as such, is totally incompatible with Marx's theory of alienation.

Stage 2: the construction of historical materialism

Marx set out to eradicate this tension; to marry two seemingly incompatible elements – Hegel's constructivist philosophy with materialism – in a series of notes written in 1845 which Engels later entitled the *Theses on Feuerbach*.[4] The *Theses*, which are at one level a critique of Feuerbach's materialism, also constitute a major transition in Marx's work, in which the duality between subject and object, being and consciousness are rejected as leading to either idealism or a defective materialism. He begins in Thesis I:

> The chief deficiency of all materialism up to now (Feuerbach's included) is that objectivity, reality, the sensible world is conceived only in the form of the *object of observation*; not however as sensible human activity, practice, not from the aspect of the subject. Hence, in opposition to materialism, the active side [was] developed in abstract fashion by idealism which naturally does not know of real sensible activity as such. Feuerbach appeals to sensible objects – ones really distinct from thought-objects, but he does not conceive human activity itself as activity *which belongs to the objective world*. . . . Hence he does not grasp the meaning of revolutionary; of practical, critical activity.[5]

This, the first of the eleven theses, heralds many of the major themes. The strength of Feuerbach's materialism lies in its acceptance of a real world independent of thought. Its major deficiency is to conceive this reality as objects given to experience. The assumption is that the social world is already constituted prior to man's experience of it and is simply apprehended through sense perception (observation) as if social relations existed apart from those who live them. Marx contrasts the *passive* subject of empiricism with the *active* or constructivist aspect of idealism (rationalism) but, simultaneously, rejects that position also as developing 'the active side' in an abstract fashion. That is to say, rationalism allows that social reality is constructed, but it is constructed not through practical activity but in thought. The two sides of the dualism – giving primacy to either the subject or object – have their strengths but also exhibit unacceptable weaknesses. On the one hand, men are seen to make their social worlds, but only in their heads, and on the other hand, man is viewed in the context of a real, material world, but is merely a passive reflector of its conditioning facts.

For Marx, then, materialism is acceptable only if it can eradicate both sets of weakness, and it can do this only if material reality is seen not as an object or thing external to and constraining upon the individual, but as an *objective activity* constituted through social practice. Material reality is both the practical accomplishment of real men and women and a condition of their activity. Marx is arguing that social reality is neither an external conditioning object nor a subjective projection: the dualism is dissolved.

In Thesis III Marx turns his attention more directly to the materialist position as applied to society:

> The materialist doctrine about change of circumstances and education forgets that circumstances are changed by men and the educator must himself be educated. Hence it must sunder society into two parts – of which one is superior to society.
>
> The co-incidence of the changing circumstances and of human activity or self-change can be conceived and rationally understood only as a *revolutionary practice*.[6]

The doctrine which is here rejected by Marx is a commonplace of modern empiricist sociology: a doctrine which suggests that it is the environment, natural or social (and in this particular example, education), that determines what we are. People are made by circumstances. Such a doctrine, Marx argues, ignores the fact that if people change, circumstances must have changed, and circumstances, such as education, are changed by people. In effect, Marx is here rejecting a materialist essentialism whereby some given material condition 'superior to society' is seen as determining social relations. It is particularly important to stress that Marx clearly and insistently rejected such materialist explanations because he is so often criticised for adopting that very position. Empiricist interpreters of Marx are particularly prone to criticise his materialist *essentialism* and, consequently, his economic determinism (we return to this below).

Marx resolves the tension that exists between constructivist idealism and objectivist materialism through the concept of *practice* or *practical activity*. First, by conceiving of men's social relations as their real practical activities he wishes to suggest that men are always constructing their social relations and social beings in the course of their everyday activities – the social is not something outside of and constraining upon these activities. Practice, then, stresses the 'active side'. It follows that when Marx refers to the material basis of society he is also referring to the material aspects of practice and not to some determining material object or objects such as the machinery employed in production. Marx's materialism emerges fully, therefore, when he argues that strategic among men's and women's practical activities is productive activity; the means through which life is sustained in human societies. The material bases of society are the *social* relations of production. Marx's materialism, therefore, is not a philosophical materialism, asserting primacy of matter, but a sociological materialism asserting the primacy of productive activity and relations (including relations to nature).

However, following from his strictures as outlined above, the relations of production cannot be a given, material condition *of action*, 'superior to society' and determining of its social relations. They are themselves the product of 'self-changing' human activity and, therefore, historically variable. Thus, far from arguing that the material conditions of social life are universal and given (i.e. determined by biological nature or natural environment), Marx argues that the material conditions themselves change and are changed by people. Before looking in more detail at the significance of this historical variation (i.e. Marx's *historical* materialism) it is important to point out that the Marxian critique of Feuerbach and associated writings opens the door to what has become a major development in modern Marxism – the various forms of subjectivist, humanist and phenomenological Marxisms.

Among the crucial effects of Marx's *Theses on Feuerbach* was the displacement of the empiricist concept of experience, as a source of knowledge, with that of practice. The source of men's knowledge of the social world was not to be found in the passive observation of objective conditions but was a consequence of men acting on and in the world. This simple displacement has enormous effects, not least in transforming the rules determining what constitutes valid knowledge from the controlled observation of facts to effective action (underlying Marx's concern with the relationship between social theory and political action). This view of science as an active accomplishment which changes its object (society) rather than being conceived of as a reflection of what exists, is merely one aspect of an overall theoretical project which emphasises the primacy of action in the construction of social reality rather than the conditioning effects of social structure on behaviour.

Humanist and subjectivist forms of Marxism have taken this emphasis in Marx as the authority for their own theoretical projects which were constructed initially in the 1920s and 1930s as a reaction to orthodox Marxism, which was increasingly dominated by the 'official' positivist version of Marx being laid down in Stalinist Russia, transforming historical and dialectical materialism into the iron laws of history and nature. It also flourished with the rise of fascism in Germany, as mounting state terror undermined assumptions about the necessarily progressive nature of technology and positivist science. The new humanism found in the writings of the Hungarian philosopher Georg Lukács,[7] Karl Korsch,[8] the Frankfurt Institute of Marxist Studies under Max Horkheimer,[9] indicating a new enthusiasm for Hegel and influenced by the phenomenological philosophy of Edmund Husserl,[10] was reinforced by the rediscovery of important elements from Marx's early writings.[11]

Central to the construction of a subjectivist Marxism has been the notion of man as the subject-creator of his own history. Man is to be distinguished from the animals as a self-conscious, self-creative being with the capacity to continuously reconstruct his relationship to nature and other men. Man is not subjected to the determinism of a natural order, because of his capacity to increasingly control nature in terms of his own purposes or intentions. This creativity is expressed in the unique human attributes of language and tools. A variety of modern Marxisms have been constructed from this point of view – on the basis of a subjectivist strategy – the major schools being phenomenological Marxism, existentialism and critical theory.[12]

The Italian philosopher Enzo Paci has recently attempted to synthesise the phenomenology of Edmund Husserl and Marxism, taking from Husserl the view that the social world is constructed through men's cónsciousness (see the discussion of Husserl in Chapter 5) and intentionality.[13] It is man's subjectivity that implies his freedom. Man, in having the capacity to construct his own social world, also has the capacity to construct it in line with his own intentions and needs. As a consequence, Paci argues, knowledge that treats people as objects has an alienating effect. Their subjectivity and potentiality for freedom are suppressed by the effects of such knowledge.

Such phenomenological interpretations of Marx characteristically involve a shift from Marx's own focus of analysis, the critique of political economy, in which production relations are seen as the strategic location of historical forms of domination, to an attack on positivist science and its naturalist doctrine. The latter is seen as alienated knowledge, viewing man as fatalistically determined by 'natural' forces such as the market, technology, social structure, etc. According to Paci, positivist science has reduced people to objects in an objectified world and in so doing has itself become an instrument of domination. Science and technology, which were created by men as the means of liberation from nature have increasingly been used for non-human ends; that is, ends that involve a loss of intentionality and a suppression of creative reason.

What Paci adds to Husserl in order to relate him to Marx is the claim that consciousness must be related to what he calls pre-categorical 'living-needs'. He criticises Husserl for a failure to develop an understanding of any relationships beyond language and consciousness. In order to live, he argues, man must *begin* by satisfying the most elementary economic needs. Consciousness is then dependent and conditioned by 'the binding character of the precategorical economic structure'.

For phenomenological Marxists such as Paci, Marx's development toward an increasingly focused critique of the economic order of capitalism was a distortion of his earlier focus on practice and alienation and its concern with the essential subjectivity of man. This later development in Marx has led to forms of Marxism that, like positivist science, have reduced man to the status of a determined object, so losing sight of the phenomenological project of returning to man a consciousness of his historical goals.

The choice that Paci offers between subjectivism (phenomenology) and empiricism (positivist science) is, however, a choice that Marx rejected in the construction of his historical materialist project. For, while in his critique of Feuerbach Marx shares with phenomenology the rejection of empiricism through the displacement of the concept of experience with that of practice, stressing that all social reality including knowledge of it is a human accomplishment, he nevertheless forecloses on the phenomenological project in two fundamental senses. First, practice is not reducible to consciousness. In the *Theses* Marx speaks of 'real sensible activity', 'which belongs to the objective world', not of a purely interpretative process as do the phenomenologists. In the real world, all practices, all relationships, have material aspects. Marx wishes to distinguish between real people acting in the world, transforming it through both interpretative and material means, and the phenomenological abstraction, consciousness, as the vessel of the real. Just as he rejects a philosophical assertion of the universal primacy of matter so he rejects a philosophical idealism asserting the primacy of consciousness. For Marx, Paci might be viewed as compounding error upon error by asserting both the primacy of consciousness and the primacy of precategorical economic forms arising out of universal material needs. For Marx, the material bases of men's activities are always specific historical conditions, not universal ahistorical conditioners.

This brings us to the second element of Marx's rejection of a phenomenological approach: the historical aspect of his materialism. Men make themselves, Marx argues, 'but not in circumstances of their own choosing'. Men always act in historical contexts which condition the potentialities of action; the circumstances of action are always already constituted by the prior activities of men. It is this historical dimension that distinguishes Marxian theory from phenomenology, for it is the theory of the changing historical conditions of action that becomes the focus of Marx's analysis of society.

As Marx wishes to assert a constructivist position (that people construct their social world) while, at the same time, retaining historical materialism as *the* form of explanation (that productive relations are strategic to the understanding of social relations in general), is it the case that the attempt to dissolve the subject–object dualism merely leads to confusion and incoherence when these principles are applied to a theory of society? This tension in Marx's theoretical project certainly gives rise to antithetical interpretations and criticisms of his work.

Perhaps the most continuous and influential critique of Marx is that which casts him as a crude materialist and economic determinist. Such a critique finds it difficult, of course, to account for the position adopted by Marx in the *Theses on Feuerbach* and must entirely neglect the central place given by Marx to the concept of practice. For it is clear from this that Marx's materialism cannot be a crude philosophical materialism which locates the determinate aspect of men's social relations in a pre-given material order. As we have seen, for Marx there is no pre-given order, and as we shall see, no such pre-given objective order exists in the natural world, let alone the social. He rejects the universal abstractions such as 'nature' and 'man' on which such doctrines are based. Rather, as we have already shown, Marx identifies as material those relations into which men enter in their 'practical activities', and in particular those relations that are conceived of as being crucial to the sustaining of any social life: the social relations of production (involving human relations and relations with nature). It is at this point that Marx's materialism is secured and his substantive theory of society emerges. He argues that among all those material relations/ practices engaged in by men, their productive relations are strategic in explaining the structure and transformation of social formations. Much of the criticism of Marxian theory centres on the determining role he assigns to production relations. We can easily dismiss the view of Marx that characterises him as claiming that man is a creature of his material conditions of life. His rejection of Feuerbach and philosophical materialism eliminates the force of any such claim. He is not replacing the universal abstraction of the market with that of production, for central to his historical thesis is that the

forms or modes of these *social* relations of production are historically variable and have different historical effects. Production relations take on different historical forms such as primitive communism, slavery, feudalism and capitalism and are, therefore, trans-
formable through men's actions as well as explaining them. Nor
is it the case that Marx identifies production relations as *the*
sole material condition of a social formation, for all practical
activities have a material aspect, including the production of knowledge, whether scientific or ideological, so the distinction between
the mode of production and social formation is not a material/non-
material distinction. Marx's form of explanation is not essentially
that of material conditions having non-material effects, but of one
strategic set of men's practices having determinate effects on others.
A Marxian concept which undoubtedly confuses this issue is the
infra-structure/super-structure distinction, which at times is used by
Marx in a way that suggests that there is a determinate relation
between a material base and a superstructure of ideas. However, in
its more precise usage in Marx[14] the distinction has more in common
with Freud's unconscious/conscious distinction. The superstructure
again is referred to in various ways but includes two major elements: 'the legal and political superstructure', that is, the agencies
of the state – police, army, courts, etc.; and ideological forms of
consciousness. What distinguishes this 'political', 'legal', 'ideological' superstructure from its 'base' is not its immateriality but its
existence as *consciously* constructed practices. The distinction is
between a 'hidden' base which can be known only through science,
and the visible appearance of a social formation in institutional,
regulatory and official forms. The superstructure is 'the official
active and conscious expressions of the economic structure of
society'.[15]

The significance of this relationship between the 'hidden' structure and its 'appearance' we will return to below. The point we wish
to stress here is that the distinction is not that between material and
non-material elements, despite the fact that Marx identifies the
base as an economic structure. This reference to the economic
brings us to the most common criticism of Marxian theory; namely,
that Marx is guilty of positing a naïve monocausal theory in which
economic relations are the sole determinant of social formations.
While it is clear from the above quotation that Marx often made
statements about the relationship of the economy to the superstruc-

ture which are difficult to construe in any other way, it is also clear that the general import of his developing theoretical project is not reductionist in this crude sense.

First, in his specification, Marx distinguishes between the forces of production (i.e. anything that can be utilised in producing a material use-value, such as tools, human labour-power, and natural resources) and the relations of production (i.e. the relations of connection and separation between men and women and between people and the means of sustaining life). It is this second set of relations that comprise, for Marx, what he calls the economic structure, and what is crucial to these *social* relations are the relations of power that exist between those who have the capacity to use or exploit the forces of production and exclude others from so doing, and those who are excluded, yet are engaged in the production of value. Central to Marx's conception of the economic, therefore, is a social relation of power which through its ramifications, he argues, is strategic to an explanation of those systems of domination that characterise historical social formations. It is, then, the strategic significance of this relationship of power within production relations, which is expressed as a process of appropriation, whereby the non-producers appropriate surplus from the producers, which sets the limits and conditions the processes of development within a social formation. Equally, the forces of production, including the forms of technology and the utilisation of natural resources, are subject to the limitations and potentialities created by the relations of production; the point being that Marx rejects, as we have seen, a materialism that would reduce social relations to the determinants of nature or technology.

In attempting to formulate what Marx means by economic determinism, it is also important to point out that in his analysis of the historical modes of production it is only in capitalism that this strategic relationship of power is secured through economic relations or institutions. It is characteristic of capitalism that this relationship of power, through which surplus is appropriated, takes an economic form – where, for example, labour itself becomes a commodity freely exchanged for wages in the market, and where surplus is also realised through the production of commodities for exchange and calculated in the form of business profits, and where a significant location of power is the business enterprise itself. This *dominance* of economic power is, according to Marx, a peculiarity of capitalism, not a universal feature of society. Whereas under capitalism appropriation is an economically mediated process taking the form of surplus value arising out of the exchange of commodities, under feudalism the direct appropriation of surplus labour is mediated by political and religious institutions. The feudal serf, unlike the capitalist wage-earner, was not entirely separated from the means of production, in so far as he held land, the possession of which was protected by custom. The lord, however, as owner of the land, appropriated value directly in the form of 'surplus' labour through systems of corvée (periods of unpaid labour on the lord's land) or payments in kind. Feudalism was, then, a mode of production in which the process of appropriation took a political form; the manorial unit and its place in a hierarchy of lord–vassal relations involved the personalisation – through the fief – of political institutions through which the relations of production were controlled; a system of domination ideologically sustained by the Church which was itself integrated into this political system.

Even while arguing that political and religious institutions were dominant in medieval Europe, Marx retains his 'economic determinism' by claiming that it is the economic structure that conditions the power of lord and Church. This position is clearly brought out in Marx's response to critics who claimed that while it may be true that the economic structure is determinant in 'our own times where material interests are preponderant', this was certainly not the case for the 'middle ages, dominated by Catholicism, nor for Athens and Rome, dominated by politics'.[16] Marx's reply is instructive:

In the first place, it strikes me as odd that anyone should suppose that these well-worn phrases about the Middle Ages and the ancient world were unknown to anyone else. One thing is clear: the Middle Ages could not live on Catholicism, nor could the ancient world on politics. On the contrary, *it is the manner in which they gained their livelihood which explains why in one case politics, in the other case Catholicism, played the chief part*. For the rest, one needs no more than a slight acquaintance with, for example, the history of the Roman Republic, to be aware that its *secret history* is the history of landed property.[17] (our italics)

The distinction that emerges as Marx attempts to refine his position on economic determinism is between an economic structure that sets the parameters for possible developments of a social formation, and 'dominant' structures or practices that play 'the chief part' in the social formation. This distinction has been raised to a fundamental principle of 'Marxist science' by the contemporary school of Althusserian Marxists who distinguish between what they call 'determination in the last instance' and 'the dominant instance';[18] arguing against the view that there is a simple causal determinism posited between, say, economic structures and political practices, such that political relations can always be explained by reference to, or 'reduced to', economic relations. Rather, politics are 'relatively autonomous', and as is the case in modern capitalist social formations, where the state plays such a significant role in mediating economic relations, may become the 'dominant instance', the most significant location of class conflict. Nevertheless, it remains the economic structure and the contradictions that characterise its development that explain why the state becomes such a significant agency and under what conditions political practice becomes autonomous. To use an analogy, then: while the economic structure of a particular historical epoch determines the rules of the game it does not determine how the cards will fall or how each player will play his game.

Stage 3: the critique of humanism and science as critique

A major controversy surrounding Marx concerns the significance of his commitment to science as the only valid and progressive form of knowledge. While, as we have seen, subjectivists stress the anti-positivist elements in Marx, it is possible to find in sociological textbooks a characterisation of his position which distinguishes his early philosophical leanings from his increasingly positivist view of science and concern with empirical enquiry.[19] It is not unknown for Marx to be categorised along with Durkheim and Comte as one of the positivist founding fathers of sociology. It is not at all difficult to discover grounds for such a characterisation in Marx's own writings. Indeed, the very commitment to materialism involves a constant emphasis on the need to comprehend that concrete material reality. Likewise Marx's rejection of philosophy, idealism, abstraction and mysticism is often taken to imply a positivist position, stressing the primacy of the real world and observation as the basis of gaining valid knowledge of it:

Sense perception must be the basis of all science. Only when science starts out from sense perception in the dual forms of sensuous consciousness and sensuous need – i.e. only where science starts out from nature – is it real science.[20]

Later in the same text:

Natural science will in time subsume the science of man just as the science of man will subsume natural science: there will be one science.[21]

It would be difficult to find in the positivist literature a more thoroughgoing assertion of positivist beliefs. There is the claim that perception is the basis of knowledge. There is the doctrine of naturalism in the assumption that the social and natural sciences are sciences in the same sense, and there is even the Comtean vision of the eventual unity of all sciences. An important source for such views is *The Poverty of Philosophy*,[22] a highly polemical attack on the socialist Proudhon, whom Marx castigated as a metaphysician and utopian, claiming that he reduced real relations between people to abstracted categories. Proudhon, argued Marx, reduced history to a realisation of categories rather than the product of human activity. The consequence of this polemic, in which Proudhon was viewed as an impoverished Hegel, was to distinguish science from philosophy, the concrete from abstraction, empirical analysis from utopian imaginings. Unless we should conclude from the source of the above quotation that this positive view of empirical science is a product of Marx's early, 'immature' thought, its parallel is readily found in the later writings. Describing his own methodology, in the preparation of *Capital* Marx claims: 'The concrete . . . is the point of departure in reality and hence also the point of departure for observation and conception.'[23] Again Marx appears to be stressing the empiricist basis of his scientific project: both observation and, significantly, conception or theory are rooted in a concrete reality. Such claims as these have provided the authority for the construction of empiricist projects in Marxism and have also provided positivist sociology with the justification for its identification of Marx as a founding father, although the latter tend to use such an identification to show how Marx's substantive theory of capitalist society fails to stand up to positivist standards of verification and procedure.[24] The incorporation of a 'failed' Marxism into positivist sociology has been paralleled by the 'triumphant' empiricist version which came to dominate the 'official' brand of East European Marxism, characterised by the Frankfurt School and other humanist locations as a 'dull, dogmatic, mechanistic theory', based on a simplistic economic determinism and cobbled to a positivistic view of science as inherently neutral and progressive.[25] In short, until very recently the dominant Marxist project has been an empiricist one, assimilated to the hegemonies of both East and West. Until the late 1960s contrary interpretations were still small voices.

There is in the empiricist version of Marx, however, a fundamental contradiction; that is, between the Marx who stresses, in the context of his critique of philosophy, the primacy of observation and the concrete real world, and the Marx who equally vigorously and consistently refers to man's experience of his social world as ideological and alienated. We are asked to accept, at one and the same time, that experience is the source of both valid, scientific knowledge, and illusion.

In order to account for Marx's attempt to resolve this incoherence, we must first return to his attempt to dissolve the subject–object dichotomy in the *Theses on Feuerbach*. As we have argued, the *Theses* are not merely the attempt to recast solutions to the problem of what the nature of social reality is (through the concept of practice); they also imply a conscious avoidance of both the empiricist and rationalist solutions to the problem of how we can gain knowledge of that reality. For the dissolution of the subject–object dichotomy also questions the fracture between theory and observation. Observation within an empiricist strategy depends, according to Marx, on the notion of an experiencing subject as the mediator between reality and knowledge of reality; a subject who merely contemplates an external object. Through the concept of practice Marx suggests that knowledge is itself a social activity through which human beings at one and the same time constitute their world *and* know it. Theory, then, does not stand outside of social reality, reflecting upon it, it is part and parcel of the ways in which such reality is constituted. To reverse the image, 'facts' are not the external 'things' the social world is made up of; they are themselves practices and constituted by practice, including theorising about them.

Because Marx believes scientific knowledge to be an aspect of our constructive practices, it is conceived simultaneously as an attempt to account for and explain practically constituted social relations and a potential for transforming them. It is in this sense that science is conceived of as 'critical' – it is an intervention in the social reality it seeks to explain – and because science does not merely reflect the ways in which people conventionally represent to themselves their social reality (ideology) it is a revolutionary practice.

In this attempt to overcome the subject–object duality and so avoid the drift into an empiricist position, Marx's project drifts into a second field of tension. For in stressing that science is an aspect of man's social practices he seems to be drawing a radical distinction between the social and natural sciences; that because men construct their own social relations, science relates to social reality in a quite different way from that of the natural world, which remains an external objective reality. Yet in the quotations above he appears to be asserting the doctrine of naturalism: that social science is, in all major respects, identical in its methods and procedures to the natural sciences. However, this seeming coincidence with the positivist doctrine of naturalism only exists because Marx has turned the doctrine on its head. The passages quoted above which appear to underline Marx's empiricist drift are put in proper perspective by a concluding and surprising sentence:

The social reality of nature and *human* natural sciences or the natural sciences of man are identical expressions.[26]

It is in this passage, in which the very distinction, natural/social, is rejected, that Marx unequivocally reasserts his constructivist strategy. According to Marx it is not only the social world that is a product of human practices, it is also nature and the natural sciences. He rejects the view that nature exists as an external, objective condition of social beings. Natural science is not a reflection of such an objective world given to experience; it is itself an aspect of man's living-in-the-world. All science is a social practice through which men construct their reality. The social sciences are equivalent to the natural sciences not because social relations can be construed as objective things in the same way as physical phenomena, but because we socially construct our relations to the natural world. Because men *act upon* nature; nature itself is socialised and science is a significant means toward that outcome. The history of the relation between man and his natural environment is one in which nature itself is progressively transformed from an alien force determining our actions into a socially constructed reality reflecting our socially constructed needs.

For Marx, then, natural science is progressive in so far as it humanises nature, involving the transformative capacity of action. Human beings do not merely reflect upon the natural order of things, they act upon it, control it, give it social meaning. Now, paradoxically, Marx conceives of social science in the same way. But what can it mean to talk of sociology, for example, as *humanising* society; as socialising society? It is here that the concept of alienation becomes central to Marxian thought, for alienation refers to those conditions in which we experience our social relations as an external, objective force determining our actions – society, like nature, becomes a *thing* over which we have no control. That which is the product of our actions becomes a condition of our actions. The naturalist doctrine in social science far from reflecting Marx's own view is one that he rejects as itself a form of alienation, by not only asserting that nature is an objective, autonomous realm but in extending that view to *society* as something standing outside of and determining the actions of people. For sociology to become a non-alienated form of activity, it would have to become a practice which 'humanised' society in a dual sense. First, it would need to conceive of social relations as constructive practices rather than structural determinations of actions, and as a constructive practice itself sociology would necessarily have the effect of liberating human beings from such alienated forms. The consequence for Marx in constructing such a theoretical project is the rejection of abstractions such as society, nature, man, etc., as universal conditions of action. There is no universal form of 'nature' acting upon 'man', because the relations between human beings and nature are continually changing, and nature itself is thereby changed. There are no universal characteristics of 'man' which determine his social relations, because those social relations are constructed by people in varied historical situations – we are an outcome of our own actions. There is no universal super-actor called 'society' acting upon 'men', merely the historically varied social formations the elements of which are the changing relations between people. In *Capital*, for example, Marx's critique of the classical political economists focuses on the way in which they treat the market as a universal abstraction having a nature-like force to determine our activities. The consequence, he argues, is that such a conception of the market has the ideological force to subordinate us to a fatalistic view of our situation. Action becomes ineffective in the face of market forces that have the appearance of being something other than the actions of people engaged in exchange relations.

Stage 4: the hidden reality and the role of abstraction

Marx's later work, and particularly *Capital*, is of prime importance in our attempt to outline Marx's substantialist project. Interpreters of his work have consistently remarked on the extent to which the later works have involved new departures in Marx's thinking. Empiricist interpreters have focused on a claim that the metaphysical elements are increasingly eradicated as Marx turns to a scientific concern with the more concrete problems of the economy. Subjectivists have viewed this development as retrograde, in that Marx's increasing focus on the economy is at the expense of a concern with ideological forms and consciousness, and the determinist aspect of Marx begins to outweigh his earlier emphasis on practice and the construction of social reality. Finally, Althusserian Marxists have adopted a position that suggests that, rather than a change of emphasis or a refocusing of interest, the later work involves a complete break with what went before; that *Capital* and associated texts established what amounted to a new science based on new concepts, which finally divorced Marx from the subjectivists and empiricists who held in common a view of society that placed the *abstract* subject at the centre of history and science.

While accepting the general point that important departures are to be observed in Marx's later works, we do not accept the view that there is a discontinuity involved, whether from metaphysics to science or from a constructivist to a determinist project. We wish, in fact, to stress a continuity – that is to say, the later works include Marx's confrontation with the central tension of his theoretical strategy. As we have already outlined, this tension results from the rejection of the empiricist separation of the real, external objective world and knowledge of it as the product of experience. Marx accepts the reality of the external world but rejects the empiricist conception of knowledge, both because knowledge as a practice is involved in constructing that reality and because knowledge of it is not simply given to experience. How then is it possible to know reality? How can we make valid statements about it? In his critique and analysis of political economy Marx deliberately confronts himself with this problem, and in so doing develops the concept of abstraction to take its place alongside that of practice and critique as central to the Marxian resolution of the problem of knowledge.

Marx shares with the empiricist sociologist a belief in the positive role of science in so far as it extends the capacities of men to think their social reality:

> The reform of social consciousness consists *entirely* in making the world aware of its own consciousness, in arousing itself from its dream of itself, in explaining its own actions to it ... our whole aim can only be to translate religious and political problems into their self-conscious human form.[27]

Science for Marx *is* the 'self-conscious human form' and this early formulation sketches his view that science must somehow break through the experience of reality as a 'dream of itself'; beyond, that is, *appearance*, to an underlying and concealed reality, so expanding men's consciousness of their own reality. In *Capital* he asserts: 'All science would be superfluous if the outward appearance and the essence of things directly coincided.'[28] The reality that Marx identifies as the object of scientific knowledge is not, then, and cannot be, a straightforward observation of the empirical world, because the phenomenal forms in which the social world is given to experience 'disguise the relations they express'. As a result, any attempt to gain knowledge on the basis of constructing categories derived from empirically observed relations, as the empiricist sociologist does when constructing models of the family or bureaucracy or types of deviancy, must be scientifically inadequate.

The problem that arises for Marx is, how do we get beyond the phenomenal forms to these underlying realities which they are said to express? Hw can we know a reality that is, by definition, hidden? One of the most influential and innovatory developments in Marxist scholarship in recent years has been the 'discovery', aided by the publication and translation of *the Grundrisse* (Marx's preparatory notebooks),[29] that *Capital* is an essay in methodology as well as an analysis of capitalism and critique of political economy. It is a methodology that takes equally seriously both method of enquiry and method of presentation. It is the latter emphasis, which views science as existing in texts that are themselves social practices and define their own relations to other social practices or realities, that has provided an impetus to the development of Marxist interest in linguistics[30] and the manner in which social reality is constructed and understood as discourse: that social sciences are systems of discourse, of writing and reading and the criteria which are used in achieving both. This emphasis on the text as a method of presentation has, then, led to a plethora of projects claiming Marxian pedigree, in which the method of enquiry, the content of the analysis has been subordinated to the analysis of forms of discourse when society itself is viewed as a text or re-presentations.[31]

The method of *Capital* hinges on two concepts: critique and abstraction. As a critique of political economy it has a dual significance, in so far as the specific criticisms of the writings of Smith and Ricardo expose not only internal contradictions in these works but these contradictions express the workings of a generalised social ideology which identifies social reality as those phenomenal forms which the observer experiences.

> The vulgar economist's way of looking at things stems from . . . the fact that it is only the direct form of manifestation of relations that is reflected in their brains and not *their inner connections*.[32] (our italics)

It is the relationship between these phenomenal forms and their inner connections that poses for Marx the problem of abstraction. What he is at pains to avoid in both his method of investigation and of presentation is the form of abstraction that he sees as characterising the 'vulgar economist' or the empiricist position: that is, a process of abstraction from complex, concrete reality which produces more and more general, abstract and transhistorical categories, so raising what are merely *attributes* of real, concrete, historically imbedded, phenomena to universally applicable categories. Thus market exchange is raised to the status of a universally applicable generalisation by economists. Paradoxically, for Marx, abstraction both begins and ends with concrete reality, for the 'inner-connection' is itself a real social relationship, but one that can only be arrived at through imaginative theorising and critical abstraction. It is a process that, far from leading to increasingly 'abstracted' universal categories, identifies the underlying real social relations which characterise a specific historical mode such as capitalism.

The analysis of capitalism begins with agreement with the 'vulgar' economist that 'the economic cell-form' of bourgeois society is commodity exchange. Bourgeois wealth presents itself in commodity form; it is the way in which the world is represented in people's experience, and as capitalism develops such experiences gain 'the stability of a natural self-understood form of social life',[33] confronting the observer as empirical fact.

The starting-point for abstraction, however, is the critical observation that this reality expresses a contradiction. If the capitalist relations present themselves as processes of commodity exchange – i.e. the exchange of equal values – how is it that a surplus, in the form of a profit, can be generated through such exchanges of equivalents? This question sets the Marxian process of abstraction into motion.

The undoubted difficulties entailed in following the Marxian logic of presentation here is that commodity relations are both real, concrete relations in capitalist formations – the way in which people act in relation to one another – *and* an ideological representation. There is nothing false or illusory about such relations. These are the lived relations but, to put it crudely, we are living a lie, which expresses itself as the contradiction between the appearance of equivalent exchange and profit. The process of abstraction (to simplify) leads Marx to the identification of an underlying reality which explains this contradiction: a relationship of appropriation, in which labour is exploited.

Marx argues that if different kinds of goods represent qualitatively distinct and incommensurable values for use (i.e. the values of a pork chop and a painting are incommensurable), how is it that they can be exchanged as though they are commensurable in quantitative terms (as measured by money)? Such exchange is possible only if these use-values have some common basis; if there is a common source of value. He concludes that the only common and concrete source of value is the labour-power expended in their production. Therefore, Marx argues, returning to the contradiction in exchange relations, if a surplus is generated through exchange, that surplus can have its real source only in labour and, therefore, must represent value which is not paid to labour for the labour-time expended in its production. Thus, in the process of commodity exchange, one commodity – labour – does not receive equivalent value through the payment of wages. Labour as a commodity only appears to receive a wage for labour expended – the reality is an appropriation of surplus value which accrues to capital in the form of profit, so providing the dynamic of capital accumulation which created the conditions for industrialisation.

It is, then, for Marx, this social relation of the appropriation of surplus value that constitutes the underlying reality of capitalism. This 'hidden' relation is not conceived of as an abstracted attribute of more concrete relations, but is itself a real, concrete social relation. What distinguishes capitalism from other historical forms of domination is that labour is expropriated through the operation of economic mechanisms while remaining formally free. The economic relation, that between labour and capital, is none the less a relationship of power which, Marx argues, is strategic in conditioning capitalist social formations – creating conditions for class formation and the forms of class struggle or conflict, state formation and legal forms, etc. The very cast of its power relations are, at all levels, mediated by this underlying social relation of appropriation. Critical abstraction is, Marx argues, necessary in order to identify these 'hidden' relations which are none the less concrete and real.

This form of abstraction has important consequences for the question of determinism, in the sense that the relation between the social relations of appropriation and relations of commodity exchange is not conceived of as that between real and illusory things. Market or distributional processes are real processes through which, for example, class relations are formed and reproduced. The significance of such a conclusion for sociology is that it undermines the conventional division in class theory, between those who espouse Marxian theory by locating the determinants of class position solely in production relations, and those who follow Weber in claiming that classes have their origins in market relations or distributional processes. The method of abstraction adopted by Marx suggests that market relations are significant in processes of class formation while remaining conditioned by the form of appropriation – the relations of production. The relation of capital to labour is the strategic relation of power, but the particular features of class formation and struggle are the historical outcome of many processes, which include the market strategies of specific occupations, as well as the emergent structures and specific activities of the state.

The intimate relationship between abstraction and critique that emerges in the methodology of *Capital* re-emphasises that Marxian theory is a critique of ideology, or to put it another way, a critique of forms of understanding based upon experience, and as such involves a critique of subjectivism as a theory of knowledge. The process of critique is crucial to the process of theorising those social relations that are strategic to an explanation of the social formation as a whole. It is a process that does not render the empirically observed world irrelevant or illusory, for it is only through the ideology critique – through identifying the contradictions in phenomena as represented to experience – that the process of abstraction is possible at all. Furthermore, it is only by way of the reverse process – that is, explaining the existence of such observed phenomena by means of the abstractive identification of such an underlying reality – that the explanatory power of the theory can be demonstrated. Finally, because the theoretical structure, so created, is also an aspect of men's practices, it is conceived of as an instrument of social and political action capable of revealing its explanatory power in its capacity to transform social relations. This last point is crucial for an understanding of how Marx attempts to overcome what we have earlier identified as the core tension of substantialism, namely the problem of validation. For while it is true that Marx retains the empiricist link between theory and the empirical world as a source of its validation, it is also true to say that he does not regard this link as one in which theory merely reflects that reality in a neutral fashion and is open to empirical testing on the basis of purely empiricist canons of procedure. For if science is an aspect of our practical living-in-the-world then the criteria of what is valid theory must be linked to the potentiality of action. The adequacy of theory must, then, according to Marx, be linked to its adequacy in informing action, and in particular, political action. For Marx, then, theory does not become political as a result of political activists using it for political purposes; it is in itself a political activity. Its scientific validity resides in its capacity to change the world. The concept of practice has, therefore, a dual significance in Marx's project. Not only is it central to his attempt to reconstruct materialism as a viable strategy – the practices of human beings constitute social reality – but it is also crucial to the way in which Marx attempts to solve the problem of validation – how we know social reality. This latter issue constitutes a field of tension in Marx's substantialism and we will return to it in Chapter 6.

Conclusion

While it is clear that Marx's substantialist strategy involved a rejection of the basic tenets of empiricism, subjectivism, and rationalism, it is also the case that the critical method he adopted involved a continuous dialogue with one or other of these alternative strategies, resulting in the adoption, in a modified form, of what he took to be their positive contributions. He accepts the empiricist characterisation of reality as a material objective set of events, while rejecting its associated nominalism and the claim that knowledge is rooted in experience. He aligns himself with subjectivism in viewing the social as a project of human constructive activity, while rejecting the assumption that such activity is entirely reducible to an interpretative process. Finally, he accepts the constructivist position of the rationalist, Hegel, while rejecting what he regarded as his abstract idealism.

In the process of constructing his own project, then, Marx continually exposed his substantialism to the counterclaims of the alternative strategies, and it is this ecumenism that helps to explain both the criticisms that seek to expose the contradictory nature of Marx's writings, and the capacity of his writings to generate so many differing schools of Marxism, each of which has found it possible – with textual authority – to reconstruct Marx from quite different strategic viewpoints. We would argue that many such reconstructions undermine what is of greatest value in Marx, and that is the extent to which his substantialism constituted a *dialogue*, as a result of which his project was forced to come to terms with other strategic claims. Marxists have tended to interpret these confrontations as exemplifications of Marx's critical method; exposing the ideological content of all that went before, in order to reject it. The consequence has been to underplay the significance of the dialogue, and its effects on the development of Marx's own project.

As we have already suggested in the introductory chapter, and will pursue at some length in the concluding chapter, it is through the medium of such dialogue that the inherent problems of each strategy may be overcome. We do not argue that Marx has provided such solutions; rather that, in attempting to displace the dualism, material/ideal and subject/object, he pointed to the possibilities of theoretical advance. In fact, as we will argue in the concluding chapter, practice, the concept we have identified as crucial to Marx's resolution of substantialism's tensions, eventually fails to solve the problem of validation, and creates its own problems for Marxist analysis.

5
Rationalism

In this chapter we will pursue further our analysis of the four theoretical strategies identified in Chapter 1, through a detailed consideration of the work of Emile Durkheim, who, we will argue, is the major representative of the rationalist tradition in sociology. The content of this chapter is very much affected by the fact that existing sociological texts mistakenly present Durkheim as a founding father of modern positivistic sociology.[1] Because our view of Durkheim is unconventional, we have, in what follows, found it necessary to show not only the extent to which Durkheim's project depended on a rationalist strategy but, at the same time, to establish the credibility of our case by way of a rather more detailed exploration of the original texts than has been the case in earlier chapters.

In keeping with the chapters on empiricism, subjectivism and substantialism, however, we will explore the internal contradictions of the rationalist strategy, the effects of which are represented in the drift towards empiricism which certainly can be found in Durkheim's work. These elements of empiricism are, however, a product of the tensions that emerge within his rationalist project rather than a defining feature of Durkheim's project in social theory.

We have argued that each of our four alternative strategies is the result of presenting, in abstract, the fourfold parameters of theoretical discourse and should not be confused with the work of actual social theorists such as Durkheim. For although all theorists must seek solutions to the dilemmas of knowledge – what is the nature of reality and how can we know it? – and make such choices within a structured set of possibilities (i.e. the strategies), nevertheless, it is both possible and likely that any given theorist, such as Marx,

Weber or Durkheim, will, in confronting common issues, construct a theoretical project that is an amalgamation of various assumptions underlying more than one theoretical strategy. In other words, such a theorist cannot be 'boxed' within the confines of one such set of strategic assumptions, but rather will be found to drift towards the corner of a box (as depicted in our diagram, p. 23) and pass into an alternative box. This, it will be argued, is the case with Durkheim, whose predominantly rationalist strategy not only suffers from the contradictions internal to that strategy but also exhibits tensions associated with the ways in which his rationalism is infected by certain empiricist elements. In order to follow this argument the reader must continually bear in mind the distinction we are making between the abstract theoretical strategy and the concrete theoretical project, the latter relating to both individual theorists and schools of theory. In summary, then, the strategies contain within themselves the seeds of their own dynamic, including the drift into alternative strategies. As a result, any given theorist will reflect this movement, which in turn means that their works are unlikely to prove an uncomplicated representation of any one strategy, or exhibit only one set of tensions, but are more likely to exhibit overlapping fields of tension deriving from both strategy and project. We will be arguing in our concluding chapter that it is the capacity of a theorist to construct a project on the basis of a dialogue with the alternative strategies that determines his creativity and interest.

What follows will, then, illustrate the effects of these dynamics at work within rationalism and within the writings of Durkheim, which, despite his commitment to a rationalist strategy, have given rise to modern schools of Durkheimian sociology that are centrally committed to an empiricist strategy. In developing this analysis we will be attempting more than a straightforward description of what happened to Durkheim's insights and findings at the hands of his 'followers'; rather, we will be tracing a structural process, involving the 'collapse' of a theoretical strategy as a result of its own internal contradictions as well as the incoherence of Durkheim's theoretical project. The chapter should function not only as an account of sociological rationalism but should also help us to understand why the major representative of rationalism in sociology failed to provide a lasting framework for sociological theorising and research.

What we shall say about Durkheim is none the less based on the view that his work can be treated as a whole – a number of commentators, notably Talcott Parsons,[2] have discerned a radical break in Durkheim's work, from the 'positivism' of the early books to 'idealism' in his mature work (empiricism to rationalism, in our terminology). It is our view that while Durkheim's concerns manifestly changed over time, centring more on those problems associated with religious belief, and while his work became more mature and articulate – reflected in numerous changes of crucial terminology – he nevertheless remained the same thinker with the same *strategy* throughout his active intellectual life, however internally incoherent that strategy may have been. We will not engage in a chronological description of his work or a detailed analysis of any one example, such as *Suicide: A Study in Sociology*. Many such studies of great merit and insight already exist.[3] Our major interest in Durkheim is as an example of the rationalist strategy in sociology.

Rationalism as a theoretical strategy

Let us first consider how rationalism typically resolves the problems arising out of the question: what is the nature of social reality? Two central tenets of rationalism must be grasped here: first, that society is a *real* and *general* phenomenon; it is a thing-in-itself which stands 'outside' of, and is independent of, all those elements that make it up, such as individuals, their consciousness, and their circumstances. Second, the *real* and *general* reality which constitutes the social is made up of ideas – it is an ideal reality. Thus, while rationalism shares with substantialism a view of reality as general, it departs from it in regarding such general structures as ideal rather than material in content. What are the implications of such presuppositions? First, as society is viewed as a general entity that governs all individual manifestations, it must not be confused with such individual events. That is to say, society should not be equated with, or confused with, the circumstances and conditions (whether spatial or temporal) with which individual human beings interact (i.e. physical environment such as climate, or social environment such as technology). Nor must it be reduced to the states of consciousness with which individuals enter these relations (i.e. needs, motives, reasons, understandings). It is these latter presuppositions and their implications that distinguish rationalism from both empiricism and subjectivism, for the empiricist regards social reality as made up of unique, individual events, while the subjectivist regards the social as the product of individual understandings and consciousness. For the rationalist then, society 'determines' the consciousness of individuals and the ways in which such consciousness relates to the circumstances and conditions that are encountered. If the empirical world is the sum of these conditions, circumstances, and consciousnesses, and as such is given to our experience as observers, it follows that society which lies behind and determines such phenomena, is somehow independent of the empirical world and is not immediately given to observation.

It also follows that while social reality is an ideal reality, these ideas are not to be equated with or confused with the thoughts of individuals, or the ideas we have of it (prevailing ideas). Rationalism does not reject the existence of material objects interacting with one another in time or space; rather, it asserts that such phenomena do not constitute *society*, which is a structure of ideas that itself determines the particular relations of such objects. It is this ideal structure, society, that explains the phenomenal world.

Given the way in which rationalists conceive the nature of social reality, what are the general presuppositions that answer the question: how do we know such a reality? Because rationalists believe that social reality is made up of ideas – that is to say, has the same character as our own thought – and because they also believe that the empirical world of objects is a reflection of (to be explained by) this ideal reality, they conclude that the *direct* examination of thought is the only route to knowledge of the real world. This examination, it is claimed, goes beyond mere subjective impressions which we as individuals gain as a result of our experience in the world (i.e. ideas in the conventional sense). Rather, they set out to reveal the structure of mind itself; those 'innate ideas' which are shared by all human beings by virtue of their status as human beings. These ideas are then prior to and independent of the experiences any particular human being may have of the world about him. It is these shared ideas (universals) that lie behind, govern, and explain the phenomena of the social world. To examine the underlying 'hidden' structure of ideas (as against the superficial features of individual consciousness) is, *ipso facto*, to examine reality itself. Put simply, while the empiricists, for example, 'look at' the world in order to know it, on the grounds that what they can see or might see is all that exists, rationalists 'think' about the world in order to know it, on the grounds that behind the world that can be 'seen' or is given to the senses, there lies a world of thought; a structure that is innate, universal, and shared. Sociology, which is committed to or influenced by a rationalist strategy often focuses on such features of social life as language, myth, ideology, symbolism, etc.; for the varieties of human language, for example, would be expected to conform to a common underlying structure, the very capacity to learn and use language being an expression of the universal structure of mind which all humans share.

It will be clear that commitment to a rationalist strategy will also involve a rejection of empiricist measures of what constitutes a true or valid statement about the world, for to show that a statement can be empirically justified is merely to assert the coincidence of superficial experience or consciousness, without ever explaining why such coincidence exists. If we accept the rationalist view that reality is constituted by ideas, then the ultimate criterion of validity is that properties and definitions should be consistent, and not characterised by a logical contradiction. If reality is ideal then it must conform to canons of logic. From the point of view of a fully rationalist strategy even the criterion that a theory should conform to the empirical world is an example of logical consistency. We know a thing to be true because logic, that ultimate structured property of pure thought, tells us that it is so, and not for other possible reasons, such as we have observed it, or others agree with us that it is so, or God has revealed it in our dreams.

A characteristic of rationalism which sets it apart from empiricism is the way in which the strategy deals with the relations between fact and value. The empiricist strategy insists on a radical distinction between fact and value, claiming that there can be no objective knowledge that entails a value judgement. That this is not the case for rationalism derives from the fact that the rationalist strategy does not distinguish between an observable world about which we can be certain, and an unobservable, 'transcendental' world, about which we can know nothing other than what faith dictates. For what the empiricist considers to be the unknowable realm, of faith, religion and metaphysic, is for the rationalist the reality that can and must be known in an objective fashion – for rationalists, fact and value are fused in one reality, and to dismember them is to distort that reality fundamentally.

The reality of values suggests, then, that the rationalist strategy leads to an ethical absolutism – that is to say, certain values are part of what it is to be a social being – rather than the ethical relativism that results from the empiricist strategy. This is a feature of rationalist strategy that is of particular importance in Durkheim's work, for his concern to establish what he calls 'a science of morality',[4] while making sense in terms of a rationalist strategy, appears nonsensical in the context of the conventional view of Durkheim as a founder of empiricist sociology.

Durkheim's theoretical project

If the above propositions represent a concise statement of the rationalist strategy, then it is not too difficult to show that Durkheim was an exponent, and representative, of this school (in describing his own position he used the phrase 'sociological rationalism'[5]), and that an examination of his works is *ipso facto* an examination of rationalist sociology. Let us pursue both these objectives in considering Durkheim's major works more closely.

No one reading Durkheim can for long remain unaware of his hostility towards individualistic explanations of social phenomena. Among the targets of his attack were the utilitarians of the nineteenth century, such as Bentham, James and J. Stuart Mill, and Spencer. According to these thinkers human society was no more than a nexus of co-operative exchanges between individuals, each of whom had, on balance, a greater incentive to remain in such exchanges (society) than they did to leave them. The essential features of social life and its varying historical forms were explained by reference to the enduring dispositions of individuals, such as their need for food, and the conditions of exchange in which they happened to find themselves. These conditions would more or less dispose them either to form alliances with others or alternatively to prevent others from entering such alliances. For the Utilitarians, society.was nothing more than a shorthand term describing the actions of individuals, and it was this nominalism that Durkheim went to such lengths to attack. As far as Durkheim was concerned the very existence of 'individuals', to say nothing of their capacity to form enduring relationships of exchange, presupposed the existence of a 'moral order' (society).

With this point in mind let us consider Durkheim's most famous work, namely his *Suicide: A Study in Sociology*, a work that is commonly regarded as a 'model' of scientific inquiry in the social sciences. According to social analysts who were the predecessors or contemporaries of Durkheim (and many social theorists today) suicide was a discrete act committed by an individual against himself. The cause of such an act was to be found in prior conditions which were 'external' to that individual, such as the climate, or whether or not the individual was 'unemployed'; or antecedent conditions which were 'internal' to that individual, such as his racial characteristics, or whether or not he 'believed' that suicide was a 'good thing'. Although such theorists differed on which of these factors they regarded as most important, some preferring variations in climate, and others diet or moral condition, all agreed that suicide was indeed 'caused' by such factors or some combination of such factors, and that the suicide rate in any given society was the outcome. Such explanations were not, and are not, confined to the scientific community. A priest, or a Christian, might provide an essentially similar account, claiming that suicide was an event 'caused' by the individual's 'disobedience' or 'sinfulness'. In all such cases suicide is conceived of as an individual phenomenon caused by some other equally individual phenomena. Such phenomena might be 'external' or 'internal' to the individual; 'environmental' or 'hereditarian', to use Durkheim's terms.

The possibility that suicide was dependent upon causes that lay outside of this individual/phenomenal world just did not occur to Durkheim's nineteenth-century predecessors, for they all adhered to the basic assumptions of empiricism, that reality is made up of particular phenomena like climates, racial groups, diets, poverty and wealth, and that causality was largely a question of the interaction between them. The possibility of looking for causes in some social reality other than these individual phenomena would not merely involve a change in the theory, but a radical change in basic assumptions about the nature of social reality – in our terms, a shift to an alternative theoretical strategy.

It is important to grasp that the essence of Durkheim's approach to suicide was not that he added to the existing list a new factor called 'the social factor' (for most theories were already 'social' in this sense). Rather, he scrapped the whole machinery of thought or strategy that generated such multi-factor approaches in the first place. Durkheim argued, and this was his central point, that both the conditions under which the suicidee found himself (for example, his wealth or poverty), *and* his state of mind at the time of the act (for example, his attitude towards suicide), were 'caused' by some *third* entity called 'society'; an entity that was in no way reducible to, or coterminous with, such 'factors'. Indeed society was not a 'factor' at all. Society was above the world of mere 'facts' and 'factors', and yet it had to be understood if they were to be accounted for in the first place. What was more, it was real; more real than the 'facts' and 'factors' ('individual manifestations' in Durkheim's words) which it caused.

At this stage we need to consider the nature of Durkheim's commitment to realism. Durkheim's realism entails more than a commitment to the view that social phenomena exist independently of our perception of them, for this is a view that the utilitarians and empiricists could themselves easily accept. More important for Durkheim is the claim that society is more than the sum of its parts – it is a whole, or thing-in-itself. In the conventional interpretations of Durkheim this claim is made to sound rather trite and unexception-able – society, like the human body, is more than the various organs and parts that make it up. However, Durkheim's application of such a view to society has quite surprising implications. Let us consider what his claims are again. First, society is a thing-in-itself, a whole, which has its own spatial and structural characteristics – i.e. it exists somewhere – and has a particular form, but it is not the same thing as those parts that make it up (institutions, beliefs, individual actions, etc.). Society must not, he urges, be confused with these observable, individual phenomena. Society is a thing, continuous and enduring over time, which determines the entire realm of observable social phenomena. Although society would be impossi-ble without these corresponding phenomena, or 'individual man-ifestations', it is none the less absolutely necessary, according to Durkheim, to make the conceptual distinction between them. He suggested that even if all the phenomena of action and beliefs ceased to exist, 'society' would somehow remain intact. The signifi-cance of the conceptual distinction between whole and part, be-tween 'society' and its 'individual manifestations', resides in the fact that while society is a condition of the individual parts, these same institutions, beliefs and acts do not constitute a condition of society. Durkheim's position is not, then, akin to the thesis of the 'emergent' properties of structure favoured by empiricists, although he did, on occasion, argue along such lines.

That Durkheim had such a 'holistic', 'mystical' and 'teleological' view of the nature of social reality, and that such a view contravened more or less every principle adhered to by the nominalistic/individualistic scientists of his own time, and indeed today, has been fully recognised by one of the major figures of modern sociology, Talcott Parsons. In discussing Durkheim's distinction between 'society' and its 'individual manifestations' Parsons wrote:

> One possible line of solution to this problem has given rise ... to the prevailing interpretation of Durkheim's position on the problem of 'social realism'. It is that *only* objective data such as legal codes and suicide statistics are empirically observable. But by Durkheim's own testimony these do *not* constitute the social reality; they are only *manifestations* of it. *What, then, is it?* Since it cannot be observed, it would seem to be a metaphysical entity. And since *only* observable things are capable of scientific treatment, this metaphysical entity is not a proper object of science. It is a psychic entity, a 'mind'. In so far as minds *are* observable at all it is obviously only the minds of individuals. The 'group mind', on the other hand, is merely a metaphysical assumption; its employment is scientifically unsound.[6] (our emphases)

Whether or not Parsons is correct in describing Durkheim's 'social realism' as 'unscientific' is not, at present, the issue. What is at issue is Parsons's correct view that 'social realism' involves a belief in an unobservable reality which is 'over and above' and irreducible to the social phenomena which are at hand (legal codes, suicide statistics, individual minds). He is also correct in identifying Durkheim's position as an unqualified 'social realism' in the sense that he (Parsons) defines it. To use a well-worn metaphor, while most people would describe and explain the events on a billiard-ball table in terms of the immanent properties of the balls, their material composition, and the resistance and friction of the table cloth, the cushions, and other balls, Durkheim would argue that the totality of such things and events was caused by 'something' that stood, quite literally, 'outside' of the billiard table altogether. It is only by realising this rather stunning fact about social realism that we can ever understand exactly what Durkheim meant when he described social reality as '*sui generis*', 'external', and 'independent of its individual manifestations'.[7] We would argue, then, that Durkheim's theoretical project only makes sense once we adopt an 'extreme' interpretation of these much discussed words and phrases – 'extreme', that is, in the view of those who are eager to 'save' Durkheim and so include him among the founding fathers of empiricist sociology. It is our contrary view that Durkheim's sociology represents a quite different strategy of theorising about the social, and one that is often discounted as 'unscientific' and 'metaphysical'. Those who accuse Durkheim of 'metaphysics',[8] 'essentialism',[9] and 'sociologism'[10] are in this sense quite right in what they say, for he was indeed guilty of these, and many other, 'sins', if 'sins' they be. The sins of the father are, in this case, defined by sons who have fundamentally departed from his way of thinking. Let us now look at the idealism of Durkheimian sociology.

To an idealist the whole of reality, and therefore the whole of social reality, is, ultimately, 'ideal'. The term 'ultimately' is important because only a very small minority ot idealists (known as Solipsists) deny the existence of the material world; they merely argue that 'behind' such a world lies another, more important, level of reality, namely the level of mind. Now the mind, or ideal reality, of which the material world is a determinate consequence, may be no more than a particular 'presence' found in all, or some, of the material particles that make up the world. Thus we may speak of human beings as 'possessing' minds, and may couple this view with the view that such minds 'determine' or 'govern' the behaviour of such humans. This is the case with most modern idealists, such as symbolic interactionists of the George Herbert Mead school. Symbolic interactionists regard the human mind as irreducible to the human body. Indeed they see the mind as determinant of many bodily functions and attributes, as in the case of social stigmatisation. Alternatively, it may be argued that Mind, with a capital 'M', is a distinctive reality in its own right, and that the minds of individual human beings, like their corresponding bodies, are mere 'reflections' of this fact, and that Mind, therefore, is 'external' to all of the particular minds and bodies that exist in the phenomenal world. This is where that crucial difference between nominalism and realism comes in again, for it should be clear that while a nominalist (who is at the same time an idealist) would hold to the first position (that mind is an attribute of individuals), a realist would hold to the second position (that Mind is outside of both minds and bodies). It follows that any social theorist who is at the same time a realist and an idealist must believe that society is essentially a structure of objective ideas: that is, a reality in its own right which stands outside of the phenomenal world, including the no less phenomenal world of individual minds, or consciousnesses.

The view of society as essentially an objective structure of ideas irreducible to phenomena, is indeed central to Durkheim's position. Although Talcott Parsons mistakenly thought that Durkheim arrived at this view of social reality only towards the end of his life, he none the less characterises Durkheim's project with an accuracy and precision that cannot be bettered:

> Society has become the thing the Idealist philosophers are talking about. It consists as Durkheim says 'Exclusively of ideas and sentiments', and not, it may be further said, merely of 'ideas', but of The Idea, for the categories are the very matrix out of which particular ideas (the minds of individuals) are formed. It consists not merely of 'representations', but of Ideas in the technical philosophical sense. Society becomes not a part of Nature at all, but, in Whitehead's phrase, of the world of 'Eternal Objects'.[11]

If Parsons is right, then, Durkheim stands in a well-known philosophical tradition represented by Plato and Hegel, called 'objective idealism' (idealistic realism). In our own terms, 'objective idealism' is a theoretical strategy which sees social phenomena, that is institutions, beliefs, and individual actions, as a series of 'reflections', or, in Durkheim's telling phraseology, 'individual manifestations', of an objective Mind. To establish the point that this strategy was central to the construction of Durkheim's theoretical project let us allow him to speak for himself.

In his first major work, *The Division of Labour in Society*, Durkheim argues that the willingness, and capacity, of individual men to form differentiated but interdependent relationships with each other – i.e. to divide their labours – is dependent neither upon their individual motivations (i.e. their desire for 'happiness'), nor upon the material conditions in which they find themselves (i.e. scarcity of resources due to demographic pressures).[12] As Durkheim says at the outset: 'The division of labour can be effectuated only among members of *an already constituted society*.'[13] (our emphasis). In other words, 'society' determines the willingness and capacity of men to co-operate with each other, rather than the other way around, as the Utilitarians thought. However, what is the nature of this determinant of the division of labour, if it is neither the willingness of individual men to co-operate, nor the environmental pressures making such co-operation necessary? Similarly, what is this society if it is not the division of labour itself, which clearly it cannot be, for 'an already constituted society' exists before the division of labour? Durkheim defines 'society' as follows: 'What we call society is a more or less organised totality of *beliefs and sentiments* common to all of the members of the group.'[14] (our emphasis). Durkheim could hardly be clearer, and this in an early work which Parsons considers to have been written before Durkheim's 'idealism' had manifested itself.[15] Another way of phrasing this sentence would be to say that 'society' is a 'group mind' (Parsons's phrase), or that it is a 'collective consciousness' (Durkheim's phrase). It follows, then, that if 'society' is 'a more or less organised totality of beliefs and sentiments', or 'collective consciousness', the fact that the division of labour sometimes develops, but sometimes does not, must be due to a particular condition of this collective mind. This is precisely what accounts for such a variation, according to Durkheim. 'The progress of the division of labour is in direct ratio to the *moral* and dynamic density of society.'[16] (our emphasis).

What the exact nature of 'moral and dynamic density' is, is not directly pertinent to our present argument. What concerns us here is that 'moral and dynamic density' refers to some condition of the prevailing *'zeitgeist'* (timespirit), some collective attitude which, however it manifests itself at the individual level, is conducive to 'the progress of the division of labour'. 'Society', then, is not a structure of undifferentiated/independent, or differentiated/-interdependent individuals or 'persons', for such structures are an effect of society. Rather it is a structure of 'ideas and sentiments' which are more or less morally and dynamically 'dense'. Durkheim has completely reversed the conception of ideas common to materialist sociologies, and, what is more, he has done so without identifying ideas as a property of individual minds, as is the case with modern 'action' approaches to sociology.

Returning now to *Suicide: A Study in Sociology*, we see that Durkheim's conception of social reality as ideal has remained unchanged. In this work he locates the 'causes' of suicide in what he variously calls 'the social environment', or the 'social milieu', but he does not conceptualise this 'environment', or 'milieu' in the usual way, as a factor or condition. He defines it as follows: 'The social environment is *fundamentally* one of common ideas, beliefs, customs, and tendencies.'[17] (our emphasis). This definition is almost identical to that found in *The Division of Labour*. Again, we need not consider the details of Durkheim's explanation of suicide, we need only point out that the 'suicido-genic currents' which lie 'behind' the actual rates of suicide are essentially states and conditions of the collective consciousness, just as 'moral density' was also one of the states explaining the division of labour. The famous concepts of 'egoism', 'altruism', 'anomie' and 'fatalism', which lie 'behind' the complex of events that make up the suicide *rate*, are, without doubt, states of collective mind. They point to systematic fluctuations in the delicate condition of the collective *zeitgeist*, and are only secondarily the property of individual minds.

The Rules of Sociological Method, Durkheim's next major work, is taken up with the problem of 'social facts', their nature, and the proper methods to be used in 'adjusting our conceptions in conformity with their nature'.[18] It is, in other words, a basically epistemological work. By defining 'social facts as things', and in turn defining those 'things' by the threefold criteria of 'constraint', 'generality', and 'independence from a simple act of the will', Durkheim makes clear the basically realist character of his sociology. However, what has been ignored or made less clear by the modern interpreters of Durkheim is that the 'things' of which he writes are not to be confused with the 'things' of empiricist science, i.e. the material objects of sense perception. By virtue of the three criteria by which they are to be recognised and defined, such 'things' cannot be material sense objects. 'Things', in the empiricist sense of that word, are, as Parsons rightly points out, 'merely manifestations of social reality'. They have none of the defining characteristics which Durkheim attributes to them, namely constraint, generality, and independence from the will. 'Things' in the empiricist sense do not constrain (there are many possible ways of reacting to a given circumstance), nor are they general ('things' by definition are particular), and nor are they independent of the will (an object can be transformed, moved, or blown apart). It is not unreasonable to conclude, then, that Durkheim was using the term 'thing' in a different and technical manner, although his choice of that term has perhaps led to the greatest single confusion in the history of sociology, for it has enabled generations of sociologists to see Durkheim as 'the founding father' of empiricism.

However, what concerns us in this section is Durkheim's idealism, that is, whether or not the 'things' of which he speaks, and which he regards as the basic subject matter of sociology, are essentially 'ideas'. That a 'thing' can be an 'idea', or an 'idea' a 'thing', may, at first sight, seem strange and contradictory. However, the case being made out here entirely depends on this linkage, for if 'things' turn out to be 'facts' in the conventional usage of that term – i.e. material objects and events – then Durkheim was certainly not an idealist, or, perhaps worse, he was an extremely muddled thinker.

The identity of 'things' and 'ideas' is made clear in the *Rules* by the constant reiteration of definitions that make the 'ideas'/'things': 'things'/'ideas' association extremely self-evident, to say the least. To take but one of these definitions: 'Individual minds give birth to a *being*, psychological if you will, but constituting a *psychic individuality of a new sort*.'[19] (our emphasis). It is inconceivable that a nominalist or a materialist could use phrases such as 'being' and 'psychic' in this fashion to describe social reality, whereas to realists and idealists such language would come quite naturally. Meanwhile, in *The Elementary Forms of The Religious Life* Durkheim's idealism takes on a maturity of expression that would have done credit to the great idealistic philosophers of the past; the last section of the book echoes Plato himself. As the more detailed arguments of the *Elementary Forms* will be taken up below, it will be sufficient at this stage to establish once more the essentially idealist character of his thinking. Talcott Parsons, it will be remembered, was in no doubt about Durkheim's idealism in *Elementary Forms*. In evaluating the relevance of various philosophical positions as a basis for sociological analysis Durkheim makes the following unambiguous point: 'There is one division of nature where the formula of idealism is applicable almost to the letter: this is the social kingdom. Here more than anywhere else, the idea *is* the reality.'[20] (our emphasis). He continues, 'Social life, in all of its aspects, and in every period of its history, is made possible only by a vast symbolism.'[21] And in a vein which flows almost word for word from Plato: 'Each particular consciousness is only the reflection of the Universal Consciousness.'[22] Finally, in his conclusion, he reasserts his idealistic view of the nature of social reality: 'Collective forces are *entirely* psychical; they are made up *exclusively* of objectified ideas and sentiments.'[23] (our emphasis).

We have been forced to belabour the point that Durkheim is an idealist, for two reasons. First, it is one of the strange features of the intellectual history of sociology that, in the Anglo-Saxon world at least, Durkheim has been fairly consistently presented as one of the 'founding fathers' of orthodox, empiricist sociology; a school of thinking that has been aggressively materialistic, in arguing that ideas are the epiphenomena of social structures; and nominalist, in arguing that general terms like 'society' are merely hypothetical devices which are ultimately reducible to individual phenomena. Our argument is, then, that Durkheim has been presented to us in a distorted fashion, and that the effect of this distortion has been to underplay and to write out of the history of sociology the important role that rationalism has played in its development. For Durkheim the rationalist strategy was the necessary starting-point for a viable sociology, for in stressing the objective reality of ideas he wished to distinguish the reality of the social world from that of the physical world and, at the same time, wished to counter the Utilitarian reduction of social phenomena to its individual manifestations; only in this way could the distinct reality of the social – *sui generis* – be sustained, and only through such a strategy could the realm of sociology as a distinct descipline be justified. One of the effects of squeezing Durkheim into the sociological orthodoxy (despite the obvious difficulties of doing so) has been, then, to exclude the major contribution of sociological rationalism from consideration. It has become a submerged tradition, which unlike the other three strategies considered in this book has remained unnoticed in the sociological theory texts. No major classification of sociological theory emerging since Parsons produced his own set of converging traditions, has even contained it.[24]

Emergent tensions in Durkheim's theoretical project

In consideration of how Durkheim viewed the nature of social reality, it has been a relatively simple matter to reveal the basic tenets of the rationalist strategy employed in his efforts to construct a theoretical project in which a viable sociology was possible. The problems arise, however, when we begin to consider how Durkheim answered our second fundamental question: how can we know this social reality? In short, the tensions in Durkheim's work arose out of his epistemology. From the discussion of rationalism above you will remember that the rationalist theory of knowledge starts from the assumption that social reality is basically conceptual (i.e. mind-like). From this it follows that the minds of individuals, including sociologists, are manifestations or copies of this reality; as Durkheim says: 'Each particular consciousness is only a reflection of the Universal Consciousness.' It follows, then, that theoretical activity which seeks to 'know' or apprehend the structures that lie behind and explain the world of empirical phenomena – the individual manifestations – has as its object 'structures of thought'. The process is entirely *rational*; knowledge is gained by constructing theoretical models which replicate those conceptual structures that cause the empirical world to be as it is. Rationalist theory does not, therefore, depend on any observational input for its construction. Indeed, it is the task of 'rational' analysis to purge individual thought of those elements that are acquired by virtue of lived experiences (as the concept of the State conjures up 'images' or 'pictures' of monarchs and armies, tax men and judges in the mind of the individual). Although the empirical world is the object of explanation (i.e. we set out to explain why suicide is more frequent among Protestants than Catholics), it does not itself provide the conditions for explanation. Such conditions must be sought in structures of necessity – of mind or society – which are not empirical at all. Thought, rather than observation, is the high road to Truth.

In the attempt to discover whether Durkheim followed such a rationalist strategy we must distinguish between what Durkheim *said*, what he *meant*, and what he actually *did*. In other words we must recognise the tensions that arise in Durkheim's work by showing the disjunctions between his writings on epistemological matters, the logic which seems to inform such writings, and the actual methods he used in discovering the many 'laws' which he undoubtedly thought he had discovered (i.e. laws regarding the progress of the division of labour, laws regarding the causes of suicide, and so on). We will hope to show in carrying out this comparison that the rationalist strategy remains the major thrust in Durkheim's work despite the problems and tensions that are generated in his attempt to come to terms with empirically based science.

Durkheim's first rule for sociological inquiry is that: 'All precon-ceptions must be eradicated .'[25] In other words, the sociologist must approach his object of study with a mind open to an infinite range of possibilities regarding its nature and variations. He must not start off by assuming that society, say, is essentially a structure of co-operation, or that religion is a belief in the supernatural. Dur-kheim launched continual tirades against those theorists who, for example, took definitions for granted, showing the erroneous con-sequences that followed from such closed minds. Durkheim, then, clearly advocated that scientists, and in particular sociologists, should have what is popularly called 'open minds'.

A problem that has arisen in the interpretation of Durkheim is that this view is perfectly consistent with both rationalism and with a form of empiricism known as inductionism, which was extremely popular during the nineteenth and early twentieth centuries. Al-though rationalists regard it as impossible to 'open' one's mind to the extent that it is devoid of all thought, they none the less argue that it is possible to rid one's thought of all that which is the product of personal experience, so 'getting at' the impersonal and universal structures which characterise all thought. To 'open' one's mind, in Husserl's terms for example, is to 'bracket' out the personal ele-ments in order that the impersonal may be revealed to the subject.[26] For a rationalist, then, the act of producing an 'open mind' is rather like polishing a mirror, so that the end result is a 'clear', 'pure', undistorted reflection of the real. Durkheim's central 'golden rule' is, therefore, in keeping with a rationalist strategy.

However, 'open minds' are also advocated by those empiricists who argue that the mind operates rather like a film which is blank until it is exposed to experience of the world, which then becomes imprinted upon it. They thus advocate an approach of pure recep-tivity towards the factual world (the scientist uses new film every time), claiming that knowledge arrived at by means other than this is not 'scientific'. The question remains, did Durkeim advocate the 'open mind' approach to knowledge in the social sciences for rationalist or empiricist reasons? An examination of *The Rules of Sociological Method* suggests that the latter is the case, and that, as most commentators have agreed, Durkheim was pursuing an em-piricist strategy. Indeed this empiricist strategy would appear to be rather simple and straightforward, and can readily be summarised in the following – often quoted – sentences:

Instead of proceeding from ideas to facts, one must proceed from facts to ideas.[27]

He continues:

The subject matter of every sociological study should comprise a group of *phenomena* defined in advance by certain common external characteristics, and all phenomena so defined should be included within this group.[28]

In other words, sociologists should start from the 'facts', and then create simple classifications of them according to their 'external characteristics'. If they also follow the rule that

The comparative method is the only one suited to sociology[29]

then sociologsts will have the means, through identifying 'concomitant variations' between societies and institutions and over time, to then identify those 'ideas' that Durkeim suggested are the end-product of the scientific process. For, as is suggested in the quotation above, the sociologist should move from 'facts' to 'ideas' and not vice versa.

That Durkheim retains his commitment to realism becomes clear when we ask what is the status of classificatory terms and definitions that must be produced, in advance, by the sociologist, and what is their relationship to the 'ideas' that are the 'end' of analysis?

Since the definition in question [the provisional one which groups the phenomena] is placed at the beginnings of the science, it cannot possibly aim at a statement concerning *the essence of reality*; that must be attained subsequently.[30] (our emphasis and brackets)

What is clear from this is that such definitions and categories are not direct descriptions of reality, but are terms that provisionally group phenomena as an aid to scientific discovery of those 'essential ideas' that do constitute social reality. What he advocates, then, is an inductive process through which 'essential ideas' are emergent from provisionally grouped facts. For example, an array of suicide statistics can, without preconceptions, be provisionally classified in terms of the systematic variations exhibited when correlated with a range of indices such as income, class, religion and race. It is from such a provisional analysis that the explanatory concepts of 'egoism' and 'anomie' emerge, revealing their truth in their capacity to make sense of the accumulated data.

This is what Durkheim said in *The Rules of Sociological Method*, and there can be little doubt that his strategy does represent a form of empiricism; but a form that since the philosopher Hume even inductivists have rejected, and that empiricists generally have rejected in favour of the hypothetico-deductive method. Since Hume, inductivists have sought not for 'essential ideas', but merely 'probabilities', and since Popper's (1963) general critique of inductionism this form of empiricism has largely been abandoned.[31] In the *Rules*, then, Durkheim advocates a form of inductivism that draws its inspiration from the sixteenth-century philosopher of science, Francis Bacon, who did indeed talk of inducing 'eternal forms', or what Durkheim would call 'essential ideas', from the facts.

Happily for Durkheim we cannot let matters rest at this point, for his theoretical project overall is more complex than this suggests, and the tensions in his work are more creative than a simple contradiction between a realist ontology and empiricist epistemology might suggest. For there is little doubt that in his sociological analyses elsewhere Durkheim does not use the methods he advocated in *The Rules* and, what is more difficult to show, *The Rules* do not even accord with the whole drift of what he took to be the nature of sociology. This last point appears to be straining our argument rather; that whatever Durkheim said, he actually meant something else. We are certainly arguing that Durkheim's writings on method are discordant with his general strategy, and particularly with his view of what the nature of social reality was. In order to understand such a discrepancy it is important to realise that Durkheim was writing in the context of the increasing dominance of natural sciences and the belief that science was the product of empiricist method. As a result, all social scientists, whatever their strategy for social science, had to accommodate the claims of the natural sciences. This not only created tensions in Durkheim's work but was particularly manifest in Weber, as is shown in Chapter 3. Let us now look briefly at the question: what did Durkheim actually mean?

As we have suggested, Durkheim's view of what the nature of

social reality is, is incompatible with an inductivist view of how we can know reality. For example, if one accepted the nominalist view that reality is no more than the infinity of discrete phenomena which are encountered through the senses or observation, it would be reasonable to proceed in the way that Durkheim suggests in the hope that the observer will eventually reach some certainty on the existence of recurring patterns between such phenomena. This is what induction advocates. However, it will be remembered that Durkheim believed that social reality should not be confused with its 'individual manifestations', i.e. the phenomena. Social reality must be conceived of as a reality *sui generis*, that is, over and above, and independent of, the phenomenal realm altogether. It follows, then, that Durkheim was expecting the inductivist method to do something that it was never designed to do; that is, 'reveal' invariant structures of a reality that is non-phenomenal in character – for example, the 'suicido-genic currents' which 'cause' people to commit suicide. It should be fairly evident that no amount of detached 'gazing' at suicide statistics will ever reveal a 'current' of 'anomie' or 'egoism'. Such observation will only reveal patterned or non-patterned relations among the phenomena themselves, i.e. between suicide rates. It is also clear that only some distinctly mental operation will bring to light such 'realities' as 'anomie' and 'egoism'. For these are not 'facts' in the empiricist/inductivist sense at all. They are facts in the Durkheimian sense. They are 'things', and 'things' are 'general' and 'independent of their individual manifestations'. We must, therefore, conclude that despite what Durkheim said in *The Rules* he could not have followed the inductivist method, for such a method cannot be used to go beyond particular observations. We will return to this discrepancy between preaching and practice in a moment.

The centrality and force of Durkheim's rationalist strategy is most clearly expressed in two of his later works, *Primitive Classification*, which he wrote with Marcel Mauss,[32] and his *Elementary Forms of the Religious Life*. In these works Durkheim forcefully argues that there exist in all societies basic categories of thought. These categories, which include such concepts as class, cause, effect, time, space, substance, force, necessity, accident, etc., are found in all religions as well as science. The universality of such categories, he argues, indicates that they are isomorphic with social reality itself. However 'primitive' or 'elementary' the religion for example, it contains beliefs which are themselves a 'dim perception' of such reality.

> It remains *true* that our nature is double; there really is a particle of divinity within us because there is within us a particle of the great ideas which are the soul of the group.[33] (our emphasis)

In other words, human beings are unavoidably constrained to think 'objectively', if only because the beliefs within them (i.e. the belief in the soul) reflect the reality that is outside them (i.e. the structure of social life). The obvious centrality of such claims in Durkheim's later work suggests a strategy that is quite different from the empiricist road that he appears to follow in *The Rules*. It follows that the method of sociology must be to distil from human thought those essential structures that fundamentally characterise it; to find within historical examples, such as primitive religions, those basic categories that structure all social institutions. By doing this, sociologists would necessarily arrive at what is 'true', for these categories mirror social reality. Such a conclusion brings us to the very core of the rationalist strategy, which places the human intellect at the centre of its project. For the rationalist, the human intellect is the high road to reality – it reflects reality – whereas inductivism shows little but contempt for men's intellectual powers, which have merely the capacity to distort the experience of facts. We may conclude, then, that Durkheim's apparent empiricism is a tension and inconsistency in his work which is generally committed to a rationalist strategy.

We now return to the preaching/practice discrepancy touched upon earlier and to our final problem in this section: what methods did Durkheim actually use in arriving at the famous generalisations which constitute the substance of his major works? First, it is clear from his analyses that Durkheim did not use the method of induction. He did not 'induce' that there were two types of solidarity – organic and mechanical – from a series of observations of legal systems; nor did he 'induce' propositions regarding the four types of suicide (egoism/altruism/anomie/fatalism) from observations of suicide statistics; nor did he 'induce' the 'elementary forms of the religious life' from observations of the rites of the Australian Aborigines. As we have already argued, such induction was impossible, even if desired, because Durkheim wished to reveal a reality that was not reducible to observable phenomena – this is, in effect, the major tension which his stated empiricism, in *The Rules*, creates.

Nor did Durkheim attempt to do the reverse, namely pluck theories out of the air on the grounds that they seemed a 'good idea' at the time, only subsequently testing them against the facts. In other words, Durkheim was no more an unconscious or 'sleep-walking' adherent of hypothetico-deductivism than he was a conscious adherent of the inductivism of his own day. He was no forerunner of 'modern' empiricism. Modern empiricism, that is hypothetico-deductivism, differs from nineteenth-century inductivism in claiming that science should begin with theories and not end with them; advocating that hypothetical theories should be confirmed or falsified against the facts. Such modern forms of empiricism would for Durkheim commit the same 'sin' as that which he identified in the empiricism of his own day – that is, it confuses theoretical concepts which are supposed to describe general structures, with their individual manifestations. For modern empiricism is based on the assumption that there is an identity between the general theory and the individual phenomena or facts. If this were not so, the notion of testing, of confirming or falsifying, would not make sense. The modern empiricist, using Durkheim's theory of suicide, is forced into a process known as operationalising: that is, of transforming, say, the general concept 'anomie' into its 'individual manifestations' or discrete phenomena, i.e. respondent statements to the effect 'I am unhappy at work'. The empiricist using the hypothetico-deductivist method necessarily fuses the general concept with the individual event, a process that for Durkheim was an error of the first magnitude.

Durkheim did not test his theories against the facts, for as has often been pointed out, whenever facts appeared to refute Durkheim's theory he could without embarrassment appeal to the common rationalist axiom that 'facts' meant different things according to their context or structural location. A classic example of this is mentioned by Douglas in his *Social Meanings of Suicide*.[34] In discussing the low suicide rate among educated, middle-class Jews, Durkheim is confronted with the potentially embarrassing finding that in this case education seemed to have the opposite effect to what it normally had, i.e. in increasing the propensity for suicide. Durkheim's response was to reject the empiricist notion that education could be used as an indicator (of anything), for, according to Durkheim, what it indicated depended on its 'meaning', its context. In other words, individual events have no reality of their own.

That Durkheim would have been appalled at the operationalism characteristic of modern empiricism – i.e. intelligence is what intelligence tests measure – is made clear in his discussion of religious categories, and the origins of language:

> In the first place, the roots [of language] are general; that is to say they do *not* express particular things and individuals, but *types*, and even types of an extreme generality. They represent the most general themes of thought; one finds there, as though fixed and crystallised, those fundamental categories of the intellect which *at every moment in history* dominate the entire mental life, the arrangement of which philosophers have many times tried to re-construct.[35] (our emphases)

To Durkheim the categories of reason 'transcended experience', and their object was not the phenomenal world at all, but rather the world that lay 'behind' it. Such a reality could not be 'induced' from the facts, for reasons we have seen, nor could such a reality be turned into or confused with such facts. Durkheim, then, was most definitely not a hypothetico-deductivist – unconscious or otherwise.

Much of our argument has been negatively posed in rejecting the conventional view that Durkheim was in his attachment to 'social facts' a founding father of empiricist sociology. In presenting this alternative view of Durkheim as a rationalist thinker it is also necessary to present more positive proofs. This proof can be found in Durkheim's use of a method referred to as 'argument by elimination'. While commentators have generally viewed this as a surprising polemical quirk in Durkheim's work, of secondary significance in his attempt to develop an empiricist methodology, in fact it should be viewed as of central concern, being *the* method of rationalist science.

The central significance of the method of 'argument by elimination' can best be illustrated through a consideration of *The Elementary Forms of the Religious Life*, although it is a method found in all his major works. Durkheim's intention in this book was clearly stated in the first chapter, entitled 'Subject of Our Study'. On page eight he writes:

The study which we are undertaking is therefore a way of taking up again, but under new conditions, the old problem of the origin of religion.[36]

In the same chapter he also writes:

How is it possible to find, underneath the disputes of theology, the variations of ritual, the multiplicity of groups, and the diversity of individuals, the fundamental states characteristic of religious mentality *in general*?[37] (our emphasis)

In the attempt to find these general 'categories' underlying the varieties of religious experience he assumes that there are only two ways in which this question can be answered: either the categories of religious experience arise out of the experiences of individuals in diverse and variable social and historical conditions, or they are present in the minds of all individuals and are thus not affected by time, place, and history.

The first position he describes as 'nominalism', and the second as 'realism'. It is as though Durkheim were saying to the reader: 'things, including "religious categories", must come from either the *outside* (nominalism), or from the *inside* (realism)'; just as a psychologist might argue that 'intelligence' must derive either from 'environment', or from 'heredity'. This is a perfectly reasonable and logical point to make, in the sense that, stated in this way, there is no other place they could come from. Even an argument that the categories come from both, in no way detracts from the correctness of the either/or form in which the question is posed. However, Durkheim goes on to argue that any attempt to 'reduce' the categories of religious experience to either 'heredity' or 'environment' ('nominalism'/'realism') will render the respective positions self-contradictory. The argument by which he substantiates this claim need not concern us here, for the point is that he eliminates all attempts to explain religion by reference to some aspect of phenomenal reality, i.e. environment or heredity. Now, such elimination is not the result of any empirical test, but is the product of showing the logical contradictions inherent in such positions. The result of this methodological procedure is to ensure that his reader is receptive to what is the only other alternative available, namely that the religious categories are part of a reality 'outside' both the environment and the heredity of human beings. That reality is, of course, 'society'. Indeed, in *The Elementary Forms*, as Parsons has noted, 'society' turns out to be an ideal reality, 'a universal consciousness'.[38] No alternative conclusion is possible, because the 'argument by elimination' involves Durkheim not in rejecting a list of inadequate theories or hypotheses, but in rejecting *all possible alternatives*. His own theory remains the only possible one, by force of logic, not fact. This conclusion is arrived at before he has considered one piece of empirical evidence; before he has observed anything.

Once again the metaphor that compares the rationalist method to that of 'polishing a mirror' is apposite – polish it long enough, and only the 'reflection' of reality is left, for all impurities impeding clear vision have been wiped away. After 'polishing his mirror' in the first chapter of *The Elementary Forms* the remainder of the book is given over to a complex, rather erudite 'filling out' of a conclusion which he has already arrived at by reason.

In short, the strategy exemplified in *The Elementary Forms* is a rationalist strategy. It proceeds not by way of positive assertion, nor by showing that the thing to be demonstrated is 'consistent with the facts', but by leading the reader along a logical route which finally admits of no alternative but to accept the truth of what the author wishes to demonstrate. This is the classic method of rationalism, known from Socrates onwards as either 'dialogue' or 'dialectic'. It is clearly the central method of Emile Durkheim's sociology, for if we were to extract the 'argument by elimination' method from his works, we would be left completely in the dark as to the source of his ideas. He certainly did not derive them from any 'facts', for they existed before 'facts' were ever considered.

The final criterion we can use in assessing the centrality of rationalist strategy in Durkheim's work is that of system. To what extent was Durkheim, in his study of such diverse phenomena as the division of labour, social integration, the law, the state, social pathology, suicide, the professions, religious beliefs, etc., applying *one single system* of interrelated concepts? If such a system existed, what was it? Briefly, it can be summarised as follows.

'Society' is a hierarchical structure of 'ideas' that 'exists' in its own right, *sui generis*, and that generates, and/or implies, the totality of social phenomena, including even the very physical structure of human beings and their most intimate and personal motivations. In its 'normal' condition such a structure is 'organic': that is, it is characterised by 'organic solidarity', or 'moral density'. This condition involves a delicate balance between collectivism (or the 'principles' of generality) on the one hand, and individualism (or particularity) on the other. However, for reasons that Durkheim never successfully theorises, the structure of 'normal' society might lurch into one of two 'pathological' states: that is, toward 'mechanical solidarity', or alternatively toward 'contractual solidarity'. These conditions are 'pathological' only where they are 'excessive'. These principles are to be found in 'normal' or organic states of society.

Social change, then, proceeds through a series of 'oscillations' between these extremes, although in the long run there is a definite tendency for organic solidarity to realise itself. However, change can never be anything other than the 'realisation' of these pre-existent structural principles. The division of labour can never develop or progress beyond its susceptibility to one of the two 'pathological' states – i.e. excessive collectivism or excessive individualism. Thus while Durkheim conceives of the possibility of social reform and social movements creating the conditions to overcome such pathology – for example, through the creation of occupational communities – he does not follow Marx in believing that the principles of social organisation can be radically transformed. For Durkheim, communism would be subject to the same pathological tendencies as capitalism. In fact, he argued that both are characterised by imbalance – pathological conditions of individualism or collectivism.

That such states are 'pathological' is evidenced by the rate(s) of suicide, for in Durkheim's 'system' excessive collectivism generates high rates of 'altruistic' and 'fatalistic' suicides, and, conversely, excessive individualism generates high rates of 'egoistic' and 'anomic' suicide. The very 'will to live' which Darwinians and empiricists would simply take for granted is, for Durkheim, a social product dependent upon organic solidarity.

Organic solidarity is, then, a condition of balance between the order that comes from the fact that life has 'meaning', and the creativity and initiative that come from the fact that that same life is an object of doubt and scepticism.

Finally, the three types of society (organic, mechanical and contractual) correspond to a series of religious beliefs and rituals. A 'normal' religion is one that recognises the reality of 'forces' and 'powers' (Durkheim's terms in *The Elementary Forms*) which are beyond the control of individuals, and yet conceptualises those same forces and powers as being embodied in human beings. Such a religion 'constrains' men, yet at the same time enlivens their day-to-day existence by creating an 'effervescence', without which they would die of 'emotional deprivation'. Pathological religions, by comparison, are either purely 'transcendental' or 'secular', the one deifying the idea, the other deifying phenomena. The 'true religion' which has been responsible for all that is 'best' and 'progressive' in human society (liberty, knowledge, prosperity, justice, etc.) is *humanism*, that is the worship of Man as God, and God as Man.

It is our argument that this world view which Durkheim held throughout his intellectually productive life was independent of any of the particular studies he carried out. It was a system of thought which existed before he looked at one suicide statistic or considered a single legal code. This is not to suggest that there was no development in Durkheim's work; that the world view did not become more systematic and consciously articulated as he worked through versions of its implications. Rather, we would argue that there is no radical 'break' in his work of the kind Parsons claims. That despite the misplaced attempt to claim inductivist principles in his methodological writings, this *a priori* system is further indicative of the rationalist tenor of Durkheim's work, and his attempt to create a rationalist project within the discipline of sociology. In this he is certainly closer to the most famous of modern rationalist philosophers, Hegel, who was writing earlier in the nineteenth century, than he was to the empiricists with whom he is conventionally classified.

A full exposition of Durkheim's rationalist strategy also involves an identification of the criteria of validity used when evaluating the 'truth' of his own or others' statements about the social world. For as we have argued above, rationalism is necessarily wedded to logic as the primary criterion of what is certain. As we have also seen, the idealist character of rationalism makes an 'appeal to the facts' irrelevant, as the 'meaning' of facts is not given in the facts themselves, but always requires interpretation, which in effect 'reveals' the underlying objective logic of the world – i.e. the interpretative act is not a process in which the subject/actor *gives* meaning to the 'fact' (see Chapter 3 on Subjectivism). The rationalist act of interpretation is guided by logic, because the world is fundamentally logical: being a reality of ideas, it shares with ideas a structure of logic. Thus, while the underlying structure of logic may permit an enormous variation in possible worlds, any actual empirical world will be consistent with the world of logic.

In the nineteenth century it was typical of social theorists such as Comte, Marx, and Spencer, to present their own positions by means of a refutation of previous, competing systems of thought, as well as an assertion and exposition of their own. Thus Marx 'refuted' Hegelianism, Utopianism and Utilitarianism, as part of the process of constructing historical materialism (see Chapter 4). However, these fathers of social science seldom discussed the formal criteria on the basis of which their systems should be accepted as 'true', relative to those they had 'refuted'. In the twentieth century, however, such discussions have become commonplace, even compulsory. It is now accepted that strict conformity to such formal rules of 'proof' is the hallmark of the scientificity of a theory.[39] Other, taken-for-granted, criteria of science have collapsed long since. For example, at times it seemed sufficient for Marx to simply establish his 'materialist' credentials in order to prove himself as 'scientist', in opposition to idealist ideology. From this point of view Durkheim resembled nineteenth-, rather than twentieth-century thinkers. At no point does he seem to doubt the scientific status of his own theory, and at no point does he contemplate the possibility that 'science' may well give rise to alternative competing theories to his own. Those theories that Durkheim refuted in good nineteenth-century fashion – most particularly Utilitarianism (which in his view included the works of Comte, Spencer, Mill *and* Marx) – he never regarded as science. According to Durkheim, 'science' dealt with 'things', whereas Utilitarianism, and other forms of 'sociology', dealt only with phenomena, or, as he would call them, 'individual manifestations'. Because science dealt only with universalities and necessities, and because the phenomenal world was inherently one of caprice and accident, those who focused upon the latter were not 'scientists'. We cannot turn to Durkheim's writings for an answer to our question, 'why prefer one theory over another?', for the simple reason that there were no other theories to choose from. Durkheim had consigned all alternatives to a dustbin labelled 'non-scientific'. While such a method may be deplored, few social theorists are guiltless when it comes to its use.

Why then does Durkheim expect us to accept *his* theory? A

'symptomatic reading' would appear to suggest that he seeks validation largely, if not entirely, on the grounds that alternative theories are logically inconsistent, whereas his own is not. For example, in *The Division of Labour*, Durkheim rejects utilitarianism on the grounds that even if we accept its premises, those premises do not logically produce the results that we are led to expect.[40] We must 'prefer' Durkheim's theory because, unlike the others, it does not produce such problems of logic.

It is possible, of course, that had other alternative examples of Durkheimian 'science' existed, Durkheim would have found it necessary to have evaluated such alternatives to his own theory by reference to facts. We must imagine a Durkheimian who confronted Durkheim himself with a theory which, while it was based on the same set of assumptions, nevertheless came to quite different conclusions. The question is, would the relative adequacy of these two Durkheimian theories be determined by reference to the facts, the significance of which they had both agreed upon? Even in this case the answer, drawn from Durkheim himself, must be 'no'. For each Durkheimian would have to produce logical arguments regarding the significance of the 'facts', as well as logical arguments to prove which of the theories was most consistent with the assumptions on which both were based. As Durkheim never considered the possibility of using criteria of validation other than 'facts' (empiricism) or 'logic' (rationalism) – they were outside of his intellectual horizons altogether – and as 'facts' were not the criterion for reasons given at length in this chapter, then it follows that whenever questions of preference arise the Durkheimian must fall back on logic. Once more, then, we find that Durkheim stood firmly in the rationalist camp.

Finally, we come to the rationalist assertion of ethical absolutism, or, in more contemporary terminology, the possibility of 'critical theory'.[41] The possibility of 'critical theory' within the rationalist strategy is a position that contrasts strongly with the empiricist view of the fact/value relationship. According to empiricists, all possible statements regarding the world have as their referents either the empirical facts of experience (as in the statement: 'Leicester University has 4,200 students') or the realm of absolute values (as in the statement: 'God is all Goodness'). Now, whereas the first class of statement can be checked for its objectivity – that is, it can be checked against what it refers to (i.e. the number of students attending Leicester University) – the second statement cannot. For the referent of the statement 'God is all Goodness' is neither 'God' nor 'Goodness', nor even the 'is' relationship between them. The referent is the state of mind of the person who makes the claim. The statement is purely subjective, even if it accurately describes the subjectivity of the person who says it. According to empiricists, entities such as 'God', or 'Goodness', do not exist at all, for they are not phenomenal. Alternatively, if they do exist, they are inherently unknowable, for being non-phenomenal they cannot impinge upon the senses, which are the only sources of knowledge. Knowledge of them, therefore, is 'pure opinion'. 'Facts' and 'values', then, belong to separate realms of discourse, there being no intrinsic relationship between them. In more practical terms, this means that while 'scientists' may legitimately be accepted as experts in the field of facts, when it comes to 'values' all judgements are of equal value. Thus scientists are in no position to claim pre-eminence when it comes to judgements about what is good or best in the field of politics or religion. For the empiricist, when it comes to value judgements, therefore, we are in a democratic world in which the capacity of judgement is distributed equally, and judgements are of equal value.

Rationalists, however, do not hold this view. As far as they are concerned, so-called 'judgements of facts' are only possible in association with 'judgements of value' which, in turn, must be consistent with the 'facts'. For it is values that produce such 'facts', and 'facts' are, quite literally, evidence of them. 'Facts' and 'values', then, presuppose each other, and each is as knowable (rationally) as the other. The question of God's existence and His attributes is a rational question, in the same way as in the question of how many students attend Leicester University. While empirical observations are vital to the settlement of the latter question, they presuppose a rational adjudication of other matters, such as 'what is number?' and 'what is a student?'. Also, adjudication of the former question entails some empirical corroboration, such as the observation of 'facts' consistent with God's existence. The empiricist distinction between objective facts, on the one hand, and subjective value, on the other, does not, then, operate in rationalism, although rationalist strategy does distinguish between judgements relating to *actuality* as against *potentiality* – a split that cuts across the fact/value dichotomy.

According to rationalists there are statements that describe an actual world, and these would include both of the above statements relating to Leicester University and God. There are also statements that describe a possible, or potential world, and these would include such statements as: 'perfect squareness is symmetrical', or 'the classless society would be a just society'. Within a rationalist strategy both statements are equally the province of science; both are, potentially at least, objective.[42] So while empiricists stress that science is neutral when it comes to matters of value, rationalists believe that science has both the right and the responsibility to legislate on such matters. Thus a potentiality is both a judgement of value and a claim that it has an objective 'right' to exist because its existence is quite consistent with reality. Judgements of value (although the term is a misnomer to rationalists) are being made from the point of view not of 'subjectivity', but from the point of view of a 'potentiality' which is as knowable as the actual world.

There can be little doubt, then, that Durkheim was not one of the founding fathers of an objective/detached empiricist sociology of the kind outlined. Durkheim himself claims: 'There are not *two* faculties of judgement. Judgements of fact bring values into play, and judgements of value have facts as their basis.'[43] In fact Durkheim's rationalist strategy allowed him to make many 'practical' proposals for the re-organisation of society, and to do so on the grounds that such policy proposals were not mere opinions, but were grounded in, and consistent with, reality itself. Durkheim's 'science or morality' consisted of what we have called judgements of potentiality. For example, his proposals that modern society should practise a form of 'humanistic' religion, and should be organised along the lines of some kind of occupational pluralism, merely express the fusion in Durkheim's work of values and objective reality. He argues that if organic solidarity is to realise itself in the modern world (and organic solidarity is the real form of human sociation), then recognition must be given to the inviolability of human occupations, and the sacredness of human individuals. These are both statements about objective reality, as far as Durkheim is concerned, and yet include what empiricists would call value judgements.

When Durkheim wrote about 'a science of morality', he meant what he said, namely that 'morality', which had hitherto been the province of priests, poets, sentimentalists, and off-duty scientists, should in fact be the province of scientists. Social scientists could treat morality and ethics in the same way as physicists treat atoms and molecules.

Durkheim and the Durkheimians

To have argued, as we have done, that Durkheim adopted a rationalist strategy in the attempt to found sociology, is to adopt a position that is by implication rejected by most of those English-speaking social thinkers who have, since Durkheim's time, regarded themselves as Durkheimians, or who have presented Durkheim as a major figure in the development of sociology. We are forced into the position of claiming that, for the most part, the Durkheimians have not followed their master. Paradoxically, it also follows that the theorist we have presented as representing one of the four major strategies in sociology has had little direct influence on the development of the subject; that it is the failure of rationalism to gain any significant hold on sociology that helps us to understand why it is that the non-rationalist elements in Durkheim's work are stressed rather than the central rationalist stance. A source of rationalism that has been of much greater influence on sociology, is Marxist schools, which have emphasised the central significance of Hegel for Marx's project. For example, the Frankfurt school of 'critical theory' specifically adopted the rationalist strategy of fusing statements of fact and value, claiming that social science must necessarily adopt a critical stance, to become a 'science of morality'. The failure of the Durkheimian project to gain a foothold in sociology is, in part, the failure of the rationalist strategy itself and the nature of its internal contradictions and tensions.

The central tension characterising the rationalist strategy in sociology arises out of the claim that social reality is a general and ideal phenomenon standing outside of, and independent of, all those individual elements or circumstances that make it up. How is it that this ideal level of reality has an effect on the material conditions and circumstances that make up the phenomenal world? How does this reality, make up of thought (literally *im*-material), produce effects on a world that is indisputably material? To use an example, how does the mind produce affects on the body, when these are two different orders of reality? A further and important extension of the problem is, how do general qualities such as the 'collective conscience' affect individual consciences?

This problem about the nature of reality rapidly becomes a problem of how we know reality, when we ask the rationalist on what grounds he assumes that knowledge of the individual mind is necessarily knowledge of the collective and thus of reality itself. A rationalist assumes this to be the case because, like Durkheim, he believes that the collective mind determines the individual mind, causing it to be like *it* is. Because the individual mind is a 'reflection' of the collective, then knowledge of it constitutes a direct route to knowledge of the hidden reality behind it. But if, as we have already said, these two levels of reality are severed from each other, how will knowledge of individual minds be anything other than know-ledge of individual minds? If this is the case, then rationalism, which presents itself as 'objective' sociology, is, in reality, another form of subjectivism, for its theoretical productions have no other referent than that of the mind that produces them. The response to this problem has been varied, and different schools of contemporary social theory have come to represent these different possibilities. Very briefly, there are those theorists like Karl Jung[44] and Alister Hardy[45] who have remained loyal to the idea of an irreducible 'Collective Mind', although in order to 'solve' the problems just mentioned, both have moved into the realms of 'mysticism', that is into notions of 'acausality', 'seriality', and 'psychic contagion', in order to deal with the question of 'contact'[46]. It is interesting to note that both writers belong to disciplines other than sociology, even though both admit their indebtedness to Durkheim and to his central ideas of a 'collective consciousness'. In sociology itself, however, the tendency has been to solve this problem in the very manner that Durkheim rejected, namely to reduce the 'collective consciousness' to some aspect or other of the strictly phenomenal world, that is to transform it into something *empirical* – merely a nominal device for the grouping of phenomena. In doing this, some of Durkheim's modern followers have mistakenly asserted that this is what he meant all along. However, it is to the credit of the major interpreters of Durkheim that they were fully aware of what they were doing in modifying the central strategic thrust of Durkheim's sociology. This is especially true of Talcott Parsons, in the United

States, and Claude Lévi-Strauss, in France, both of whom have, in very different ways, transformed Durkheim's works and sustained his influence in sociology.

Under the guiding influence of Talcott Parsons, who personally exhibited a profound understanding of Durkheim's central intentions, Durkheimian sociology underwent a sea-change in the trans-Atlantic crossing, becoming a forerunner of American structural-functionalism. Parsons himself made it quite plain that he considered Durkheim's social theory 'unscientific', in that it ascribes causal reality to an entity, 'society', which is not only unobservable, but which is not even phenomenal in the first place. Parsons's reaction was to transform the 'collective consciousness' into what it most definitely was *not* for Durkheim, namely an 'analytical device' (see Chapter 2) or 'ideal type' – that is, a construct in the mind of the scientist/observer who is thereby better able to handle the complex phenomenal reality with which he has to deal. Parsons's view in *The Structure of Social Action* was that social reality is an interaction between 'the conditions of action' and 'the orientations to action'. As such, the 'collective consciousness' loses its explanatory power, becoming an emergent property of the interaction of a hypothetical 'ego' and 'alter', who are none other than the pure individuals of the old utilitarianism, with their 'needs', and so on. In the form that structural-functionalism came to dominate both American and English sociology in the 1950s and 1960s the 'collective consciousness' ceased to be what explains the individual manifestations of social life, and itself is seen as what results from the needs of individuals and social systems. For example, religion is explained as a 'functional necessity' for social integration or individual adaptation, whereas for Durkheim, as we have seen, it could not be understood *at all* by reference to such utilitarian and 'functional' considerations. For such conventional sociology the very concept of 'collective conscience' is progressively eradicated from the discourse, giving way to the notion of a plethora of values, being the individual manifestations of a plural society. Talcott Parsons, as we have seen in Chapter 2, because he took Durkheim's sociology seriously, eventually found himself drifting much closer to Durkheim's rationalist strategy. As we have also shown in Chapter 2, it is in Parsons's later writings, when he comes to account for the evolution of societies, that his reliance on a Durkheimian solution re-emerges. In this context Parsons argues that processes of adaptive social change can only ultimately be explained in terms of the controlling effects of an autonomous cultural system. What causes societies to change is the existence of 'ultimate values' which lie outside of the social in the autonomous sphere of culture. Durkheim's external and constraining 'collective conscience' is echoed strongly here. Parsons is, however, faced with the same intractable problems in attempting to identify the origins of those values, such that he is forced at times to the conclusion that their origins are unknowable, that they are essentially religious categories. But at the same time he does veer towards a Weberian solution in suggesting that they are the product of special individuals, charismatic personalities. Here the source of social change is rooted in the unique individual: the personality with the capacity to change the world. These two solutions express Parsons's ambivalence in the attempt to go beyond the social for an explanation of social events. Ironically, it is at this point, where Parsons comes closest to Durkheim, albeit in an ambivalent fashion, that he moves furthest from the concerns of the structural-functionalism that he helped to construct. For the mainstream structural-functionalist this is the point at which Parsons's metaphysical tendencies, already hinted at by his liking for 'grand theorising', became clearly manifest.

In his native France, meanwhile, the influence of Durkheim has taken a rather different course. As C. R. Badcock said in the Introduction to his book *Lévi-Strauss: Structuralism and Sociological Theory:*

> Durkheim, while eradicating the worst effects of Comte's positivism, nevertheless retained 'society' . . . or more strictly the collective consciousness . . . as a quasi-metaphysical entity, transcending individuals and, in certain respects, inscrutable to science. For Durkheim, positivism had not created a religion of humanity, but had caused him to see human societies as possessing semi-divine attributes, and in particular as being the source of all moral values, philosophical ideas, and social norms. Apart from this, Durkheim was incapable of accounting for the origin of these collective representations, or social facts, and it is to Lévi-Strauss's resolution of this problem that we will now turn.[47]

Note the similarity of this comment to the one made by Parsons nearly forty years earlier (Chapter 2), namely the demand that non-phenomenal entities be accounted for in terms of their 'origins', and should not be given 'quasi-metaphysical' status. Just as mainstream structural-functionalism 'resolved' this problem by dissolving the 'collective consciousness' into a purely phenomenal construct on the part of the scientist/observer arising out of interaction, so, as Badcock shows in his book, the social anthropologist Claude Lévi-Strauss 'resolved' this *same* problem by turning the 'collective consciousness' into the universal properties of human cognition, and, ultimately, into the universal structures of the human brain. Lévi-Strauss takes from the Durkheimian tradition a view of social reality as a domain of ideas, symbols, and representations, whose relations are characterised by their underlying logical consistency. On the basis of such an assumption he is able to argue that *all* human cultural productions can be analysed by identifying the common problems imposed by this underlying structure – the structuralist method of analysis which Lévi-Strauss derived from the linguistics and applied to social anthropology, particularly in the analysis of myths. Such an analysis is possible only because all the diverse products of human culture and language are constrained by a collective mental mechanism – the unconscious.

In Lévi-Strauss's project, then, the unconscious takes the same place as Durkheim's 'collective conscience.' It is external and constraining, prior to all particular, individual mental contents, and providing the conditions of their existence. Unlike the Freudian term, it refers to an essentially cognitive or intellectual function. At this point one could conclude that for Lévi-Strauss reality is essentially ideal, and external to particular individual minds and social relations: that the unconscious is a Durkheimian concept.

The structural analysis of world mythologies is the attempt to uncover the universal effects of this unconscious/mind as it structures all human thought in terms of binary oppositions such as good and bad, raw and cooked, material and ideal, etc. Such dualities are, then, for Lévi-Strauss a feature of all human thought: the very capacity to think is dualistic.

Lévi-Strauss shares with Durkheim the view that reality is not to be observed in the particular events or relations of social life or consciousness of individuals, but that these are determined by a structure independent of them. However, it is when Lévi-Strauss attempts to specify the origins of this, unconscious, cognitive structure that he seemingly departs from Durkheimian idealism. He suggests that this global cognitive capacity is associated with the *physical* potentialities of the human brain. Finally, the capacity to structure experience as binary oppositions is a cerebral function. The relations of the socio-cultural realm are determined by the material conditions of thought – the brain.

Lévi-Strauss attempts to reject any outright materialism by claiming that the material and ideal realms function in association. The unconscious/mind is subject to a double determination – the structure of thought and its physical determinations – but as neither the relations of the two determinations, nor the way in which they conjointly determine the unconscious/mind are spelled out, there remains an uneasy and ambivalent assertion of a reality that is both material and ideal – a dilemma that Durkheim would have regarded as unnecessary.

While it is true to say that under the influence of Lévi-Strauss modern French structuralism has retained the more 'holistic' and 'structural' features of Durkheimian sociology, it has none the less failed to sustain the rationalist strategy as developed by Durkheim. For example, in Durkheimian sociology there is an irreducible division within the 'collective consciousness' between the 'Sacred' and the 'Profane' (two categories that for Durkheim reflected the reality, 'society'). In the hands of Lévi-Strauss the division becomes a reflection of the fact that the human brain (a phenomenal/material entity) is divided into right and left cerebral hemispheres. Now the issue is not whether, as Parsons says, some things are 'beyond empirical investigation', or whether, as Lévi-Strauss says, empirical reality is 'good to think with'; it is, rather, that any sociology that looks to functions, on the one hand, or brain circuitory, on the other, cannot legitimately be called 'Durkheimian', for in neither case is 'society' any longer a-thing-in-itself. And yet this was Durkheim's central message.

6

The Dialectic of Theoretical Practice

In the preceding chapters we have tried to show that sociology is characterised by the *co-existence* of competing theoretical projects generated by four broad strategies, each arising out of alternative answers to the same questions: how is social reality constituted?; and how can we know it? We have also shown that the existence of this common structure of thinking about the social world in no way detracts from the possibility of individual theorists developing quite idiosyncratic projects which combine elements and posit solutions drawn from more than one of these strategies. In fact, as we have argued, those theorists who do combine or synthesise the strategies appear to generate the more interesting and fruitful analyses.

In identifying four strategies of theoretical practice – empiricism, substantialism, subjectivism, and rationalism – we have, at the same time, suggested that these competing perspectives are implicated in a common structure. Any attempt to argue for the claims of one strategy, necessarily involves taking into account the alternatives, if only to reject them. For example, the subjectivists establish the adequacy of their projects by countering the claims of those, such as substantialists, who stress that the social world is an objective reality. The existence of these competing claims does not, then, imply a chaotic discipline in which dialogue between different theoretical schools is impossible, for not only do the synthesising classics of Weber, Marx or Durkheim illustrate the possibilities of a dialogue internal to each of their theoretical projects, but in a fundamental sense all theorists are involved in a common structure of choices and their competing claims only make sense in relation to the alternatives.

It should, then, be possible to consider theoretical sociology from the point of view of its interconnectedness rather than as a fragmented body of incommensurate positions; pointing to the conditions under which dialogue might be fostered rather than inhibited.

A major inhibition to such dialogue, however, is the fact that each of the four strategies is capable of generating its own criteria of what constitutes a valid statement about social events; they each attempt to establish their own brand of 'truth'. How, then, is it possible to make our claim that this dialogue is possible when the very canons of 'truth' we can apply in judging one project as against another are a matter of dispute? The remainder of this concluding chapter will confront this issue – the problem of validation – considering first the alternative criteria of validation generated by the four strategies.

Four criteria of validity

There is nothing particularly esoteric about the various criteria adduced by the strategies in determining the validity of a claim; they arise in everyday usage when we claim to know something to be the case. For example, the empiricist brand of truth is paralleled in our claims that it must be true because we have 'seen it with our own eyes' or 'have experienced it again and again'. Empiricism, however, recognises that the individual experience can be no final arbiter, as we do not always 'see' the same thing and our experience might well be unique. Thus, while focusing on experience/observation as the source of validation, the empiricist strategy has increasingly elaborated techniques of controlling observation through such means as the experiment or statistically manipulated data. These methods are ways of eliminating the distortions of individual observation and experience as well as measuring the probability that such an experience of events is likely to be repeated. When it is claimed that today we live in a 'scientific age', it is, in part, asserted that the empiricist criteria of certainty have become dominant in our culture. Little or no distinction is made between 'science' and 'empiricism'. The alternative strategies, however, reject this association of empiricism and science, as involving a mistaken view of what science is. In particular, they reject the validilty of empiricist method as applied to social science.

The first criterion of validity is, then, experience; but closely linked with this in everyday usage is a second criterion which arises when we claim, 'I know it's right, because it works', or, 'it's correct because it has been applied in practice'. In essence, this is the criteria of validity that is generated by the substantialist strategy. Substantialism, then, involves a rejection of the empiricist criterion of experience on the grounds that it presupposes a passive orientation to the world. The truth of our knowledge is not determined by taking the world as it is given in experience, but through our acting in and upon the world. For Marx, the test of a theory is not the artificially controlled experiment but its capacity to generate effective action, and there are grounds for believing that this is a view he would have applied to the natural as well as the social sciences. The criterion of truth is, then, *practice*, and for Marx there is a direct link between scientific practice and political practice. When the writings of Marx and his followers are referred to as 'scientific Marxism', the meaning and resonance of the phrase is not what an empiricist would understand by it. What is referred to is the effectiveness of Marxist theory in informing political action, not its experimental or statistical testing.

A third way in which we normally assess the truth of a statement is through its acceptability to others, and it is in the subjectivist strategy that this criteria is given pre-eminence. The criterion of agreement, or what we will call *convention*,[1] is regarded by subjectivists as crucial when determining the validity of statements about social relations, for societies are, they argue, made up of negotiated agreements which arise between interacting subjects. Thus, for many subjectivists the only way of validating a statement about the meaning of a social event is to subject it to the scrutiny of the 'members', the actors themselves, in order to discover whether they find it acceptable. For the subjectivist, then, there is no objective source of truth because the social investigator, like other members of society, is merely establishing what kind of agreements society is dependent upon and the ways in which such agreements are constituted and established. Whereas most of us, in our everyday lives, take those agreements for granted, social theory and analysis problematises them.

Finally, in our everyday activities we may reject a statement on the grounds that it is inconsistent or internally contradictory. It is often possible to identify and reject racialist claims on the basis of their inconsistency; when, for example, it is claimed both that 'blacks live off social security', and are 'coming over here taking our jobs'. The statements can be shown to have no validity, on the grounds that they are self-contradictory; both cannot be true at the same time. The criterion operating here is that of *logic*, and it is this that provides the basis for determining the truth of a statement in the strategy of rationalism.

On the face of it, there appears to be a problem in identifying the criterion of logic with rationalism alone, for it is abundantly clear that all strategies have recourse to logical coherence and consistency as a measure of validity. Empiricists construct their methods of investigation using such a criterion, while subjectivists, being particularly concerned with language-use, also invoke logical criteria in their writings. In each of these cases, however, the problem of coherence and consistency is not raised to the status of the central indicator of truth, as it is in rationalism. For the empiricist, logic is a tool of reasoning, a means of arriving at the truth of experience; for the rationalist, logic *is* the truth. The rationalist takes the view that the fact that we are able to apply general rules of reasoning to language-use is neither arbitrary nor accidental; it reflects an underlying reality. For the rationalist, logic is inherent in reality; the rules of reason or logic work because reality *is* reasonable and logical; whereas with the empiricist no such presupposition is made. Although the empiricist would accept that logic can validate the truth of 'analytic aprioris' (i.e. tautologies) it cannot do so in the case of 'synthetic' propositions which require empirical confirmation. As we have already shown (Chapter 2), the language of science does not, in the empiricist view, reflect an underlying reality, but is purely a nominal device for methodological and communicatory purposes.

Each of the four strategies we have identified do, then, generate their own criteria of validation – experience, practice, convention, and logic. But as we have already seen in previous chapters, specific theoretical projects may well combine these strategies; particular theorists have recourse to more than one of these forms of validation. Weber's whole sociological project is an attempt to construct a methodology in which both subjectivist and empiricist criteria of validation operate in a complementary fashion. We have argued that Weber's attempt to combine *verstehen* methodology, ideal-type construction, models of rational action and causal analysis, sets up a whole range of unresolved tensions in his work. Before we look in more detail at the potentialities of such syntheses we will consider the problems that are associated with each of these types of validation and their coexistence as alternative brands of truth.

The problem of incommensurability

How is it possible to judge the validity of a particular theoretical project or even a particular theory if there is no agreement about what the criteria of validation should be? The empiricist who rejects an ethnomethodological 'account' on grounds of the inadequacy of its observational control procedures, would be importing into a subjectivist project irrelevant criteria. In the same way, a subjectivist criticism of a substantialist or rationalist analysis, that their conclusions are unacceptable in so far as they exclude subjective intentions, would merely ignore the principled reasons these strategies advance for so doing. We are here describing a pattern of non-communication which is common in sociology; a pattern in which the representatives of different perspectives continually 'talk past one another', confronting each other with incommensurable points of view. The very means they have at their disposal for judging each others' contributions are different and in dispute. Can we overcome this problem of incommensurability? On what grounds should we prefer one theory rather than another? For if we can only judge the validity of a project in its own terms we have no means of making comparative judgements.

If we accept that the adoption of alternative strategic assumptions does generate incommensurate sociologies, then any claim to be able to judge the relative worth of one theorist as against another, operating within an alternative strategy, must involve the hidden claim that there exists outside of each of the projects being evaluated a superior all-encompassing position which has the capacity to subject all of its competitors to its own, and different criteria of what is truth. The philosophical discipline of epistemology – a theory of the grounds of knowledge – often makes such claims to 'superiority', while in effect merely advancing the claims of one of the alternative strategies. More often than not these are empiricist claims; the hidden criteria turn out to be those of one of the strategies being comparatively judged.

One suggested solution to this dilemma is that we should convert the problem of incommensurability into a virtue, as in the epistemological rule that 'anything goes'.[2] Thus, we might accept that there can be no absolute criteria of what truth is and, as a result, conclude that there can be no such thing as social *science*, only social *sciences* – different strategies which constitute the social world and themselves according to quite different principles, with radically different consequences for both knowledge and action. Where the solution to the problem of incommensurability accepts such relativism, then knowledge becomes a vehicle of human values, of whatever kind, and its validation remains internal to such value/action systems. Does truth, then, depend solely upon 'what you want out of life'? If the roots of rationalism lie in the desire to contemplate the harmonies and universalities of Reason, the roots of substantialism in the desire to transform social orders, the roots of empiricism in the desire to reform and improve existing social structures, and the roots of subjectivism in the desire to 'debunk' the smug certainties of those who take their own certainties for granted, then little more can be said. Surely they have a right 'to get on with it'?

It is clear from our discussion, however, that such a resolution does not prise us away from reliance on one of the strategies. The centrality of intention reminds us that in the attempt to avoid the problem of incommensurability we are increasingly pushed toward a recasting of elements that are crucial to a subjectivist project. In fact, a number of the arguments involved are expressed in the works of Marxists of the Frankfurt School, such as Herbert Marcuse, who has been influenced by subjectivism.[3] Marcuse, for example, argues that it is an important part of the activity of social theory to construct utopias; that is, to scientifically construct images of a possible future, in order to counter positivist social science which, he argues, merely reproduces, and therefore helps to sustain, what exists – the established order of society.

If any attempt to overcome the problem of relativism merely drives us back into one or other of the strategies, why do we not recognise this consequence and make an arbitrary decision to 'go for' one of the strategies on the basis of personal predilection? If we are going to be forced into such an outcome, why not, at least, enjoy the satisfactions of exercising choice? The difficulties entailed in making such a choice reside in the fact that from the point of view of their criteria of validity each of the strategies are equally deficient; who would knowingly choose failure? The problem is that each of the criteria of validation – experience, practice, convention, and logic – collapses; they cannot be fully justified *even in their own terms*. Let us consider the reasons why they are inadequate.

The failures of the criteria of validation

No consideration of the grounds on which empiricism makes its claims to validity can ignore the work of Karl Popper, for not only has Popper had a profound influence on social science, but his writings – particularly, in this instance, his book *Conjectures and Refutations* – remain the most lucid and persuasive defence of the empiricist strategy and its grounds for making valid statements.[4] Ironically, Popper would reject the label 'empiricist', partly because he would regard his work as a genuine departure from a purely empiricist 'inductivism' (i.e. the belief that knowledge is entirely the product of accumulated observations). Popper does not accept inductivism (and thus 'empiricism') for he believes that the significance he attaches to theory or 'conjectures' distances his own position from 'empiricism' proper. However, Popper remains an empiricist in our sense because he retains the belief that the only reality about which we can have any *certainty* is that reality that gives rise to sensory experience within ourselves (i.e. sense-data). He remains, in short, both a materialist (the only certain reality is made up of material things) and a nominalist (collective terms are merely shorthand descriptions of such things). How, then, does Popper go about justifying empiricism and its criteria of validation?

Popper's argument is dazzling in its simplicity. He suggests that continual debates about the sources of knowledge are a waste of time, for whether knowledge is generated by *a priori* categories (essentialism) or arises out of experience (empiricism) is of little importance. Whatever knowledge is produced from these alternative sources, and he admits the likelihood of both, it none the less remains nothing more than opinion or 'conjecture'. For example, while we may assert the self-evident logic of truths such as $2 \times 2 = 4$, and learn from our experience that all human beings have language, we have no way of being *certain* about such claims. We cannot know whether the self-evident, logical truth corresponds to anything other than what is in our minds, and we can never be sure that there is not a human being who exists, or has existed somewhere, without language. Where such conjectures come from is, therefore, a matter of no great importance because they do not have the status of 'true' knowledge anyway.

In Popper's view these opinions or conjectures only become significant elements of knowledge when those who hold them have grounds for their 'certainty'. But, he argues, as no such grounds exist, then *certain* knowledge, or truth, in the traditional sense of the word, cannot exist.

Popper believes that our opinions and conjectures come from a variety of sources, from 'inborn knowledge' and 'experience', and, by his own logic, we could not even rule out such sources as 'intuition' or 'divine revelation'. If then, our beliefs arise out of such diverse sources, none of which provides us with a basis for certainty, how do we choose between the competing claims of various forms of knowledge which may well contradict each other? Popper's answer is clear: 'We do possess criteria of truth at our disposal which, *if we are lucky*, may allow us to recognize error and falsity.[5] (our emphasis). This sentence refers us to Popper's famous doctrine of 'falsificationism', which simply states that although it is impossible for us to know that anything is true, it is possible for us to know that something is false. While we can never know that '$2 \times 2 = 4$' is always the case, or that 'all humans have language', we can know whether they are false, at least 'if we are lucky'. Either by accident or by design we may well come across a situation where we *observe* 2×2 equalling 5, 6, 7, or n (in high energy physics this has actually been found to be the case),[6] and we may well observe a human being without language. Should we do so, then we know *with certainty* that such propositions are 'false'; in which case, we have every right to act as if our opinions and conjectures were 'true', as long as they have not encountered a 'falsifying' instance and are in principle open to falsification. Those opinions and conjectures that have been subjected to a long period of exposure to deliberately designed and potentially falsifying situations, can be said to have 'stood the test', and we can act towards them with a relatively higher degree of certainty than we can toward those that, although not falsified, have not been subject to such scrutiny. It is at this point that *a priori* reasoning (inborn knowledge) and experience enter the picture, for both have a part to play in establishing these relative degrees of certainty, but only as instruments in a methodological process, and never as sources of certainty:

> The most important function of observation and reasoning, and even of intuition and imagination, is to help us in the critical examination of those bold conjectures which are the means by which we probe into the unknown.[7]

Reason (the central criterion of rationalism) can be useful in turning 'bold conjectures' into systematic theories, and in deducing from these theories a large number of hypotheses pertaining to empirical facts, which in turn can (potentially) be falsified. Between the 'bold conjecture' that 'society is God, and God is society' (which might well have been the product of a Durkheimean dream or mystic insight) and the hypotheses that 'tribal totems are collective representations' or that 'the social rate of suicide is higher among protestants than among catholics', there is a whole chain of reasoning and deduction which may well be 'rational' or '*a priori*' etc. However, the certainty that goes with falsification is always an experience; it always refers to an empirical situation such as the social rates of suicide among protestants and catholics.

For Popper, then, the process of scientific advance involves nothing more nor less than the accumulation of unfalsified theories and hypotheses, and the discarding of falsified ones. While we still may not know what truth is, we *do* know what science is, and according to Popper if sociology is to be a science then it must follow this method, because this *is* the scientific method.

It cannot be disputed that Popper's argument is a very powerful one, which has been widely accepted as the 'last word' by a whole generation of both natural and social scientists. However, the crisis in sociology which we identified at the beginning of this book, is, in part, the result of the collapse of the Popperian final solution. Although the literature on Popperian method is voluminous we need to refer to only three major and very damaging criticisms that have been made of his case. In presenting these arguments we will also be pointing to the ultimate failure of empiricism to provide an adequate basis for making valid statements.

First, Popperianism, like empiricism in general, is self-refuting. Just as empiricism's claim that knowledge has its source in experience cannot be validated through experience, so the Popperian method of falsification is based on an assertion that is unfalsifiable. The statement that absolute knowledge is unknowable, is the keystone to the whole of Popper's argument, but it is a statement of the same order as any other absolute statement; it cannot be falsified. To falsify this statement would require that we came across a piece of knowledge that was absolute, an experience that has been precluded (*a priori*) by the initial premises of the argument. Popper's argument is, then, metaphysical and essentialist; that is, unscientific in the strictly Popperian sense of that term.

Second, the argument that experience can falsify a statement, as when the discovery of a non-linguistic human being refutes the statement that 'all human beings have language', presupposes that certain features of an experience have self-evident properties which are not dependent upon the theoretical language with which they are described; that we can experience an event in a theoretically neutral fashion. Anthony Giddens presents this criticism succinctly:

> According to Popper's famous example, the universal law 'all swans are white' can never be verified, since this would demand access to the total population of swans, past, present, and future; but it can be falsified by the discovery of a single black swan. However matters are not so simple. The discovery of a black swan might not falsify the law: a swan that had been painted black, or dipped in soot, would not qualify as a falsifying instance, nor, if this were possible, would the discovery of a black animal born of the union of a swan and a black eagle, since this would probably not count as a 'swan', even if it were like a swan in other respects. What these instances show is that 'all swans are white' *presupposes theories* of origins of colour typing, and biological form, in birds. What 'counts' as a falsifying observation thus depends in some way upon the theoretical system or paradigm within which the description of what is observed is couched; and such theoretical systems are able to provide the sort of accommodation to apparently falsifying instances that I have mentioned previously.[8] (our emphasis)[8]

In other words, what takes place in the so-called process of falsification is not a simple confrontation between a theoretical proposition and an independent fact, which is 'out there' in all its pristine self-evidence, but involves an internal dialogue within theory itself about what facts mean. This point is closely linked to the general difficulty experienced by empiricism (see Chapter 2) in being able to describe the facts of experience through a theory-neutral language.

The third major criticism of Popper's argument follows from the second, and bears upon a debate concerning the process of scientific change, and the part played by the role of paradigms or the background expectancies associated with theoretical statements in such transformations. The progress of science through falsification essentially stresses the continuity of the process, whereas historians of, and philosophers of, science such as Kuhn[9] have stressed the discontinuity of scientific advance, in which some theories have been abandoned long before falsified and others have been held onto despite being shown to be false in some aspect.

While Popper agrees with Giddens's quotation that to test a conjecture requires that background assumptions about reality have to be taken for granted – that is, the empirical world is never directly confronted – he underestimates the degree to which discontinuities between such background assumptions or 'paradigms' (Kuhn) are part of the historical practice of science. How can competing conjectures be validated when the background assumptions they make about the world are radically different? Kuhn and others have argued that major changes in scientific knowledge involve radical shifts in such paradigms, changes that cannot be understood as dictated by experience because what is experienced is only possible through the paradigms at issue. As a result, the rise and fall of scientific paradigms, while bound up with the degree to which they can successfully confront attempts to refute them, ultimately are tied to matters of faith and convention, as any apparent refutation can be dealt with by making additional assumptions to 'save' the theory at risk, as in the swan example quoted above.

While Popper accepts that 'theory-free' data are an impossibility, he has none the less argued against the idea of historical discontinuity in paradigms, and argued for the idea that progress means that one conjecture is better than another because it explains *more* than its competitors. Thus he suggested that a conjecture should be rejected if one has to make additional assumptions to save it, while Lakatos maintained that a 'refuted' conjecture would only be rejected if a competitor could account for the same data and additional data not covered by the theory rejected.[10] However, these ideas, and particularly the rejection of discontinuity in scientific paradigms, involve an appeal to the idea that paradigms can be translated into a common language in order to resolve the problem of validation. This involves resuscitating precisely the point at issue – the idea of theory-neutral observation languages. It is interesting to note that in his later work Popper has attempted to save empiricist criteria of validation, by appealing to pragmatist ideas to show that continuities between paradigms – and scientific 'progress' – exist because valid paradigms are those that further human control and adaptation to the natural and social environments.[11] The dispute between Popperian and Kuhnian perspectives is a strategic dispute between empiricism and subjectivism, with the former struggling to maintain a belief in an objective empirical reality resistant to all shifts in paradigms, and the idea that progress involves a successful 'unpeeling' of that reality.

These criticisms of Popper suggest, then, that the failure of empiricism lies in the incoherence of its appeal to experience as the criterion of validity. The ultimate justification for such a criterion is made on the basis of non-experiential, arbitrary reasoning. In Popper's own terms it rests on a foundation of conjecture; mere opinion and prejudice. We have also noted the ease with which it drifts into other strategies, particularly those of subjectivism.

As we have already argued (Chapter 4), the substantialist strategy shares with empiricism a belief in the reality of an objective, material world, but rejects the empiricist claim that it can be known directly through experience. It follows that the Popperian falsification doctrine – the falsifying effects of observation – cannot operate as a source of validation. In Marxist theory, for example, our direct experience of the social world, the way in which in our everyday lives we account for our situations, is an ideological process, and therefore illusory. If this were not so, Marx argues, science would be unnecessary. It is this commitment to an objective, material world which is, at the same time, not directly accessible to experience, which we have identified as a significant source of tension in the Marxian project. How then is it possible to arrive at any certainty, on the basis of Marx's substantialist strategy?

The various schools of Marxism have attempted to resolve this dilemma in a number of ways. The fact that experience is explicitly rejected as a process mediating reality and our theories about it, has led some Marxists to drift into forms of rationalism, claiming that the real world is somehow reproduced in our theories about it.[12] Others have attempted to overcome the dilemma by importing into Marxism, subjectivist assumptions, stressing that social reality – even in its materiality – is the product of human subjectivity and that there is, therefore, no distinction to be made between our ideas about the social world and what it is.[13] Such resolutions of the Marxian dilemma have the effect of importing into substantialism alternative criteria of validation such as logic and convention. However, central to Marx's own project was the reliance on *practice* as the crucial validatory procedure, a criterion that arises out of his substantialist strategy.

Marx's rejection of experience as a means of arriving at adequate knowledge, centres on his view that knowledge rooted in experience entails a 'passive' acceptance of what is. It assumes that social reality is like nature is thought to be, an objective given, rather than an historically specific, human construction. For Marx, the only sure way of determining the validity of a truly scientific knowledge, with the capacity of revealing the underlying structures of exploitative human relations, was to test it in action. Certainty could be arrived at only as a result of people acting in the world in accordance with their theories of it. The basis for such a claim within the substantialist strategy is rooted in the belief that the reality of social life inheres in material practices, and it is only in so far as knowledge is a part of such practices that its validity is demonstrated.

This resolution of the problem of validation in Marxian theory has, however, generated a whole series of derived problems and tensions, which have created a major arena of controversy within Western Marxism. At the core of such controversy is the question: how is it possible to differentiate between ideology (the form of knowledge through which we conventionally and subjectively represent the world to ourselves) and science? Unlike empiricism, Marxist theory does not suggest that such ideological practices are continually confronting a contradicting and falsifying reality, for the experienced social reality, on most occasions, merely reaffirms the dominant ideological perspective. Moreover, much Marxist analysis suggests that these ideological practices operate to sustain and reproduce the established order of capitalist relations. In other words, ideological knowledge can itself be said to be validated as a result of its confirmatory effects within a given social order. If practice does not distinguish between the relative certainties of ideological and scientific knowledge, then what use is it as a criterion of validation?

One resolution to the problem of distinguishing between ideology and science, is the claim that the certainties of scientific knowledge reside in its capacity to transform the social world. It is suggested that Marxism is *the* social science because it has revolutionary potential which can be realised only in association with the natural carrier of its ideas: the proletariat or working class. While such a resolution distinguishes between the reproductive functions of ideology and the transformative effects of science – so more closely specifying a link between science and a particular kind of political practice – the solution to our problem is more apparent than real. The problems that it, in turn, raises are legion. For example, how does one determine what constitutes a revolutionary change? At what point can capitalism be said to be transformed? If it is argued that the considerable social changes that have been brought about in Britain over the last one hundred years have merely functioned to sustain the capitalist system, then it must also be concluded that ideology itself has the capacity to inform such change, so rendering the ideology/science distinction once again murky. Similarly, such a resolution does not allow for the possibility that science itself may play a 'reactionary' role. Where it does, it must be relegated to the status of ideology. In effect, practice as a criterion and procedure of validation fails at all points to overcome its basic incoherence; an incoherence that arises out of the untenable assumption that there is a determinate relationship between knowledge and action. Science cannot be regarded as inherently 'progressive' in all historical circumstances. Nor can science – not even Marxist science – claim to make manifest the most effective political strategy whatever the situational contingencies. Once it is admitted that the implications of knowledge for action are open-ended, then there can be no general principle; no universal certainties demonstrated in the relationship between the two.

The view that science, as a practice, will have necessary (if 'long-run') effects upon, say, political practice, is an example of the unacceptable determinism on the basis of which many critics reject Marxism, and there is little doubt that, as a procedure of validation, practice does assume a determinate link between the practice of Marxism and revolutionary road to socialism.

It should also be noted at this point that the similarities between substantialism and empiricism – sharing a belief in the existence of an external material world – have effects at the level of validatory procedures. Not only has the 'orthodox' Marxism adopted by the regimes of Eastern Europe attempted to stress the scientificity of Marxism by stressing an empiricist view of the relation between fact and theory, but a significant brand of American empiricist theory – the pragmaticism of Dewey, Mead,[14] etc. – has sought to overcome the problems of empiricism by arguing for the role of practice in the validation of theory. Pragmatism and substantialism remain opposed, however, in so far as the former is wedded to the empiricist view of social reality as made up of unique, individual events.

As we have seen, subjectivism as a strategy starts with the premise that social reality is the construction of human consciousness. Knowledge, being itself a social construct, can have recourse to only one criterion of truth, and that is what is socially agreed, or acceptable; what we have called the criterion of convention.

The way in which this criterion actually operates in different subjectivist projects, varies. In its most radical ethnomethodological expression the only source of validation is seen to arise out of a situated dialogue between members (see Chapter 3, pp. 109–12). An ethnomethodological account can be validated only in the course of a dialogue between the social investigator and the members. A less radical form of conventionalism also operates where it is claimed that the agreements that count are those that are arrived at within a community of social scientists, who operate in accordance with an agreed set of rules: the canons and methods of a discipline. This latter claim, that relative certainty is no more than what a community of social scientists take the truth to be at any given time, departs from the former, principled subjectivist perspective by endowing the scientific community with a privileged social location.[15] This claim is rejected by ethnomethodologists, for the reasons referred to in Chapter 3.

Such a subjectivist project invites us to embrace a thoroughgoing relativism, in which the truth of a statement is always relative to a particular situation or circumstance. We are asked to dispense with the empiricist crutch, that there are objective truths about society which can be known, in favour of a view which suggests that a belief in objective truth is merely one of the assumptions through which we order and give meaning to our everyday lives. The claim that the certainties of social life are essentially those that we agree to live by, has a certain commonsense cosiness about it, with the added virtue that it accords with democratic values. Unfortunately, we are again offered a solution to the problem of validation that is self-contradictory.

The fundamental incoherence undermining the subjectivist criterion of validation is that it presupposes the *conditions* of dialogue, which cannot, in principle, be determined where consciousness is given primacy in the construction of social reality. An example of this problem that underlines a basic absurdity in the position is helpfully provided by a modern subjectivist sociologist, Douglas. He argues that positivist sociologists mistakenly classify seemingly identical actions without taking into account the different meanings attaching to them. Even in the case of death, he suggests, we can only understand the phenomenon by taking into account the meanings of the actors involved.

> When some ronin of Japan or some Asian Buddhists perform actions which lead to what American or European doctors classify as death, we must recognize that this is a classification by Western doctors, not by the actors involved. Their linguistic expressions for such actions may be totally different from the ones Western observers use and certainly might mean totally different things to the actors and the significant observers of these actions within their own cultures.[16]

Now while we would admit to our cultural bias as 'Westerners', we feel bound to enquire how the meanings of dead buddhists are arrived at? Unless Douglas has developed some procedures for accounting 'beyond the grave' we are surely forced to accept that consciousness is not all; that death does have its dominion. This, perhaps trivial, example does have its serious point, suggesting that the possibility of arriving at validity through agreement requires that we specify the conditions for dialogue. Death is a condition under which dialogue can be said to end.

A less extreme example will bring home the self-contradictory nature of the conventionalist position. If a sociologist says that 'the Ayatolla Khomenie *believes* that Allah is great', this would be consistent with a subjectivist strategy, namely that human beings construct beliefs of this order. Such a statement would not, however, be acceptable to the Ayatolla, because for the Iranian leader, Allah *is* great, and the use of the qualification 'believes' completely distorts his lived experience. However, for the subjectivist to then conclude, in deference to the conventionalist criterion of truth, that Allah *is* great, would negate the fundamental subjectivist principle that no-*thing* has a property such as greatness unless human consciousness endows it with such a property – and this applies even to Allah.

In other words, subjectivists cannot have it both ways. The reliance on acceptability or convention as the criterion of validation must involve the abandonment of the premise that reality is the construction of human consciousness, at least in those cases where human actors do *not* accept that reality is so constructed. In this case the conditions of dialogue actually undermine the principled position of the strategy of subjectivism itself.

While rationalism shares with subjectivism the view that social reality is a structure of ideas, it rejects the view that that ideal reality – society – is the product of individual consciousnesses and their interrelations. Rather, society determines the consciousness of individuals, for society is conceived of as those universal innate structures of mind that lie behind, and explain, the phenomenal everyday world of human subjectivity. Because rationalists believe that the empirical world of interacting subjects is a reflection of, and needs to be explained by, this hidden, ideal reality, the only means of obtaining knowledge of such a reality is through a direct examination of the structure of thought itself; a structure of 'mind' shared by all human beings. Sociologists who are influenced by rationalism are, therefore, likely to focus on language as a central feature of social life, particularly as the enormous variety of human languages would be expected, at some deep level, to exhibit a common, underlying structure. For the human capacity to learn a language would be regarded as a manifestation of that universal, ideal structure which constitutes the reality of the social.

A commitment to the rationalist view that social reality is such a structure, also entails a view that the ultimate criterion of what constitutes a valid statement is that such statements should be consistent, and not characterised by logical contradiction. In this sense, the statement reflects reality itself, which being an ideal structure must itself conform to such canons of consistency. In short, we can accept the truth of a statement because it expresses a logic which is the underlying structure of reality itself.

Such a criterion of validity renders an empiricist appeal to the 'facts' not only irrelevant but also an impossible procedure, because all empirical events require interpretation; their meaning is not given in the facts, which themselves require explanation in terms of the underlying reality of which they are an expression. Rationalism also displaces the subjectivists' notion of interpretation as a process in which actors give meaning to events, for meaning is the relationship of the event to the underlying structure; the conditions of dialogue are already set by a structure of thought from which individual actors cannot escape.

In comparing the criteria of validation used by each of the strategies we have discussed, the peculiarity of the rationalist criterion of logic is that it is used systematically by each of the alternatives. No empiricist, substantialist or subjectist would cede to rationalism any exclusive rights in the use of logic as a criterion of validity. All agree that consistency is an important determinant or corollary of validity; without, that is, accepting the rationalist view that logic expresses the structure of social reality itself.

This general recourse to logic as a criterion of validity underlines a fundamental problem for rationalism: the fact that it is possible to conceive of a number of explanations of a social phenomenon, each of which is adequate from the point of view of the criterion of logic, yet which are none the less contradictory. How does one then determine their relative merit? There is no way of doing so, unless it is argued that one such explanation more adequately reflects the underlying logic of social reality than another. However, such a conclusion would have the effect of denying the basic rationalist claim that logic in thought reflects the logic of reality, because in this case to claim that one logically consistent explanation is better than another suggests that the connection between thought and reality does not hold universally, and the possibility of selecting between equally consistent arguments must involve using a criterion other than logic. The governing link between the world of reason and fact is broken, and the criterion fails.

Our argument that rationalism cannot sustain the necessary link between social reality and thought, on which the criterion of logic depends, is further reinforced when we consider the possibility of contradictions existing in social reality. There is a Marxist tradition and a number of sociological theories of social change that, while not rationalist, depend upon a notion of social structural contradiction: that is, a contradiction in social reality. Now, a fully rationalist strategy which claimed that consistency in thought merely expressed a consistency in social reality would be forced to exclude the idea of contradiction, not only from argument and explanation, but also from social reality itself. The result of this requirement in Durkheim's work is that while he identifies such contradictory realities as anomie, and other pathological forms of the division of labour as a characteristic of modern, industrial societies, his rationalism forces him to suggest that they are temporary and pathological phenomena. That is to say that, for Durkheim, normal social forms are indeed non-contradictory (see the discussion in

Chapter 5). Nevertheless, the result is again to sever the link between thought and reality, the problem being that if that association does not hold, then there are no grounds for suggesting that logic can operate as the sole or fundamental criterion of certainty. The rationalist criterion, in turn, fails because of the failure to establish that social reality conforms with the canons of reason; we cannot therefore be certain of the reasonableness of the social world.

Our discussion of the four criteria of validation suggests, then, that any attempt to choose between them is likely to be a rather sterile activity in so far as each criterion is confounded by self-contradiction. The problem of incommensurability is merely exacerbated. Not only do the strategies offer incommensurable guides to truth, but each guide is apt to lose his way even on his own terrain. Does the direction of our argument suggest that the only answer is a thoroughgoing relativism? There is, we would argue, a further possibility for consideration: that of synthesis. What we offer in following this line of argument is no ready-made answer, but a potential which arises out of the whole discussion of the strategies that we have developed so far.

Towards a dialectical synthesis

In the introduction to this chapter we stressed that while the structure of sociological theorising has been characterised by the competing claims of four distinct strategies, each of the particular theorists we have discussed has either elected, or has been forced, to adopt certain of the assumptions and arguments drawn from alternative strategies. This drift towards synthesis is not, we argued, coincidence, but arises out of a common structure of theoretical choices, such that any attempt to argue for the claims of one strategy necessarily involves taking into account the alternatives. For example, the discussion of Marx (Chapter 3) suggests that his intellectual career can be seen as successive attempts to confront, and take into account, what was for him both acceptable and unacceptable in each of the strategies. In this sense, therefore, each of the strategies is involved in a dialogue, spoken or unspoken; they face, as we have said, a common structure of choices and their solutions only make sense in relation to the alternatives.

It is this common structure that we now wish to emphasise. In discussing the failures of each of the strategic criteria of validation, potential solutions seemingly emerged only when criteria were combined. For example, the substantialist rejection of experience as a criterion of validity was not to eliminate 'objective' criteria, but to stress that human beings in constructing knowledge acted upon the world rather than merely reflecting it. Similarly, the subjectivist focus on convention does not undermine the significance of practice, but confronts directly the problem of the relationship between thought and action as a situational emergent. Rationalism, in turn, rejects the relativism which the criterion of convention entails, but fails to provide adequate grounds for the assertion that theories about social reality are a reflection of that reality; a problem that empiricism confronts squarely, if inadequately, in its own terms.

It is the way in which these counter-claims of validation continuously interact in the attempt to overcome internal incoherence that suggests the possibility of synthesis as the ultimate goal to be pursued. However, to suggest that synthesis is possible and desirable is not to provide any immediate answer to the problems of the social sciences, for what is implied by such a project is nothing less than a revolution in the ways in which the problems of social theory are conceived. The magnitude of such a task is best illustrated by pointing out that a genuine synthesis must supplant, in its basic assumptions and concepts, each of the strategies we have outlined, while retaining the various elements that they provide. To merely juxtapose in whatever combination the dualisms ideal/material and real/nominal, from which the strategies themselves arise, would be to court the very failures that we have pointed to as characterising their present theoretical expression. To speak of a 'genuine' synthesis is to require it to be dialectical; to transcend the dualities from which it emerges. Let us consider this notion of dialectical synthesis further.

The conditions for theoretical synthesis are built into the oppositional structure of the strategies. That is to say, the strategy that defines social reality as subjective and meaningful necessarily involves a rejection of the alternative, its objectivity. What the subjectivist and substantialist share in common is the view that such opposites are defined in terms of one another; the subject is what the object is not. In the same way, mind (ideal) is something other than the functioning of the brain (material). The adoption of one of the four strategies involves, therefore, a process in which the claim is made that one of these opposites (ideal/material) is more *real* than the other. Even in those cases where there has been an attempt to synthesise – to claim that each aspect of the duality expresses a reality – the attempt usually has the effect of subordinating one side of the duality to the other: a *reduction* of one aspect of reality into another. In the case of the materialist who claims that ideas are nevertheless 'important', we are likely to find that the claim to synthesis merely hides such reductionist activities. The alternative to systematically reducing ideas into a material reality is eclecticism; that is, a position that admits the reality of ideas, but simply leaves them 'hanging in the air', untheorised, ready to use on an *ad hoc* basis if and when an argument appears to require it.

Such theoretical practices are the result of what we will call *dualistic syntheses*; where the dualisms are never, in fact, superseded and continue to impose on the theorist a dominant strategic outcome.

The first rule of a dialectical synthesis must be, then, the theoretical recognition of a single reality which unifies the dualities, *without* eliminating them. A dialectical resolution recognises the existence of the material and ideal aspects of reality, while at the same time accepting that they are both parts of a single reality. Mind and matter remain genuine aspects of a reality that is organised as a singular system. To talk of united opposites may sound contradictory, but this is a blockage imposed upon our thinking by the flat world of the dualisms. Such contradiction dissolves once the oppositions are seen in terms of the relief-map which the dialectical resolution provides. Such a resolution would eliminate the possibility of either reductionism or the all-too-easy rejection of the dualities as 'false dichotomies' by requiring that we both recognise the validity of idealism and materialism and provide a systematic schema in terms of which their interrelations (the singular reality) makes sense.

A dialectical synthesis would involve three basic assumptions. First, the alternative realities that each of the strategies identifies have equal status. While each of the strategies attempts to impose its own monistic order upon reality, such reductionism betrays a wisdom, in so far as each strategy can only identify its own version of reality in terms of alternatives that are also true but reduced to epiphenomena. As rationalism argues, there is a structure and purpose/intentionality to social reality, but that structure is not, as it claims, abstracted reason. As substantialism asserts, there is a single reality which objectively exists, but that reality is not matter alone. Empiricism correctly points to experience as a source of knowledge, but experience is not a passive exposure to facts. Finally, subjectivity and creativity are integral to social reality, but these are not exhaustive of that reality, standing in opposition to inert, uncreative nature. The second rule of dialectical resolution, then, would be that none of the alternative elements identified by the strategies should be reducible to any other.

Finally, and this is the crucial axiom, each of the alternative strategies unites into a unified system, or totality. Thus, any attempt at synthesis that contravenes such rules by maintaining dualistic assumptions or engaging in reductionist analysis will ultimately fail as a synthesising project. Those tensions that we have identified as characterising the theoretical projects discussed in earlier chapters are, in effect, indices of such failures to synthesise. It will be useful at this point to consider two contemporary attempts at synthesis. In doing so, we will focus once again on the problem of validation while evaluating the achievement of our examples in the light of our discussion of dialectical synthesis.

Contemporary attempts at synthesis

Perhaps the best-known recent example in British sociology of a sustained attempt to construct a theoretical synthesis is the work of Anthony Giddens, exemplified by his book, *New Rules of Sociological Method.*[17] The central thrust of this work is to make the reader aware of a revolution in social theory brought about by the influence of the subjectivist tradition. In Giddens's view this tradition consists of three related strands: the phenomenology of Husserl, Schutz, and Merleau-Ponty; the philosophy of Wittgenstein, Austin and Winch; and the hermeneutic school of Gadamer, Ricoeur, Habermas, and others. In effect, Giddens claims that this broad tradition has transformed our conception of social reality and the possibility of making valid statements about it. No longer is it possible to conceive of social reality as a pre-given structure awaiting disclosure. Rather, it must be seen as an ongoing product of intentionality and reason, both of which are the products of the creative consciousness of the human subject. In his introduction Giddens makes this point clear with two unambiguous claims:

> I want to assert that social science should move out of the shadow of the natural sciences, in whatever philosophical mantle the latter may be clad.[18]

> for society is, in some sense that is not at all easy to spell out, the outcome of the consciously applied skills of human subjects.[19]

Human beings, through language, are able to reflect upon, and monitor, their own actions and those of others. They are able to continually alter the criteria by which they recognise the world, so producing new meanings within it. Society is, then, a changing nexus of interactions between human agents, what Giddens calls a 'set of reproduced practices'. Actors produce themselves and others, and are, in turn, produced by others with the self-same productive capacities.

For Giddens the task of sociology is not to explain human action in terms of a pre-given social reality, but to describe human actions in a manner that is at least consistent with the intentions and reasons of the actors themselves. This is what is called the 'double hermeneutic':

> The conceptual schemes of the social sciences therefore express a double hermeneutic, relating both to the entering and grasping of the frames of meaning involved in the production of social life by lay actors, and reconstituting these within new frames of meaning involved in technical conceptual schemes.[20]

The outcome of this task will, however, be commonplace:

> the findings of social science ... are bound to be unremarkable, since they cannot do more than redescribe what we must already know as participants in social life.[21]

It is clear from the emphasis of Giddens's argument in defining the terrain of sociology that Giddens is heavily dependent on a subjectivist strategy. However, this emphasis is to be seen as a reaction against what he believes to be the dominant tradition in sociology, that of empiricism, and the consequent failure of sociology to successfully incorporate the valid insights of subjectivism. Also, being a synthesiser, Giddens's subjectivism is fundamentally qualified by the introduction into his project of concepts drawn from other traditions. In the attempt to generate a genuine synthesis he argues that a purely 'interpretative' or subjectivist sociology is unacceptable, in so far as it fails 'to cope with the problems of institutional organization, power and struggle as integral features of social life'.[22] In order to avoid such failure in his own project he introduces the concepts of 'motive'/'interest', 'power', and 'duality of structure'. Briefly, he argues that human beings have motives of which they are typically unaware and which give them interests that they may or may not understand:

> But since men are not necessarily aware of their motives for acting in a particular way, they are not necessarily aware of what, in any given situation, their interests are either.[23]

The consequences of such a qualification of the emphasis on human intentionality and reason is, of course, considerable. The fact that human beings have interests of which they are not conscious means that social life is not just a dialogue over the meaning of events and objects, but is a practical affair in which actors pursue lines of action that others may well resist. This, in turn, means that, given the resources available to those engaged in such struggles, power will become an important determinant of the outcome of interaction, including the determination of what meanings will 'count': 'meanings that are made to count express asymmetries of power'.[24]

The net result of introducing these essentially materialistic concepts into an otherwise straightforwardly subjectivist schema, is to produce an overview of social reality which sees it as both produced by human agents while at the same time existing as a set of unintended, external conditions (motives/interests/powers) which mediate and constrain that self-same productive process. This is what Giddens refers to as the 'duality of structure', perhaps the most 'synthetic' of all his concepts:

> By duality of structure I mean that social structures are both produced by human agency, and yet at the same time are the very medium of this constitution.[25]

Giddens's synthesis can be summed up in Marx's phrase, 'men make their own history, but not in circumstances of their own choosing'. In fact, he quotes these words approvingly, as a description of his own project.

Given the central theme of this chapter – the problem of validation – we will not confront directly the question: does Giddens's central concept, the duality of structure, transcend the subject/object dualism, or merely reassert it? Rather, the question will be posed: on what grounds should we accept what he has to say in preference to the contradictory claims made by others? In so doing, we are not avoiding the central question, because the solution to the problem of structure and that of providing a synthesis of the criteria of validation are just two aspects of the same problem. For in positing the duality of structure, Giddens must also show us how we can go about obtaining adequate knowledge of it; of both its meaningful and objective aspects.

Obligingly, Giddens devotes a whole chapter – 'The Form of Explanatory Accounts' – of the *New Rules* to this question. In this chapter he explicitly rejects the standard validation claims made from the point of view of the strategies discussed above. Of rationalism he says:

> the mediation of frames of meaning cannot be treated in terms of the premises of formal logic imposed as a set of 'necessary' relations which all thought, to be rational, must observe.[26]

In opposition to the empiricist strategy Giddens makes the following comments:

> Statements which refer to 'sensory observation' cannot be expressed in a theoretically neutral observation language: the differentiation between the latter and theoretical language is a relative one, within a framework of a pre-existing conceptual system.[27]

He continues in no uncertain terms:

> There is *no way* of justifying a commitment to scientific rationality rather than, say, Zande sorcery, apart from premises and values which science itself presupposes, and indeed has drawn

from historically in its evolution within Western culture.[28] (Giddens's emphasis)

However, in view of his commitment to such concepts as motive, interest, and duality of structure, all of which imply the notion of 'false consciousness', Giddens must also reject the principles of validation favoured by the subjectivist strategy – that an observer's accounts of social life must either reproduce the actors' accounts, or at least be consistent with them. This is our criterion of convention, whereby it is claimed that an account is adequate so long as it is acceptable to those about whom it is an account. But, as Giddens argues: 'since men are not aware of their motives ... they are not aware of their interests'.[29] Their own accounts cannot, then, be an adequate representation of their own situations. The subjectivist criterion of validation cannot work within Giddens's project. In fact, Giddens's argument suggests that while it is impossible to justify an account that the actor would accept, there is equally no way of justifying an account or statement that appeals to principles lying outside of the actor's presuppositions. The former is rejected because actors' accounts are bound to involve ideologies and utopias that misrepresent the structure of power and interest, and the latter is rejected because it loses sight of the fact that 'men make their own history' and are not, therefore, merely the agents ('cultural dopes') of objective structures, which lie outside themselves. The subject/object duality provides no answer to the problem of validations, but how does Giddens resolve the dilemma that it poses?

It is difficult to answer this question because, frankly, Giddens does not appear to answer it himself, despite the chapter heading. Certainly there is no answer that can be regarded as a dialectical resolution; that is to say, one that transcends the duality that generates the dilemma, so excluding the possibility of reductionism. The hints of an answer that exist in the work, and appear to be consistent with his overall position, suggest that the problem of adequacy remains a hermeneutic problem, a matter of interpretation: 'The mediation of paradigms or widely discrepant theoretical schemes in science is a hermeneutic matter.'[30] What is suggested here is that while the dialogue between actors cannot generate valid accounts because of the distorting effects of interest and power, the dialogue that constitutes science may be a source of validity.

Just as we have suggested that the strategies only emerge in a dialogue with the alternatives, so Giddens suggests here that the 'paradigms' of science are interpretatively mediated by one another: 'While Einsteinian physics broke with Newtonian physics it nonetheless had direct continuities with it at the same time.'[31] However, while we would argue that such a mediating structure requires a conception of the whole that transcends yet incorporates its various parts, generating a system of validation that recognises the various elements provided by each of the strategies, Giddens appears to suggest that validity resides in the process of mediation itself. That is to say, to the extent that a 'paradigm' presupposes much of the contents of another – for example the continuities which exist between Newtonian and Einsteinian physics – is itself a measure of validity. The view that scientific dialogue can exist as an interpretative process and that validation is an outsome of the process itself, is to restrict the subjectivist criterion of convention, as an adequate criterion of truth, to a limited sphere of human activity – science – which, we may presume, somehow escapes the distorting influences of power and interest.

Our belief that this is Giddens's position is reinforced by the fact that he approvingly draws on Habermas:

> Truth, Habermas says ... is not to be looked for in what guarantees the 'objectivity' of experience, but 'in the possibility of argumentative corroboration of a truth claim'.[32]

For Habermas, the possibility of 'argumentative corroboration' or validation, depends on the existence of what he calls an 'undistorted speech community'.[33] Recognising the problems of distortion that can arise as the result of power and interest, he argues that such a validatory structure depends on social arrangements which ensure the free flow of linguistic criticism; permitting language to operate in a manner that is 'undistorted' by such exigencies. There would, of course, be no final solutions to the problem of knowledge emerging in such a community, because knowledge would be a continually emerging human product, subject to the potentialities of language, which is also continually reproducing itself. However, according to Habermas, such a community would be able to overcome ideological distortion, and in common with the Popperian scientific community, be capable of recognising what is false; resting content, at least temporarily, with whatever language asserts. Unlike the Popperian view, however, this outcome would be achieved not by reference to 'the facts', but as the product of a constantly changing language potential, in a social context in which the undistorted purity of the language was guaranteed.

Before we conclude that Giddens's seeming approval of Habermas in *The Rules* provides sufficient evidence for his subjectivism, we must take account of subsequent writings of relevance to the question of validation. His later critique of Habermas[34] suggests that despite the emphases present in *The Rules* he is not committed to a view that merely modifies the subjectivist strategy in such a way that a proposition would be regarded as adequate if it were acceptable to a community of scientists, whose 'unfettered' dialogue was neither subject to the illusions 'language speaks', nor to pregiven constraints outside language. Perhaps more significant for this synthesising project is his essay on Positivism and its Critics.[35]

Two issues emerge from Giddens's critique of positivism. How, given the failure of falsificationism, may we construe the relationship between theory and reality, and how may the seemingly intractable problem of meaning-variance or incommensurability be overcome?

Giddens accepts that Popperian falsificationism fails because scientists for the most part assimilate anomalies arising in given theories unless and until a better theory emerges, and that the latter can occur without 'any refutations leading the way'. Moreover, the idea that science *progresses* through falsification makes the unwarranted assumption that only a *finite* number of theories about the world are possible and that the possibility of subjecting them to comparative tests provides the objective basis of scientific advance. Without this prop, falsificationism would face the stark choice between a pragmatic subjectivism – i.e. a theory has some pay-off even though there are others available which are no more or less refutable – or a return to the empiricist idea that one theory is better than another because it can be shown to reflect the world more accurately; an idea already rejected by Popper.

To escape this impasse Giddens turns to the network theory formulated by Hesse.[36] Giddens suggests that scientific theory involves a network of statements that cannot be divided into theory on the one hand, and observation language on the other, but which connects with the object world via 'knots'.

As far as we can see, this rather vague metaphorical term, 'knots', refers to the existence in theory of clusters of statements about the world which are a product of the combined processes of observation and theorising, and which involve a particular way of connecting our concepts with the real world. What is to be observed, indeed what *is* observable, is defined by this cluster of relationships and the network that stems from it. On the basis of such an analogy, then, neutral observation statements about the world are impossible, for 'knots' are the dense points of a network that itself is in process of transformation as the statements and techniques of science change. Thus, 'what is observable and what is theoretical can only be distinguished in a pragmatic and relative way'.[37]

While the idea of network is used by Giddens to render redundant the empiricist distinction between theory and observation, he is also aware that if his own position is to move beyond the relativism of Kuhn's version of scientific change, then network theory must be complemented by a *realist* view of the objective world, otherwise the charge of subjectivism stands. Yet it is in explicating what such a realist project entails that Giddens's analysis remains tentative and undeveloped.

Having disposed of the distinction between theory and observation language, Giddens confronts the problem of relativism or incommensurability. The problem is resolved by claiming that scientific practice has already 'dissolved' it. Thus Giddens suggests that in science, as in everyday life, the grasping of alternative realities is not an intractable hermeneutic problem but one that we manage quite successfully. In science, it is the case that competing theories can be made to be comparable in ways that allow for their truth claims to be judged. The possibility of such an exercise is, however, asserted rather than demonstrated. In addition, Giddens suggests that the scientific practice of comparing theories is secured by the standards of critique that are institutionalised in science and that are not to be identified with falsificationist epistemology.

Giddens realises that these two arguments, even if they could be demonstrated, say little about the relationship between theory and reality, but only about the relations between different meaning frames and how science interprets them. Giddens also is aware that in order to show how theory and reality connect, his projected realism must be spelled out. However, rather than embarking on such a project he returns to a critique of empiricism, indicating those errors that realism would have to avoid in order to provide an acceptable basis for validation. The critique centres on what he regards as empiricist and discredited views: that competing theories can be compared by appealing to a bedrock of neutral observations; that the idea of correspondence itself may be observationally defined; and the notion that there is an object world independent of language. None of these ideas, argues Giddens, is necessary to a superior model of validation. Howerver, we are never presented with the superior version. Network theory is the road toward such a goal, but network theory itself does not logically entail a commitment to realism (although it is compatible with subjectivism), and Giddens does not show how a reformulated realism could become, in association with network theory, the basis for a system of validation. Giddens's attachment to realism is, to say the least, extremely tentative and unexplicated. The consequence is, that what he *actually* provides in his account of validation is further indication of his subjectivist predilections concerning scientific discourse, already suggested in *New Rules*. His way out of the relativist impasse which results from the subjectivist critique of empiricism, rests itself, in large part, on subjectivist premises, despite his attempt to match his substantive stress on the unacknowledged conditions of action with a commitment to an unexplicated realism.

We now turn to an equally influential and even more recent attempt at synthesis presented by Bhaskar in his book, *The Possibility of Naturalism*.[38] Bhaskar, a philosopher with particular interests in sociology, starts from a remarkably similar position to that of Giddens, namely the opposition between a naturalistic positivism and an anti-naturalist hermeneutics, but unlike Giddens he does not reject out of hand the natural science model of the social sciences. Remember Giddens's assertion: 'the social sciences should move out of the shadow of the natural sciences, in whatever philosophical mantle they may be clad'.[39] Bhaskar differs, in attempting to provide the natural sciences with 'a philosophical mantle' that renders them more amenable to social scientists, including those who accept the force of subjectivist arguments.

According to Bhaskar, positivistic naturalism suggests that there is no difference between the natural and the social sciences, as both seek to explain and/or predict and control an invariant/law-like order between events, whether natural or social. Clearly Bhaskar's 'positivistic naturalism' is identical to our 'empiricism'. On the other hand he identifies what he calls an 'anti-naturalistic hermeneutic' tradition, which argues that while the natural sciences look for an invariant/law-like order between events, the social sciences do not, and nor can they. This is so because human beings consciously interpret their world, and are not, therefore, the simple products of such 'events' as heredity and environment. Human beings do not, then, obey laws in the same way as natural objects do, and, as a result, observers of their behaviour can only describe historically and situationally contingent meanings of their actions. Social scientific knowledge, then, is not, strictly speaking, 'scientific' in the objective/explanatory sense of the word, but merely a common-sense reproduction of the commonsense meanings that shape and determine the social world. Again clearly, Bhaskar's 'anti-naturalistic hermeneutics' is identical to our 'subjectivism'.

It is at this point that Bhaskar moves in a genuinely 'dialectical' direction, for instead of seeking to somehow piece these two strategies together, as does Giddens, he transcends them in terms of a third position which at the same time retains elements of each. He achieves this by pointing out that both positions share a view of natural science: namely, that it seeks to uncover invariant relationships between events. According to Bhaskar this is where both positivism and hermeneutics go wrong, for science is not, and never has been, of this character. Once we change our view of what natural science is, he argues, then the objections to an integration of the natural and social sciences disappear. This 'third' position, which allows for the possibility of naturalism, he calls 'transcendental realism'.

According to Bhaskar, natural science involves a fundamental distinction between events that belong to what he calls a 'transitive realm' – the actual world of relations between objects/phenomena, which is accessible to an observer through sense-perception – and an 'intransitive realm' – which is equally real but is accessible only through theoretical construction and experimental manipulation. The intransitive realm is constituted by a hierarchy of law-like, necessary, and generative mechanisms, which explain the events of the transitive realm. This hierarchy of generating mechanisms includes, in the biological realm, the DNA code; in the chemical realm, the table of elements and their conjunctures and permutations; and in the physical realm, the structures of atomic and sub-atomic matter and energy fields. That science operates in this way, and not according to empiricist principles according to which scientists merely seek for an order among observables, is testified to by the existence of the *experimental method*, which presupposes that no order among observables *is* immediately apparent. It is only when such observables are deliberately removed from their normal contexts and conjunctures that the 'hidden' order of the intransitive realm becomes apparent. It becomes apparent that the order in nature is not between things and events, but between 'pure' generalities uncontaminated by time, space, and context. Thus, the scientist is interested in the properties and effects of 'friction' in an abstract/general sense, and not in the actual events that take place in his own car engine. That such an intransitive realm is 'real', and not a mere figment of the observer's theoretical imagination and constructions, is testified to by the assumptions that necessarily underlie the use of experiment in science in the first place.

> The analysis of experimental activity shows that the objects of scientific investigation are typically structured and intransitive, that is irreducible to patterns of events, and active independently of their identification by men.[40]

In other words, the assumption of the truth of transcendental realism is the condition for the existence of science in the first place, and all scientists are transcendental realists even if they protest that they are empiricists:

> Now it follows from my argument that scientists, when they are practising science, are implicitly acting on transcendental realism.[41]

It should by now be clear that Bhaskar's transcendental realism has much in common with our substantialism, for both see theoretical constructs not as arbitrary/nominal groupings of events, but as referring to 'real' structures which underlie the empirical world, and explain it. Also, for Bhaskar, such structures are material, as he rejects the rationalist view that the transcendental realm consists of pure ideas. 'Transcendental realism' could well be renamed 'transcendental materialism', or, as we would prefer, 'substantialism'.

Once such a view of science is accepted, argues Bhaskar, the divorce between the natural and social sciences claimed by the anti-naturalists – including Giddens – disappears. Transcendental realism is, then, also applicable to the social sciences, admittedly with qualifications, but with just those qualifications that enable it to overcome the subjectivist objections to naturalism. The basic intransitive/transitive opposition also holds for the social sciences, for just as the understanding of natural events involves the assumption of the hidden reality of generative structures, so too does the condition for the existence of social events involve the assumption of the *sui generis* reality of transcendental social structures. In both cases the explanans is the hidden structure of the real, and the explanandum is the eventful world of natural/social phenomena, in this case individual actions:

> For the predicates designating properties special to persons all presuppose a social context for their employment. A tribesman implies a tribe, the cashing of a cheque a banking system.[42]

Bhaskar qualifies the application of transcendental realism to the social sciences by arguing that whereas in the natural world events depend totally upon the hidden structures that generate them, this is only partially the case for the social world. Social structures, unlike natural structures, are dependent for their 'reproduction' and 'transformation' on the individuals/events whose actions they otherwise determine. Although society is '*sui generis* real' it differs from natural structures in the following ways:

> (1) Social structures, unlike natural structures, do not exist independently of the activities they govern;
> (2) Social structures, unlike natural structures, do not exist independently of the agents' conceptions of what they are doing in their activity;
> (3) Social structures, unlike natural structures, may be only relatively enduring (so that the tendencies they ground may not be universal in the sense of space-time invariant).[43]

In other words, social structures, which are 'relations of production', act as a determinant framework for action, and a set of constraints upon its possibilities, even though the 'reproduction' and 'transformation' of such structures is continuously contingent upon the 'skilled performances' and creative potentialities of the actors themselves, for whom, therefore, determination is limited, even though freedom is never unlimited. From this perspective, which differs from Giddens only in its emphasis upon the hidden/intransitive nature of social structures, Bhaskar develops a critique of other sociologies, particularly with reference to their conceptions of the individual/society relationship. He outlines three perspectives: the 'atomistic' (which includes both our subjectivism *and* empiricism); the 'collectivistic' (which includes our rationalism and those forms of substantialism that do not make his qualifications, i.e. economic determinism); and 'dialecticism' (a term that he uses, ironically, to designate those theorists, like Berger and Luckmann,[44] who talk of an 'interaction' between the two). This critique is worth following, for it brings into relief the character of his own position.

Of atomism – that is the strategy that sees social structure as no more than the sum total of individual actions – he says that the condition for the existence of any statement made about individual behaviour presupposes a social structure *sui generis*: i.e. speech presupposes language, kings presuppose kingship, and so on. He adds further that 'individualism' presupposes that the 'individual' remains a metaphysical entity unless it too is reduced to its individuals, i.e. cells, DNA, and so on.

Collectivism, on the other hand, is that strategy that sees social structures as exclusively and totally determining of individual behaviour. He points out that such a project fails to recognise the significance of language for human action and relations. It is the existence of language that makes it impossible to conceive of social actors as the 'cultural dopes' that collectivism has reduced them to. Finally, he points to a third position, dialecticism, which argues that while society determines individual behaviour, individuals in turn react back on society and change its course and character in ways not necessarily immanent within it. For this position, probably because Bhaskar is concerned that it might be mistaken for his own, he reserves special scorn

> On Model III, then, society is an objectification or externalisation of man. And man, for his part, is an internalisation or re-appropriation in consciousness of society. Now I think that this model is seriously misleading. For it encourages, on the one hand, a voluntaristic idealism with respect to our understanding of

social structure and, on the other, a mechanistic determinism with respect to our understanding of people. In seeking to avoid the errors of both stereotypes, Model III succeeds only in *combining* them. People and society are not, I shall argue, related 'dialectically'. They do not constitute two moments of the same process. *Rather they refer to radically different kinds of thing.*[45] (our emphasis)

In other words, society is not simply made up of individuals, even with the proviso that their actions produce 'emergent properties', because society is a structure *sui generis*. Nor is society a determinant whole, controlling individuals like a master puppeteer, for individuals are 'skilled actors', capable of 'reproducing' and/or 'transforming' social structures in ways that make social structures non-universal/historical entities. And finally, social structures and individuals do not 'interact', because to conceive of them in this way is to view society as the outcome of a compromise between determinism and free will, a view which ignores the crucial difference between individuals, as transitive 'objects' and social structure, as intransitive.

Given Bhaskar's reformulation of the similarities and differences between natural and social science, and their objects of study, it follows that social science can, and must, produce objectively valid statements about the social structure/individual relationship, but in ways that recognise the distinctive features of the latter. For example, social science cannot utilise the experimental method, because while natural systems are closed/repeatable, social systems are open/unrepeatable. A corollary of this is that social scientific knowledge is both historically specific – dependent upon prevailing modes of production – and at the same time 'emancipatory'.

The emancipatory potential of social science is, for Bhaskar, a necessary product of its realist character. Social science is emancipatory, he argues, because the intransitive realm of social reality is itself open to transformation (human beings can act upon it to change it). Social science knowledge is an important part of this transformative process, because by revealing those 'hidden' structures, through its explanatory procedures, it at the same time reveals the potentialities for change as well as the contingency of its own explanatory statements. Such realist explanations mean that if:

one is in possession of a theory which explains why false consciousness is necessary then one can pass immediately without the addition of any extraneous value judgements, to a negative evaluation of the object (generative structure, system of social relations or whatever) that makes that consciousness necessary.[46]

In other words, such knowledge, by revealing the contingent nature of the social structure, de-mystifies those ideologies that assert that the conditions of human action have the status of universal, invariant, nature-like laws. Transcendental realism has, then, the capacity to explain the conditions under which ideology operates as false consciousness; a capacity that is used by Bhaskar as one of the criteria of what distinguishes objective theory from ideology. It is in the formulation of such criteria that Bhaskar sets about answering the central question of this chapter: Why should we prefer one theory in preference to the alternatives available?

Bhaskar presents a number of criteria which distinguish between what he calls theory (T)–the real order of things as apprehended in thought – and ideology (I)–the supposed order of things that typical lay actors use in living their lives. Briefly, Bhaskar argues that T is to be preferred because (i) it explains all that I explains, and more; (ii) T explains the conditions for the existence and transformation of I (the point made above), whereas I does not do so in relation to T; and (iii) T conforms both to the general criteria of scientificity (transcendental realism) and to the specific criteria of social scientificity, whereas I does not.[47] It is clear that these rules of validation depend entirely on the force of Bhaskar's argument concerning transcendental realism which lays down the general criteria of what scientificity is. If we can accept his view that transcendental realism genuinely transcends the alternative strategies (and we would point out here that the main thrust of Bhaskar's polemic is directed toward only two of the strategies we have outlined), then the criteria of preference would hold. Let us reconsider the argument overall.

Bhaskar argues, then, that where scientific procedures are fundamentally dependent upon experimentation there also exists the necessary assumption that an intransitive reality underlies those successions and conjunctures that characterise actual events. This argument seems unobjectionable, for unless we assume the existence of such a necessary order we do not need experiments in order to reveal it; we can, with the empiricists, take the immediately experienced events to be the only order (or lack of it) that exists. The fact that natural science procedures do imply realism does not, however, establish transcendental realism, for experiment may well represent a false way of gaining knowledge, even in the natural sciences. By refusing to engage in the kind of *a priori* justifications of science adopted by rationalists (which he explicitly rejects), Bhaskar leaps from the actual practice of modern science to the construction of a hidden reality which such practices presuppose. This is an unacceptable procedure because it takes as self-evident that which is problematic in the first place. The presuppositions of scientific practice cannot be taken as substitutes for reality itself, without further argument. Scientific practice could be wrong. As the whole of Bhaskar's case depends upon making this leap, he ends up on very shaky ground, because while transcendental realism may be correct, it remains *unfounded*. The same problem arises when Bhaskar attempts to establish the conditions for a realist social science. He argues that the language of description used by social science (concrete/historical social science as it is practised today) presupposes the reality of generative social structures – i.e. speech presupposes language, kings presuppose kingship, to use his own examples. Once again, consistent with his method, he starts out from actual practices and then constructs an intransitive model of the structures that such practices presuppose. However, just as experiment presupposes the *thought* of transcendental realism, rather than its reality, which cannot be so established, so the language of social scientific description presupposes the *thought* of society *sui generis*. However, subjectivists have always been aware of this point, for no one doubts that speech would be impossible without language. But this does not establish the 'transcendental' reality of language, for maybe the speaker merely *thinks* that what is in fact his own creation (language) is really an external reality forced upon him from the outside.

The main point that emerges from this discussion is that Bhaskar – a realist and materialist – appears to share the problems we have already identified as facing substantialism. That is, given substantialism's rejection of sense-data and logic, how is it possible to acquire knowledge of the underlying structures which it assumes to be there. Bhaskar fails to overcome this problem, for he merely assumes the existence of an intransitive realm on the basis of existing practices in the natural and social sciences. He does not identify such a reality directly, he accepts its existence on the basis that natural and social scientists act *as though* it were there. Experiment and speech become the arbitrary starting-points for a chain of reasoning that, while persuasive, presupposes what it sets out to prove in the first place.

Let us now move onto what Bhaskar calls his 'transformational model of social activity', which he summarises, by way of analogy, as follows:

> The rules of grammar, like natural structures, impose *limits* on the speech acts we can perform, but they do not determine our performances.[48]

and which he states more formally, thus:

> people do not create society. For it always pre-exists them and is a necessary condition for their activity. Rather society must be regarded as an ensemble of structures, practices and conventions which individuals reproduce or transform, but which would not exist unless they did so. Society does not exist independently of human activity (the error of reification). But it is not the product of it (the error of voluntarism). . . . It is important to stress that the reproduction and/or transformation of society, though for the most part unconsciously achieved, is nevertheless still an *achievement*, a skilled accomplishment of active subjects, not a mechanical consequence of antecedent conditions.[49]

Now the question arises, from where does Bhaskar derive this notion of society, from what historical 'givens' and/or *a priori* assumptions is this structure generated? This is a legitimate question, because Bhaskar requires that theory, unlike ideology, should be able 'to explain itself to itself'. It appears, however, that this notion arises, quite literally, out of thin air, and has the status of a 'taken-for-granted'. It does not, for example, arise out of any serious confrontation with those natural scientists who do *not* accept that nature consists of events that are a 'mechanical consequence of antecedent conditions', but, rather, have developed a view of nature not too different from Bhaskar's view of society. According to physicist Paul Davies, the indeterminacy principle of quantum field theory *does* mean that natural systems are dependent on the reproductive and transformative activity of 'individuals', and that because the *probability* of order in nature is so low, we are forced to assume the existence of conscious/communicatory and even teleological properties in inanimate nature.[50] In other words, while Bhaskar's dualism between nature and society and the natural sciences and the social sciences *does* confront the radical naturalism of the positivists, and even the anti-naturalism of the hermeneutic's view of nature, it does not confront the emerging anti-naturalism of modern physics. Bhaskar, then, seems unaware that the natural sciences are no longer entirely committed to the 'Newtonian paradigm', a failing he shares with both positivists and subectivists, as we have seen in our earlier discussion.

Just as Bhaskar fails to confront an emergent anti-naturalism in the natural sciences, which would break down his natural/social science dualism, so too does he fail to confront the views of those substantialists who cling to the view that society is a structure that makes individual behaviour 'a mechanical consquence of antecedent conditions'. The anthropologist Marvin Harris[51] is a case in point, for in his work *Cannibals and Kings* he argues that whole ranges of human activity – for example, human sacrifice, cannibalism, meat-eating and vegetarianism, and even religious taboos – are rigidly and mechanically determined in accordance with principles connected with population/resource/ecology ratios, and that social structures do in fact *determine* individual activities right down to the smallest and most intimate details. On what grounds should we reject such mechanical materialism in favour of Bhaskar's transcendental realism? Bhaskar's answer is that natural action, the action of inanimate and animate objects up to the level of the human, can be differentiated from human action by 'intentionality'. Thus he says:

> Human action is characterised by the striking phenomenon of intentionality. This seems to depend upon the feature that persons are material things with a degree of neuro-physiological complexity which enables them not just, like the other higher order animals, to initiate changes in a purposeful way, to monitor and control their performances, but to monitor the monitoring of

these performances and to be capable of a commentary upon them. This capacity for second order monitoring also makes possible a retrospective commentary upon actions, which gives a person's account of his own behaviour a special status, which is acknowledged in the *best practice* of all the psychological sciences.[52] (our emphasis)

Once again we find Bhaskar appealing to existing practices to substantiate his transcendental claims: i.e. experimental practice presupposes transcendental realism *therefore* transcendental realism is true; human self-descriptions presuppose society *sui generis therefore* society *sui generis* is true; and so on. Here, we have: 'the best practice of all the psychological sciences' recognises that human behaviour depends 'upon a feature' that is unique to humans, therefore humans have a unique feature called 'intentionality'. This is not a systematic generation of a case of the kind that Bhaskar seems to require in his 'explanatory criteria' for the separation of theory from ideology, but simply an argument from 'authority', and existing authority at that. This is from someone who claims that social scientific explanations are necessarily 'emancipatory'. Our argument here is not that Bhaskar is wrong, but that his arguments do not provide a secure basis for transcendental realism, nor do they live up to the criteria he himself adduces as the bases on which we should prefer one theory as against another. Bhaskar fails to confront those sociologists, anthropologists, psychologists and biologists who, while engaged in the 'best practice' of their sciences, firmly believe that hierarchical/deterministic models of human action, which start with the structure of DNA and end up with the phenotype in its environment, are perfectly adequate explanatory/descriptive models of the human, including its supposedly unique capacity 'to monitor the monitoring' of its performances.[53] No one, to our knowledge, suggests that the structure of language determines what is actually said, but many have argued that what is actually said *is* determined by a *compounding* of language structure, along with motivational states, learned responses, and environmental conditions, and that an exhaustive/explanatory model along the lines of Newtonian mechanics *is* possible. Marvin Harris, for example, is one such:

I insist that on the evidence of prehistory and history that the force which cost/benefit considerations has exerted on religious beliefs and vice versa has *not* been equal. Religions have generally changed *to conform to the requirements of reducing costs and maximising benefits* in the struggle to keep living systems from falling; cases in which production systems have changed to conform to the requirements of changed religious systems regardless of cost/benefit considerations *either do not exist, or are extremely rare.* The link between the depletion of animal proteins ... and the practice of human sacrifice and cannibalism ... demonstrates the unmistakable causal priority of material costs and benefits over spiritual beliefs.[54]

Writing this in 1977, Harris is in effect saying: 'Come back Engels all is forgiven.' There is a definite sense in which Bhaskar rules such arguments out of court, in the name of transformationalism, by simply not including them in his 'best practices', just as he would presumably rule out of court the theoretical constructions of a physicist who did not use the experimental method to arrive at them. Of course Bhaskar may well be right, and the mystical drift in modern physics and the mechanistic drift in modern social science *is* ill-grounded, but we cannot assume this to be the case on the basis of Bhaskar's undialectical approach to the construction of his own project.

We may conclude, then, that Bhaskar's project fails because his, admittedly subtle, transcendental realism is established not on the basis of its conformity to the requirements of the dialectic, but on the basis of arguments that appeal to existing practices, which are themselves underived, and which, on examination, turn out to be extremely problematic. Unresolved in Bhaskar's project is the material/ideal duality. This is so because his justification for transcendental realism depends on a series of assumptions about the nature of reality that find their authority in the 'best practices' of natural and social sciences. That is to say, a material, objective reality exists because it is *thought* to exist. We would argue that a dialectical strategy can only emerge on the basis of a confrontation with, and retention of, each of the synthesisable elements found in the four strategies, and not just those projects that have been prejudged on *a priori* grounds to be the 'best'. As a synthesis, then, Bhaskar's project is, as yet, not exhaustive of the elements that would go to make up a conception of the singular reality.

The way ahead

This brief consideration of limited aspects of Giddens's and Bhaskar's arguments, while critical of their attempts at synthesis, should not be taken as entirely dismissive. Both theorists illustrate the more positive developments in social theory to the degree that they recognise that synthesis is crucial to its development, and that this necessary task arises out of the failures of the alternative strategies to solve fundamental problems in their own terms. Synthesis is the goal suggested by both the interrelatedness and failures of the strategies.

Our grounds for criticising Giddens and Bhaskar arise out of the arguments presented above, that an adequate synthesis would take a dialectical form. That is to say, the dualisms that structure the strategic alternatives would be transcended by a singular conception of reality that would nevertheless recognise the reality of such oppositions (for example, the material and ideal). Dualisms may be construed as 'false dichotomies' where they remain unincorporated into a conception of the whole. Such dualities are false where a sense of social reality is achieved by dint of subordinating one such aspect of social reality (for example, the ideal) to another (for example, the material). This process of reductionism effectively undercuts any conception of a single social reality by making the claim that one aspect of reality is more *real* than another. Giddens's synthesis fails in its attempt to provide a basis for validation, by succumbing to a subjectivist reductionism, while Bhaskar's failure lies in the inability to transcend the material/ideal dualism except by way of a sleight-of-hand in which existing thought is taken for the proof that such a material reality exists.

In reaching such conclusions about these theoretical projects, we are adopting what might be called dialectical rules of judgement as a means of evaluating theory. They are dialectical because they involve criteria that do not presuppose the validity of any one theoretical strategy. Rather, they require that a synthesis transcend the dualities that generate the strategies in the first place. We cannot, however, present as a conclusion to our argument such a dialectical resolution of the dilemmas of social theory. There is no such resolution available to be presented. We are here merely presenting a goal. Such a resolution has still to be thought; to be worked toward. It is a task that must be the work of generations of social scientists who are forced by the failure of one strategy or another to seek a resolution.

In this text we have set ourselves a more limited task; not to resolve the problems of contemporary sociology, but to clarify what those problems are, to explain why the different attempts to resolve them have failed, and to suggest the criteria that any synthesis would have to meet – namely, the transcendence of the two fundamental axes of social theory, subject/object and material/ideal. We have argued that the seeming fragmentation of social theory can be understood, as a structured set of responses to the fundamental questions we pose ourselves about the nature of the social world – what we have called the strategies. It has also been argued that the seemingly endless varieties of sociological perspectives cohere around these four alternative strategies, with the more fruitful and insightful theoretical projects combining elements of a number of these strategies. Having claimed that theory was structured in terms of these four alternative strategies, we went on to suggest that the strategies, in fact, comprised a common structure of thinking in which one set of answers to the problems of what social reality is and how we know it, was arrived at only through confrontation and *dialogue* with the alternatives. That is to say, each strategy implies the alternatives. It was this common structure and interdependence that led to the conclusion that an adequate solution to the problems was only likely as the result of some kind of synthesis of the alternative strategies, particularly as each strategy could be shown to fail to justify itself in its own terms. In the course of this book we have, then, moved from the conventional characterisation of sociology as a fragmented and incommensurable set of perspectives, to a position where we are able to argue that the fragments were in fact a unified structure of theory in exhibiting a tendency towards synthesis.

Finally, it was argued that the conditions for a successful synthesis of the strategies were dialectical, in which the alternative aspects of reality and related means of knowing it both retained their force but were at the same time transcended by the recognition of a singular reality. It is the foreshadowed and potential unity of the strategies that, we would argue, presents the most exciting goal in sociology and one that the founders of the discipline directed themselves toward. In formulating the dialectical rules of judgement we provide no substantive answers to the major questions facing the discipline, but we do, we believe, provide a means of evaluating emergent syntheses, even if only negatively. However, such rules, in an elaborated form, might also be regarded as a guide to the construction of syntheses, because they are, above all, made up of statements that should be genuinely acceptable to theorists operating within the assumptions of each of the four strategies that structure social theory, for no social theorists can escape the dialogue – its complementarities and oppositions. The solutions to the problems of theorising about the social are, then, already present in the structure of that dialogue.

Notes and References

1 Theoretical sociology: the conditions of fragmentation and unity

1. Peter Winch, *The Idea of a Social Science* (London: Routledge & Kegan Paul, 1958); Aaron Cicourel, *Cognitive Sociology* (Harmondsworth: Penguin, 1972); Harold Garfinkel, *Studies in Ethnomethodology* (Englewood Cliffs, New Jersey: Prentice-Hall, 1967).
2. Thomas S. Kuhn, *The Structure of Scientific Revolutions*, 2nd edn (Chicago: University of Chicago Press, 1970).
3. For recent alternative attempts at classification, see Russell Keat and John Urry, *Social Theory as Science* (London: Routledge & Kegan Paul, 1975); Ted Benton, *Philosophical Foundations of the Three Sociologies* (London: Routledge & Kegan Paul, 1977); Gibson Burrell and Gareth Morgan, *Sociological Paradigms and Organizational Analysis* (London: Heinemann, 1979); A. Dawe, 'The Two Sociologies', *British Journal of Sociology*, 21 (1970) pp. 207–18; R. Robertson, 'Towards the Identification of the Major Axes of Sociological Analysis', in J. Rex (ed.), *Approaches to Sociology* (London: Routledge & Kegan Paul, 1974).
4. Talcott Parsons, *The Structure of Social Action* (Glencoe, Ill.: Free Press, 1949).

2 Empiricism

1. General discussions of empiricism may be found in L. Kolakowski, *Positivist Philosophy* (Harmondsworth: Penguin, 1972); G. Novack, *Empiricism and its Evolution* (New York: Pathfinder Press, 1969).
2. See A. Giddens, 'Positivism and its Critics', in T. Bottomore and R. Nisbet, *A History of Sociological Analysis* (London: Heinemann, 1979) pp. 237–86; Kolakowski, *Positivist Philosophy*; P. Achinstein and S. F. Barker, *The Legacy of Logical Positivism* (Baltimore: Johns Hopkins Press, 1969); C. G. A. Bryant, 'Positivism Reconsidered', *Sociological Review*, 23 2 1975; R. Bernstein, *Restructuring of Social and Political Theory* (Oxford: Blackwell, 1976) pp. 1–55.

3. Metaphysics may be viewed either as meaningless, as in Ayer's empiricism, or as meaningful but non-scientific as in Popper. See A. J. Ayer, *Language, Truth and Logic* (Harmondsworth: Penguin, 1971); K. Popper, *Conjectures and Refutations* (London: Routledge & Kegan Paul, 1963).

4. On these variations in empiricist explanation, see E. Nagel, *The Structure of Science* (London: Routledge & Kegan Paul, 1961); C. G. Hempel, *Aspects of Scientific Explanation* (Glencoe, Ill.: Free Press, 1965); A. Ryan, *The Philosophy of the Social Sciences* (London: Macmillan, 1970); R. Keat and J. Urry, *Social Theory as Science* (London: Routledge & Kegan Paul, 1975) pp. 9–22, 67–87; T. Benton, *Philosophical Foundations of the Three Sociologies* (London: Routledge & Kegan Paul, 1977) pp. 46–77.

5. See Trent Schroyer, *The Critique of Domination: Origins and Development of Critical Theory* (New York: Braziller, 1973).

6. This has led, in recent years, to a number of attempts to reconstruct the bases of sociological theorising: see A. W. Gouldner, *The Coming Crisis of Western Sociology* (London: Heinemann, 1971); Bernstein, *Restructuring of Social and Political Theory*; Keat and Urry, *Social Theory as Science*; Benton, *Philosophical Foundations*; and A. Giddens, *New Rules of Sociological Method* (London: Hutchinson, 1976), *Central Problems in Social Theory* (London: Macmillan, 1979) and *A Contemporary Critique of Historical Materialism* (London: Macmillan, 1981).

7. On these points see R. Bhaskar, *A Realist Theory of Science* (Leeds: Leeds Books, 1975) and *Possibility of Naturalism* (Brighton: Harvester, 1979).

8. On conventionalism and problems of theory-neutral observation languages, see Bernstein, *Restructuring*, pp. 4–7; Keat and Urry, *Social Theory*, pp. 46–65; Benton, *Philosophical Foundations*, pp. 73–6.

9. On Skinner, and problems of Behaviourism generally, see B. F. Skinner, *Verbal Behaviour* (London: Methuen, 1957) and *About Behaviourism* (London: Cape, 1974); N. Chomsky, *Language and Mind* (New York: Harcourt Brace Jovanovich, 1968); A. Koestler, *Ghost in the Machine* (London: Hutchinson, 1967); S. Mennell, *Sociological Theory: Uses and Unities* (Sunbury: Nelson, 1974) pp. 9–13.

10. That positivist explanations rely on their capacity to predict and control their subject-matter has been stressed by those writers in the traditions of critical theory: see B. Fay, *Social Theory and Political Practice* (London: Allen & Unwin, 1975); J. Habermas, *Theory and Practice* (London: Heinemann, 1974).

11. D. and J. Willer, *Systematic Empiricism – A Critique of a Pseudo-Science* (Englewood Cliffs: Prentice Hall, 1973); C. Wright Mills, *The Sociological Imagination* (Oxford University Press, 1959) pp. 60–86, and 'The Ideology of Social Pathologists', in Wright Mills, *Power, Politics and People* (Oxford University Press, 1967) pp. 525–52.

12. R. Blauner, *Alienation and Freedom* (Chicago: University of Chicago Press, 1964); J. E. T. Eldridge, *Sociology and Industrial Life* (London: Nelson, 1971) pp. 139–96.

13. D. and J. Willer, *Systematic Empiricism*, pp. 34–43.

14. J. Irvine, I. Miles and J. Evans, *Demystifying Social Statistics* (London: Pluto Press, 1979) pp. 87–110.

15. D. and J. Willer, *Systematic Empiricism*, pp. 63–72.

16. On hypothetico-deductivism see P. Cohen, *Modern Social Theory* (London: Heinemann, 1968) pp. 1–17; Keat and Urry, *Social Theory*, pp. 9–13; M. Lessnoff, *The Structure of Social Science* (London: Allen & Unwin, 1973) pp. 12–31, 75–109.

17. See W. Pope, *Durkheim's Suicide: a Classic Analysed* (Chicago: University of Chicago Press, 1976).

18. G. Homans, *The Human Group* (New York: Harcourt Brace, 1950); J. O'Neill, *Modes of Individualism and Collectivism* (London: Heinemann, 1973).

19. T. Parsons, *The Structure of Social Action*, 2 vols (Glencoe, Ill.: Free Press, 1937). For recent sympathetic critiques of Parsons, see: S. Savage, *The Theories of T. Parsons: The Social Relations of Action* (London: Macmillan, 1981); K. Menzies, *T. Parsons and the Social Image of Man* (London: Routledge & Kegan Paul, 1977); G. Rocher, *T. Parsons and American Sociology* (London: Nelson, 1974); Z. Bauman, *Hermeneutics and Social Science* (London: Hutchinson, 1978) pp. 131–47; H. Bershady, *Ideology and Social Knowledge* (Oxford: Blackwell, 1973).

20. *Structure of Social Action*, Preface, pp. v–ix.

21. Bershady, *Ideology and Social Knowledge*; Savage, *Theories of T. Parsons*; Bauman, *Hermeneutics*.

22. T. Parsons, *Toward a General Theory of Action* (Cambridge, Mass., 1962) and *Working Papers in the Theory of Action* (Glenco, Ill.: Free Press, 1953); Rocher, *T. Parsons*, pp. 28–51.

23. This point provides the central theme of K. Menzies, *T. Parsons and the Social Image of Man* (London: Routledge & Kegan Paul, 1977). See also J. Turner, *The Structure of Sociological Theory* (Dorsey, Homewood, Ill.: 1974).

24. T. Parsons, *The Evolution of Societies* (edited version of *Societies*, 1966) and *The System of Modern Societies* (1971) (Englewood Cliffs, NJ.: Prentice Hall, 1977); T. Parsons, 'Evolutionary Universals in Society', *American Sociological Review*, 29 (June) pp. 339–57.

25. *Societies, Evolutionary and Comparative Perspectives* (Englewood Cliffs, NJ.: Prentice Hall, 1966) p. 113.

26. See Toby, introduction to *The Evolution of Societies*, pp. 20–22.

27. S. Savage, *The Theories of Talcott Parsons: The Social Relations of Action* (London: Macmillan, 1981) pp. 105–27; also, A. Giddens, 'Power in the Recent Writings of Talcott Parsons', in Giddens, *Studies in Social and Political Theory* (London: Hutchinson, 1977).

28. Parsons, *Evolutionary Universals*.

29. N. Smelser, *Social Change and the Industrial Revolution* (London: Routledge & Kegan Paul, 1959).
30. Parsons, *Evolutionary Universals.*
31. P. Cohen, *Modern Social Theory* (London: Heinemann, 1968) pp. 47–66; C. G. Hempel, 'The Logic of Functional Analysis', in L. Gross, *Symposium on Sociological Theory* (New York: Harper & Row, 1959) pp. 271–302; E. Nagel, 'A Formalization of Functionalism', in *Logic Without Metaphysics* (Glencoe, Ill.: Free Press, 1956); S. Mennell, *Sociological Theory: Uses and Unities* (London: Nelson, 1974) pp. 141–65.
32. R. K. Merton, *On Theoretical Sociology* (London: Collier-Macmillan, 1967) pp. 39–73.
33. Ibid, p. 47.
34. Ibid, pp. 149–50.
35. Ibid, pp. 82–4.
36. Ibid, p. 106.
37. K. Davis, 'The Myth of Functional Analysis as a Special Method in Sociology and Anthropology', in N. J. Demerath and R. A. Petersen, *System, Change and Conflict* (Glencoe, Ill.: Free Press, 1967) pp. 379–402.
38. Cohen, *Modern Social Theory*, pp. 47–66. C. G. Hempel, 'The Logic of Functional Analysis' in Llewellyn Gross *op. cit.*, pp. 271–307.
39. Parsons, *The Structure of Social Action*, pp. 728–37.
40. R. Dahrendorf, *Class and Class Conflict in Industrial Society* (London: Routledge & Kegan Paul, 1959); J. A. Banks, *Marxist Sociology in Action* (London: Faber, 1970).
41. T. S. Kuhn, *The Structure of Scientific Revolutions* (Chicago University Press, 1970); K. Popper, *The Logic of Scientific Discovery* (London: Basic Books, 1959); I. Lakatos and A. Musgrave, *Criticism and the Growth of Knowledge* (Cambridge University Press, 1970); A. Giddens, *New Rules of Sociological Method* (London: Hutchinson, 1976).

3 Subjectivism

1. Z. Bauman, *Hermeneutics and Social Science* (London: Hutchinson, 1978) pp. 23–47; A. Giddens, *New Rules of Sociological Method* (London: Hutchinson, 1976) pp. 71–92.
2. E. Husserl, *The Crisis of the European Sciences and Transcendental Phenomenology* (Evanston, Ill.: Northwestern University Press, 1970).
3. Cited in T. Parsons, *Structure of Social Action* (Glencoe, Ill.: Free Press, 1968) p. 589.
4. M. Weber, *Methodology of the Social Sciences* (Glencoe, Ill.: Free Press, 1949) pp. 72–112; M. Weber, 'Science as a Vocation', in H. Gerth and C. W. Mills, *From Max Weber: Essays in Sociology* (London: Routledge & Kegan Paul, 1970) pp. 142–56.

5. Weber, *Methodology of the Social Sciences*, p. 84.
6. Ibid, pp. 171–6.
7. Ibid, p. 97.
8. M. Weber, *Economy and Society* (Berkeley: University of California Press, 1978) pp. 22–31; A. Giddens, *Positivism and Sociology* (London: Heinemann, 1974) pp. 23–31.
9. Weber, *Economy and Society*, pp. 24–6.
10. Ibid, pp. 8–22.
11. For example, T. Abel, 'The Operation Called Verstehen', *American Journal of Sociology*, 59, pp. 211–18.
12. Weber, *Economy and Society*, pp. 468–500.
13. Ibid, pp. 241–54, 1111–56.
14. Ibid, pp. 302–7, 926–39.
15. Ibid, pp. 928–9.
16. Max Weber, *The Protestant Ethic and the Spirit of Capitalism* (London: Allen & Unwin, 1968) pp. 24–8.
17. A. Schutz, *Phenomenology of the Social World* (London: Heinemann, 1972) pp. 3–20, 38–53, 57–63.
18. Ibid, pp. 63–71.
19. Ibid, p. 166.
20. Ibid.
21. Ibid, pp. 31–8.
22. Giddens, *New Rules of Sociological Method*, pp. 23–70.
23. E. Bittner, 'The Concept of Organization', in G. Salaman and K. Thompson, *People and Organizations* (London: Longmans, Open University, 1973) pp. 264–76.
24. J. C. McKinney and E. A. Tiryakian, *Theoretical Sociology: Perspectives and Developments* (New York: Appleton Century Crofts, 1970) pp. 337–66.
25. J. Douglas, *The Social Meanings of Suicide* (Princeton University Press, 1967).
26. A. Cicourel, *Method and Measurement in Sociology* (London: Collier Macmillan, 1964).
27. H. Garfinkel, *Studies in Ethnomethodology* (Englewood Cliffs, NJ.: Prentice-Hall, 1967).
28. A. Cicourel, *Cognitive Sociology* (Harmondsworth: Penguin, 1978).
29. Garfinkel, *Studies*, pp. 35–76.
30. J. Douglas, *Understanding Everyday Life* (Chicago: Aldine, 1970) pp. 80–103.
31. B. Gidlow, 'Ethnomethodology: A New Name for Old Practices', *British Journal of Sociology*, 1972, 23, pp. 395–405.
32. H. Blumer, 'Society as Symbolic Interactionism', in A. Rose, *Human Behaviour and Social Process* (Boston: Houghton Mifflin, 1962) pp. 179–92.
33. P. Attewell, 'Ethnomethodology since Garfinkel', *Theory and Society* (1974) pp. 179–210.
34. G. H. Mead, *Mind Self and Society* (Chicago: University of Chicago Press, 1962).

35. N. K. Denzin, 'Symbolic Interactionism and Ethnomethodology', *American Sociological Review* (1969) pp. 922–34.
36. Douglas, *Social Meanings of Suicide.*
37. McKinney and Tiryakian, *Theoretical Sociology*, pp. 337–76.
38. Cicourel, *Cognitive Sociology.*
39. A. Blum, *Theorising* (London: Heinemann, 1972); P. McHugh, *On the Beginning of Social Enquiry* (London: Routledge & Kegan Paul, 1974).

4 Substantialism

1. H. B. Acton, *The Illusion of the Epoch* (London, 1955) p. 271.
2. While this systematisation of the discussion to follow is presented as a series of stages having a chronological basis in Marx's work, we would not wish to suggest that Marx's development was as neatly progressive and clear-cut as the concept of *stage* suggests. He was constantly backtracking and redefining this position as well as failing to recognise the full implications of previously established solutions. The stages, therefore, should be taken as general shifts in emphasis associated with major problems confronted.
3. That this clear expression of a forthright materialism comes from Marx's later work is an indication of the problems facing any attempt at periodization. See *Capital*, vol. 1 (Harmondsworth: Penguin Books, 1976) p. 102.
4. This translation comes from Wal Suchting, 'Marx's Theses on Feuerbach: Notes Towards a Commentary (with a New Translation)', in John Mepham and David-Hillel Ruben (eds), *Issues in Marxist Philosophy* (Brighton: Harvester Press, 1979) pp. 5–34. For alternative translations see T. B. Bottomore and M. Rubel, *Karl Marx: Selected Writings in Sociology and Social philosophy* (London: Watts & Co., 1956); Karl Marx, *Early Writings* (Harmondsworth: Penguin, 1975) pp. 421–3.
5. Suchting, 'Marx's Thesis', pp. 7–8.
6. Ibid, p. 12.
7. George Lukács, *History and Class Consciousness* (London: Merlin Press, 1971).
8. Karl Korsch, *Marxism and Philosophy* (London: New Left Books, 1970).
9. As well as Horkheimer the Frankfurt School included Theodore Adorno, Herbert Marcuse, Franz Neumann, Erich Fromm, and Jurgen Habermas. See David Held, *Introduction to Critical Theory: Horkheimer to Habermas* (London: Hutchinson, 1980).
10. Edmund Husserl, *The Crisis of the European Sciences and Transcendental Phenomenology* (Evanston, Ill.: Northwestern University Press, 1970).
11. Of major importance were the 'Economic and Philosophical Manuscripts': see Marx, *Early Writings,* pp. 279–400.
12. For the phenomenological Marxism of Enzo Paci, see B. Smart, *Sociology, Phenomenology and Marxian Analysis* (London: Routledge & Kegan Paul, 1976). For the existentialists Sartre and Merleau-

Ponty, see James Miller, *History and Human Existence* (Berkeley: University of California Press, 1979); and Mark Poster, *Existential Marxism in Post-War France* (Princeton: University Press, 1975). For critical Theory, see Held, *Introduction to Critical Theory*.

13. Enzo Paci, *The Function of the Sciences and the Meaning of Man* (Evanston, Ill.: Northwestern University Press, 1972).
14. For a discussion of Marx's usage here, see John McMurtry, *The Structure of Marx's World View* (Princeton, NJ: Princeton University Press, 1978) ch. 7, 'Economic Determinism'.
15. L. Easton and K. Guddat (eds), *Writing of the Young Marx on Philosophy and Society* (New York: Doubleday, 1967) p. 350.
16. Karl Marx, *Capital*, vol. 1 (Harmondsworth: Penguin Books, 1976) p. 176.
17. Ibid.
18. See Nicos Poulantzas, *Political Power and Social Classes* (London: New Left Books, 1973) pp. 13–15.
19. See, for example, Percy Cohen, *Modern Social Theory* (London: Heinemann, 1968): 'I am well aware that the views of the early, "romantic" Marx were rather different. But I hold to the opinion expressed by Raymond Aron in his unrivalled discussion of Marx that there is little in the early Marx of value to sociology as such.' p. 79.
20. Marx, *Early Writings*, p. 355.
21. Ibid.
22. Karl Marx, *Poverty of Philosophy* (Moscow: Progress, 1976).
23. Karl Marx, *Grundrisse* (Harmondsworth: Penguin, 1973) p. 101.
24. For example, Karl Popper, *The Poverty of Historicism* (London: Routledge & Kegan Paul, 1965).
25. See ch. 1 of Martin Jay's, *The Dialectical Imagination: A History of the Frankfurt School and the Institute of Social Research 1923–50* (London: Heinemann, 1973).
26. Marx, *Early Writings*, p. 356.
27. Ibid, p. 209.
28. Marx, *Capital*, vol. III, p. 817.
29. Marx, *Grundrisse*.
30. The structuralist linguistics of Saussure and Jakobson have been influential in the work of Marxist structuralists such as Louis Althusser and Nicos Poulantzas.
31. See Colin Sumner, *Reading Ideologies* (London: Academic Press, 1979).
32. Letter to Engels, 27 June 1967, Karl Marx and Frederick Engels, *Selected Correspondence* (Moscow: Progress, 1975).
33. Marx, *Capital*, p. 75.

5 Rationalism

1. See, for example, A. Giddens, *The New Rules of Sociological Method* (London: Hutchinson, 1976).
2. T. Parsons, *The Structure of Social Action* (Glencoe, Ill.: Free Press, 1949) pp. 304–5.

3. See particularly, S. Lukes, *E. Durkheim: His Life and Work* (Harmondsworth: Penguin, 1975); and P. Hirst, *Durkheim, C. Bernard and Epistemology* (London: Routledge & Kegan Paul, 1975).

4. E. Durkheim, *The Division of Labour in Society* (Glencoe, Ill.: Free Press, 1964) p. 32: 'We do not wish to extract ethics from science, but to establish a science of ethics.'

5. E. Durkheim, *The Elementary Forms of the Religious Life* (London: Allen & Unwin, 1971) p. 19: 'The rationalism which is imminent in the sociological theory of knowledge is thus midway between the classical empiricism and apriorism.'

6. Parsons, *The Structure of Social Action*, p. 357.

7. E. Durkheim, *The Rules of Sociological Method* (Glencoe, Ill.: Free Press, 1966) pp. 13, 35.

8. Parsons, *The Structure of Social Action*.

9. Durkheim's recurrent concern with 'the essence of reality' (e.g. *The Rules of Sociological Method*, p. 42), means that Popper would undoubtedly have made this accusation had he paid attention to Durkheim's work. See, K. Popper, *The Poverty of Historicism* (London: Routledge & Kegan Paul, 1965).

10. J. Douglas, *The Social Meaning of Suicide* (Princeton: Princeton University Press, 1967).

11. Parsons, *The Structure of Social Action*, p. 444.

12. Durkheim, *The Division of Labour in Society*, book two, Chs 1 and 2.

13. Ibid, pp. 276–7.

14. Ibid, p. 129.

15. Parsons, *The Structure of Social Action*.

16. Durkheim, *The Division of Labour in Society*, p. 257.

17. E. Durkheim, *Suicide: A Study in Sociology* (London: Routledge & Kegan Paul, 1952) p. 302.

18. Durkheim, *The Rules of Sociological Method*, p. 29.

19. Ibid, p. 103.

20. Durkheim, *The Elementary Forms of the Religious Life*, p. 228.

21. Ibid, p. 231

22. Ibid, p. 270.

23. Ibid, p. 365.

24. See, for example, recent texts such as Keat and Urry, *Social Theory as Science*, and T. Benton, *Philosophical Foundations of the Three Sociologies*, which ignore this tradition of theorising.

25. Durkheim, *The Rules of Sociological Method*, p. 31.

26. For a sympathetic statement of Husserl's methodological position, see especially, M. Merleau-Ponty, 'Phenomenology and the Sciences of Man', in M. Merleau-Ponty, *The Primacy of Perception* (Northwestern University Press, 1964).

27. Durkheim, *The Rules of Sociological Method*, p. 15.

28. Ibid, p. 35.

29. Ibid, p. 125.

30. Ibid, p. 32.

31. K. Popper, *Conjectures and Refutations* (London: Routledge & Kegan Paul, 1967).

32. E. Durkheim and M. Mauss, *Primitive Classifications* (New York: Harper & Row, 1964).
33. Durkheim, *The Elementary Forms of the Religious Life*, p. 264.
34. Douglas, *The Social Meanings of Suicide*.
35. Durkheim, *The Elementary Forms of the Religious Life*, p. 76.
36. Ibid, p. 8.
37. Ibid, p. 5.
38. See Parsons, *The Structure of Social Action*, p. 444.
39. See particularly, Popper, *Conjectures and Refutations*, for an elaboration of this position.
40. Durkheim, *The Division of Labour in Society*, p. 204.
41. For a modern statement of 'critical theory', see J. Habermas, *Towards a Rational Society* (London: Heinemann, 1971).
42. A. Meinong, 'The Theory of Objects', in R. M. Chisholm, *Realism and The Background of Phenomenology* (Glencoe, Ill.: Free Press, 1960).
43. E. Durkheim, 'Value Judgements and Judgements of Reality', in his *Sociology and Philosophy* (London: Cohen & West, 1968) p. 95.
44. C. Jung, *Psychology and Religion* (London: Routledge & Kegan Paul, 1958).
45. A. Hardy, *The Living Stream* (London: Collins, 1965), and *The Biology of God* (London: Cass, 1975).
46. C. Jung and W. Pauli, 'Naturerklarung und Psyche', in *Studien aus dem C. G. Jung-Institut*, IV (Zurich, 1952).
47. C. R. Badcock, *Lévi-Strauss: Structuralism and Sociological Theory* (London: Hutchinson, 1975) p. 28.

6 The dialectic of theoretical practice

1. The term 'convention' comes from the 'conventionalism' used by R. Keat and J. Urry in *Social Theory as Science* (London: Routledge & Kegan Paul, 1975).
2. The rule 'anything goes' is taken from P. Feyerabend, *Science in a Free Society* (London: New Left Books, 1978).
3. See particularly, H. Marcuse, *Reason and Revolution: Hegel and the Rise of Social Theory* (London: Routledge & Kegan Paul, 1955), *An Essay on Liberation* (Boston: Beacon, 1969), and *Counterrevolution and Revolt* (Boston: Beacon, 1972).
4. K. Popper, *Conjectures and Refutations* (London: Routledge & Kegan Paul, 1967).
5. Ibid, p. 28.
6. Apparently, when two sub-atomic particles collide, the net result of their fusion is sometimes more, and sometimes less, than their combined masses: F. Capra, *The Tap of Physics* (London: Wildewood, 1975).
7. Popper, *Conjectures*, p. 28.
8. A. Giddens, *New Rules of Sociological Method* (London: Hutchinson, 1976) pp. 140–1

9. T. Kuhn, *The Structure of Scientific Revolutions*, 2nd edn (Chicago: University of Chicago Press, 1970).

10. I. Lakatos, 'Proofs and Refutations', *British Journal for the Philosophy of Science*, vol. 14 (1963) pp. 1–25, 120–39, 221–45, 296–342.

11. Karl Popper, *Objective Knowledge* (Oxford: Clarendon Press, 1972).

12. This has been a major thrust in the criticism of Althusser. See A. Glucksmann, 'A Ventriloquist Structuralism', *New Left Review*, March–April 1972, pp. 68–92.

13. See B. Smart, *Sociology, Phenomenology and Marxian Analysis* (London: Routledge & Kegan Paul, 1976).

14. George Herbert Mead, *Mind, Self and Society* (Chicago: University of Chicago Press, 1934).

15. The most influential source for such conventionalist arguments is Karl Mannheim, *Ideology and Utopia* (London: Routledge & Kegan Paul, 1972), who generalises this structural warranty to 'free floating' intellectuals.

16. J. Douglas, *Understanding Everyday Life* (London: Aldine, 1970).

17. Giddens, *New Rules of Sociological Method*.

18. Ibid, p. 14.

19. Ibid, p. 15.

20. Ibid, p. 79.

21. Ibid, p. 131.

22. Ibid, p. 92.

23. Ibid, pp. 85–6.

24. Ibid, p. 53.

25. Ibid, p. 121.

26. Ibid, p. 147.

27. Ibid, p. 135.

28. Ibid, pp. 139–40.

29. Ibid, pp. 85–6.

30. Ibid, p. 158.

31. Ibid, p. 144.

32. Ibid, p. 67.

33. Jurgen Habermas, *Towards a Rational Society* (London: Heinemann, 1971).

34. A. Giddens, 'Habermas' Social and Political Theory', in *Profiles and Critiques in Social Theory* (London: Macmillan, 1983) pp. 82–99.

35. In A. Giddens, *Studies in Social and Political Theory* (London: Hutchinson, 1977).

36. M. Hesse, *The Structure of Scientific Inference* (London, Macmillan, 1974).

37. Giddens, *Studies in Social and Political Theory*.

38. R. Bhaskar, *The Possibility of Naturalism* (Brighton: Harvester Press, 1979).

39. Giddens, *New Rules of Sociological Method*, p. 14.

40. Bhaskar, *Possibility*, p. 14.

41. Ibid, i, 20.

42. Ibid, p. 35.

43. Ibid, pp. 48–9.

44. P. Berger and T. Luckmann, *The Social Construction of Reality* (Harmondsworth: Penguin, 1966).
45. Bhaskar, *Possibility*, pp. 41–2.
46. Ibid, p. 81.
47. Ibid, pp. 86–7.
48. Ibid, p. 47.
49. Ibid, pp. 45–6.
50. See P. Davies, *God and the New Physics* (London: Dent, 1983).
51. M. Harris, *Cannibals and Kings* (London: Collins, 1977).
52. Bhaskar, *Possibility*, p. 44.
53. See particularly the introductory chapters to J. W. Kalat's *Biological Psychology* (London: Wadsworth, 1980) for a forceful statement of this view.
54. M. Harris, *Cannibals and Kings*, p. 154.

Bibliography

T. Abel, 'The Operation called Verstehen', *American Journal of Sociology*, 59, 211–18.

P. Achinstein and S. F. Barker, *The Legacy of Logical Positivism* (Baltimore: Johns Hopkins, 1969).

H. B. Acton, *The Illusion of the Epoch* (London, 1955).

L. Althusser, *For Marx* (Harmondsworth: Penguin, Allen Lane, 1969).

P. Attewell, 'Ethnomethodology since Garfinkel', *Theory and Society* (1974) 179–210.

A. J. Ayer, *Language Truth and Logic* (Harmondsworth: Penguin, 1971).

J. A. Banks, *Marxist Sociology in Action* (London: Faber, 1975).

Z. Bauman, *Hermeneutics and Social Science* (London: Hutchinson, 1978).

T. Benton, *Philosophical Foundations of the Three Sociologies* (London: Routledge & Kegan Paul, 1977).

T. Benton, 'Objective Interests and the Sociology of Power', *Sociology*, May 1982, 161–82.

P. Berger and T. Luckmann, *The Social Construction of Reality* (Harmondsworth: Penguin, 1966).

R. Bernstein, *The Restructuring of Social and Political Theory* (Oxford: Blackwell, 1976).

H. Bershady, *Ideology and Social Knowledge* (Oxford: Blackwell, 1973).

R. Bhaskar, *A Realist Theory of Science* (Leeds Books, 1975).

R. Bhaskar, *The Possibility of Naturalism: A Philosophical Critique of the Human Sciences* (Brighton: Harvester, 1979).

P. Blau, *Exchange and Power in Social Life* (New York: Wiley, 1964).

R. Blauner, *Alienation and Freedom* (Chicago: University of Chicago Press, 1964).

A. Blum, *Theorising* (London: Heinemann, 1972).

T. Bottomore and R. Nisbet, *A History of Sociological Analysis* (London: Heinemann, 1979).

T. Bottomore and M. Rubel, *Karl Marx: Selected Writings in Sociology and Social Philosophy* (London: Watts & Co., 1956).

G. A. Bryant, 'Positivism Reconsidered', *Sociological Review*, 23, (1975).

Gibson Burrell and Gareth Morgan, *Sociological Paradigms and Organizational Analysis* (London: Heinemann, 1979).

R. M. Chisholm, *Realism and the Background of Phenomenology* (Glencoe, Ill.: Free Press, 1960).

N. Chomsky, *Language and Mind* (New York: Harcourt Brace Jovanovich, 1968).

A. Cicourel, *Cognitive Sociology* (Harmondsworth: Penguin, 1972).

A. Cicourel, *Social Organization of Juvenile Justice* (Chichester: Wiley, 1968).

A. Cicourel, *Method and Measurement in Sociology* (London: Collier Macmillan, 1964).

P. Cohen, *Modern Social Theory* (London: Heinemann, 1968).

R. G. Colodny, *The Nature and Function of Scientific Theories* (Pittsburgh: University of Pittsburgh Press, 1970).

R. Dahrendorf, *Class and Class Conflict in Industrial Society* (London: Routledge & Kegan Paul, 1959).

C. Dandeker and J. Scott, 'The Structure of Sociological Theory and Knowledge', *Journal for the Theory of Social Behaviour* 9, 3, (1979) pp. 303–25.

P. Davies, *God and the New Physics* (London: Dent, 1983).

A. Dawe, 'The Two Sociologies', *British Journal of Sociology*, 21 (1970) 207–18.

N. J. Demerath and R. A. Petersen, *System, Change and Conflict* (Glencoe, Ill.: Free Press, 1967).

N. K. Denzin, 'Symbolic Interactionism and Ethnomethodology', *American Sociological Review* (1969) 922–34.

J. Douglas, *Understanding Everyday Life* (Chicago: Aldine, 1970).

J. Douglas, *The Social Meanings of Suicide* (Princeton University Press, 1967).

E. Durkheim, *The Rules of Sociological Method* (Glencoe, Ill.: Free Press, 1964).

E. Durkheim, *Professional Ethics and Civic Morals* (London: Routledge & Kegan Paul, 1957).

E. Durkheim, *The Division of Labour in Society* (London: Collier Macmillan, 1964, 1968).

E. Durkheim, *The Elementary Forms of the Religious Life* (London: Allen & Unwin, 1976).

E. Durkheim, *Suicide: A Study in Sociology* (London: Routledge & Kegan Paul, 1952).

E. Durkheim, *Essays in Sociology and Philosophy* (London: Cohen & West, 1968).

E. Durkheim and M. Mauss, *Primitive Classification* (Chicago: University of Chicago Press, 1963).

H. P. Dreitzel, 'Patterns of Communicative Behaviour', *Recent Sociology No. 2* (Collier-Macmillan, 1970).

J. E. T. Eldridge, *Sociology and Industrial Life* (London: Nelson, 1971).

L. Easton and K. Guddat (eds), *Writings of the Young Marx on Philosophy and Society* (New York: Doubleday, 1967).

B. Fay, *Social Theory and Political Practice* (London: Allen & Unwin, 1975).

P. Feyerabend, *Science in a Free Society* (London: New Left Books, 1978).

H. Garfinkel, *Studies in Ethnomethodology* (Englewood Cliffs, N.J.: Prentice-Hall, 1967).

H. Gerth and C. Wright Mills, *From Max Weber: Essays in Sociology* (London: Routledge & Kegan Paul, 1970).

A. Giddens, *Positivism and Sociology* (London: Heinemann, 1974).

A. Giddens, *New Rules of Sociological Method* (London: Hutchinson, 1976).

A. Giddens, *Studies in Social and Political Theory* (London: Hutchinson, 1977).

A. Giddens, *Central Problems in Social Theory* (London: Macmillan, 1979).

A. Giddens, *A Contemporary Critique of Historical Materialism* (London: Macmillan, 1981).

A. Giddens, *Profiles and Critiques in Social Theory* (London: Macmillan, 1983).

B. Gidlow, '*Ethnomethodology:* A New Name for Old Practices?', *British Journal of Sociology* (1972) 23.

A. Glucksmann, 'A Ventriloquist Structuralism', *New Left Review*, April–March 1972, 68–92.

A. W. Gouldner, *The Coming Crisis in Western Sociology* (London: Heinemann, 1971).

L. Gross, *Symposium on Sociological Theory* (New York: Harper & Row, 1959).

J. Habermas, *Theory and Practice* (London: Heinemann, 1974).

J. Habermas, *Towards a Rational Society* (London: Heinemann, 1971).

M. Harris, *Cannibals and Kings* (London: Collins, 1977).

David Held, *Introduction to Critical Theory: Horkheimer to Habermas* (London: Hutchinson, 1980).

C. G. Hempel, *Aspects of Scientific Explanation* (Glencoe, Ill.: Free Press, 1965).

M. Hesse, *The Structure of Scientific Inference* (London: Macmillan, 1974).

B. Hindess and P. Q. Hirst, *Pre-Capitalist Modes of Production* (London: Routledge & Kegan Paul, 1975).

P. Q. Hirst, *Durkheim, Bernard and Epistemology* (London: Routledge & Kegan Paul, 1975).

G. Homans, *The Nature of Social Science* (New York: Harcourt Brace, 1967).

E. Husserl, *The Crisis of European Sciences and Transcendental Phenomenology: An Introduction to Phenomenological Philosophy* (Evanston, Ill.; Northwestern University Press, 1970).

J. Irvine, I. Miles and J. Evans, *Demystifying Social Statistics* (London: Pluto Press, 1979).

Martin Jay, *The Dialectical Imagination* (London: Heinemann, 1973).

J. W. Kalat, *Biological Psychology* (Belmont, California: Wadsworth, 1980).

R. Keat and J. Urry, *Social Theory as Science* (London: Routledge & Kegan Paul, 1975).

C. Kerr, *Industrialism and Industrial Man* (Harmondsworth: Penguin, 1973).

A. Koestler, *Ghost in the Machine* (London: Hutchinson, 1967).

L. Kolakowski, *Positivist Philosophy: From Hume to the Vienna Circle* (Harmondsworth: Penguin, 1972).

Karl Korsch, *Marxism and Philosophy* (London: New Left Books, 1970).

T. S. Kuhn, *The Structure of Scientific Revolutions*, 2nd edn (Chicago University Press, 1970).

I. Lakatos, 'Proofs and Refutations', *British Journal for the Philosophy of Science*, vol. 14 (1963) 1–25, 120–39, 221–45, 296–342.

I. Lakatos and A. Musgrave (eds), *Criticism and the Growth of Knowledge* (Cambridge University Press, 1970).

M. Lessnoff, *The Structure of Social Science* (London: Allen & Unwin, 1973).

D. Lockwood, 'Some Remarks on the Social System', *British Journal of Sociology* (1956).

A. Louch, *Explanation and Human Action* (Oxford: Blackwell, 1966).

Georg Lukács, *History and Class Consciousness* (London: Merlin Press, 1971).

S. Lukes, *Essays in Social Theory* (London: Macmillan, 1977).

S. Lukes, *Power: A Radical View* (London: Macmillan, 1974).

S. Lukes, *Emile Durkheim: His Life and Work* (Harmondsworth: Penguin, 1975).

B. Malinowski, *A Scientific Theory of Culture* (Carolina University Press, 1944).

P. McHugh, *On the Beginning of Social Enquiry* (London: Routledge & Kegan Paul, 1974).

J. C. McKinney and E. A. Tiryakian, *Theoretical Sociology: Perspectives and Developments* (New York: Appleton Century Crofts, 1970).

J. McMurtry, *The Structure of Marx's World View* (Princeton NJ: Princeton University Press, 1976).

Karl Marx, *Early Writings* (Harmondsworth: Penguin, 1975).

Karl Marx, *Capital*, vols I and III (Harmondsworth: Penguin, 1976).

Karl Marx, *Poverty of Philosophy* (Moscow: Progress, 1976).

Karl Marx, *Grundrisse* (Harmondsworth: Penguin, 1973).

Karl Marx and Frederick Engels, *Selected Correspondence* (Moscow: Progress, 1975).

H. Marcuse, *Reason and Revolution* (London: Routledge & Kegan Paul, 1955).

H. Marcuse, *An Essay on Liberation* (Boston: Beacon Press, 1969).

H. Marcuse, *Counterrevolution and Revolt* (Boston: Beacon Press, 1972).

G. H. Mead, *Mind, Self and Society* (Chicago: University of Chicago Press, 1934).

S. Mennell, *Sociological Theory: Uses and Unities* (London: Nelson, 1974).

K. Menzies, *Talcott Parsons and the Social Image of Man* (London: Routledge & Kegan Paul, 1977).

J. Mepham and David Hillel-Ruben (eds), *Issues in Marxist Philosophy*, vol. II (Brighton: Harvester Press, 1979).

M. Merleau-Ponty, *The Primacy of Perception* (Evanston III.: Northwestern University Press, 1964).

R. K. Merton, *On Theoretical Sociology* (London: Collier-Macmillan, 1967).

James Miller, *History and Human Existence* (Berkeley: University of California Press, 1979).

E. Nagel, *Logic Without Metaphysics* (Glencoe, Ill.: Free Press, 1956).

E. Nagel, *The Structure of Science* (London: Routledge & Kegan Paul, 1961).

G. Novack, *Empiricism and its Evolution* (London: Pathfinder Press, 1969).

J. O'Neill, *Modes of Individualism and Collectivism* (London: Heinemann, 1973).

Enzo Paci, *The Function of the Sciences and the Meaning of Man* (Evanston, Ill.: Northwestern University Press, 1972).

T. Parsons *et al.*, *Working Papers in the Theory of Action* (Glencoe, Ill.: Free Press, 1953).

T. Parsons, E. Shils, *et al. Toward a General Theory of Action* (New York: Harper & Row, 1951).

T. Parsons, 'Evolutionary Universals in Society', *American Sociological Review*, 29, 339–57.

T. Parsons, *Societies: Evolutionary and Comparative Perspectives* (Englewood Cliffs: Prentice-Hall, 1966).

T. Parsons, *The Structure of Social Action*, 2 vols (Glencoe, Ill.: Free Press, 1968).

T. Parsons, *The Evolution of Societies* (Englewood Cliffs: Prentice-Hall, 1977).

W. Pope, *Durkheim's Suicide: A Classic Analysed* (Chicago: University of Chicago Press, 1976).

K. Popper, *The Poverty of Historicism* (London: Routledge & Kegan Paul, 1965).

K. Popper, *The Logic of Scientific Discovery* (London: Basic books, 1959).

K. Popper, *Conjectures and Refutations* (London: Routledge & Kegan Paul, 1967).

K. Popper, *Objective Knowledge* (Oxford: Clarendon Press, 1972).

M. Poster, *Existential Marxism in Post-War France* (Princeton: Princeton University Press, 1975).

Nicos Poulantzas, *Political Power and Social Classes* (London: New Left Books, 1973).

A. Radcliffe-Brown, *Structure and Function in Primitive Society* (Glencoe Ill.: Free Press, 1952).

J. Rex, *Key Problems in Sociological Theory* (London: Routledge & Kegan Paul, 1961).

G. Rocher, *Talcott Parsons and American Sociology* (London: Nelson, 1974).

A. Ryan, *The Philosophy of the Social Sciences* (London: Macmillan, 1970).

G. Salaman and K. Thompson, *People and Organizations* (London: Longman, Open University, 1973).

S. Savage, *The Theories of Talcott Parsons: The Social Relations of Action* (London: Macmillan, 1981).

B. F. Skinner, *Verbal Behaviour* (London: Methuen, 1957).

B. F. Skinner, *About Behaviourism* (London: Cape, 1974).

T. Schroyer, *The Critique of Domination: The Origins and Development of*

Critical Theory (New York: Braziller, 1973).

A. Schutz, *The Phenomenology of The Social World* (London: Heinemann, 1972).

A. Schutz, *Collected Papers* (Amsterdam: Nijhoff, 1962).

B. Smart, *Sociology, Phenomenology and Marxian Analysis* (London: Routledge & Kegan Paul, 1976).

N. Smelser, *Social Change and the Industrial Revolution* (London: Routledge & Kegan Paul, 1959).

C. Sumner, *Reading Ideologies* (London: Academic Press, 1979).

J. H. Turner, *The Structure of Sociological Theory* (Homewood, Illinois: Dorsey, 1974).

M. Weber, *Economy and Society*, 2 vols (Berkeley: University of California Press, 1978).

M. Weber, *The Methodology of the Social Sciences* (Glencoe Ill.: Free Press, 1949).

M. Weber, *The Protestant Ethic and the Spirit of Capitalism* (London: Allen & Unwin, 1968).

A. K. Whitehead, *Process and Reality* (Glencoe, Ill.: Free Press, 1978).

D. and J. Willer, *Systematic Empiricism: A Critique of a Pseudo-Science* (Englewood Cliffs: Prentice-Hall, 1973).

P. Winch, *The Idea of a Social Science and its Relation to Philosophy* (London: Routledge & Kegan Paul, 1958).

C. Wright Mills, *The Sociological Imagination* (Oxford University Press, 1959).

C. Wright Mills, *Power, Politics and People* (Oxford University Press, 1967).

D. Wrong, 'The Over-Socialised Conception of Man in Modern Sociology', *American Sociological Review* (1961), 26, 183–93.

Name Index

247

Subject Index

249